Professional Photoshop™

D1277775

Color Correction, Retouching, and
Image Manipulation with
Adobe Photoshop℠

DAN MARGULIS

John Wiley & Sons, Inc.

New York • Chichester • Brisbane • Toronto • Singapore

Publisher: Katherine Schowalter
Editor: Paul Farrell
Managing Editor: Micheline Frederick

Designations used by companies to distinguish their products are often claimed as trademarks. In all instances where John Wiley & Sons, Inc., is aware of a claim, the product names appear in Initial Capital or all CAPITAL letters. Readers, however, should contact the appropriate companies for more complete information regarding trademarks and registration.

This text is printed on acid-free paper.

Copyright ©1995 by Dan Margulis.

Published by John Wiley & Sons, Inc.

All rights reserved. Published simultaneously in Canada.

Many of the images presented in this volume are copyrighted by third parties and are used herein by license or by special permission. Readers are directed to the Notes and Credits section commencing on Page 281 for further information concerning the ownership of the images.

This publication is designed to provide accurate and authoritative information in regard to the subject matter covered. It is sold with the understanding that the publisher is not engaged in rendering legal, accounting, or other professional service. If legal advice or other expert assistance is required, the services of a competent professional person should be sought.

Reproduction or translation of any part of this work beyond that permitted by section 107 or 108 of the 1976 United States Copyright Act without the permission of the copyright owner is unlawful. Requests for permission or further information should be addressed to the Permissions Department, John Wiley & Sons, Inc.

Library of Congress Cataloging-in-Publication Data:
Margulis, Daniel, 1951–
   Professional Photoshop : color correction, retouching, and image manipulation with Adobe Photoshop / Dan Margulis
     p.   cm.
   Includes bibliographical references.
   ISBN 0-471-01873-2
   1. Color computer graphics. 2. Adobe Photoshop. I. Title.
T385.M3635 1995   94-33545
006.6'869--dc20   CIP

Printed in the United States of America
10 9 8 7 6 5 4 3 2 1

C ONTENTS

Acknowledgments   vii

Introduction: The Two Worlds of Photoshop   ix

1

Preflight: What Shall We Do with This Image? 2

Defining "Quality" **4**   *The Goals in Color Manipulation* **5**   *Should We Match the Art?* **5**   *Matching the Meaning* **6**   *Viewing Conditions: Do Our Eyes Deceive Us?* **7**   *The Sources of the Images* **8**   *You Be the Judge* **8**   *The CMYK Standard* **9**   *Four Plates, One Objective* **10**   *The Power of Curves* **14**   *Image Manipulation: What the Terms Mean* **14**   *All the Tools You'll Ever Need* **15**

2

Calibrationists and Buccaneers 21

Printing Basics **22**   *Contract Proofs* **23**   *Black and White Printing* **24**   *The Pantone Matching System* **25**   *Screens* **26**   *Paper and Dot Gain* **27**   *Color Printing* **28**   *The Colorspace Conundrum* **30**   *In CMYK, the C Is for Cockeyed* **30**   *SWOP: Setting the Standards* **31**   *Famous Last Words* **33**   *Dot Gain: The Numbers, the Newspapers* **36**   *Why Not an RGB Press?* **37**   *The Eye Is the Arbiter* **37**

3

Scanning, Screening, Resolution 41

Other File Formats **43**   *Image Sources* **43**   *High-End Scanning* **45**   *Resolution Defined* **47**   *Resolution and File Size* **48**   *What Is the Right Resolution?* **49**   *Speaking the Scitex Language* **52**   *Imagesetter and Scanner Resolution* **52**   *Olé, Have a Moiré* **55**   *Orderly Chaos: The End of Moiré?* **57**   *Moiré Control in Photoshop* **59**

4

By the Numbers: An Introduction to Curves 63

A General Approach to Correction **64** *Writing Curves: A First Step* **65** *Many Birds with One Curve* **67** *Fighting the Blues* **70** *Skin Tones in the Studio* **70** *Blending Plates for Contrast* **72** *Behold a Paler Horse* **74** *Of Values and Judgments* **76** *Can You Top This?* **77**

5

Color Correction as Horsetrading 81

How Green Is My Image **82** *Taking Inventory* **84** *Let the Sparks Fly* **88** *Its Fleece Was White As Snow* **89** *As Red As a Lobster* **90** *Old Myths and New Realities* **91**

6

Selections and Silhouettes 95

Choosing a Selection Method **97** *Avoiding the Cut-Out Look* **98** *Feathering and Saving Paths* **100** *Quick Masks and Quicker Blends* **102**

7

Local Patchwork, Sharpening, and Enhancements 107

Inspecting for Defects **108** *Minimizing vs. Eliminating Problems* **109** *Extending a Background* **111** *Focusing on the Unsharp* **113** *A Photoshop Makeover* **115** *But Why Is It Unsharp? How Photoshop Brings Images Into Focus* **116** *Photoshop on the Razor's Edge* **118** *A Fractal Facial* **120**

In Color Correction, The Key Is The K 125

The Role of Black **126**   *A Hypothetical Colorspace* **127**   *GCR: When in Doubt, Do Without* **128**   *When More Black Is Better* **130**   *Allowing Flexibility on Press* **132** *Repeatability With GCR* **132**   *The Planned GCR Correction* **133**   *The Whites of Marble* **135**   *If We Shadows Have Offended* **140**   *So Fair and Foul a Day* **141** *Methinks I Scent the Morning Air* **141**

The Unwanted Color and Why We Want It 147

And the Last Shall Be First **148**   *Where Is the Impact?* **150**   *Creating the Contaminant* **151**   *For Intensity, Think Murkiness* **154**   *Back to Three Letters* **155** *Going Against the Grain* **157**   *Sky of Blue, Sea of Green* **160**

Kodak CDs, Digital Cameras: Is the Future Already Here? 165

The End for Film? **166**   *Kodak's Initial Marketing Mistake* **167**   *The Problem in Shadow Areas* **168**   *The Views of Kodak Management* **171**   *The Same Results Every Time?* **172** *The Common Corrections* **177**   *Living With L*a*b** **179**   *Which Plate Has the Contrast?* **183** *Makeover, Digital Style* **186**   *Organizing Before the Conversion* **189**   *The B Channel Beats the Blues* **192**   *Back in the CMYK Saddle* **194**   *Local Touchup Where It Counts* **195**

On the Marriage of Images 201

The Four Deadly Sins **203**   *The Sky Is What Limits* **204**   *Using Masks to Merge* **206** *The Least Common Denominator* **207**   *A Believable Background* **208**   *Pre-Merge Retouching* **211**   *Adding by Subtracting* **212**   *Let It Be Your Secret* **215**

Keeping the Color in Black and White 217

The Fatal Flatness in B/W **218**   *Planning the B/W Conversion* **220**   *Fuzzy Wuzzy Needs Some Hair* **221**   *When "Good Enough" Isn't* **223**   *What to Lighten, What to Darken* **226**   *Balancing the Checks* **229**

Duotones 233

How Strong a Duotone Effect? **234**   *The Definition of a Multitone* **236**   *The Four-Color Black and White* **236**   *Curves, Preset and Otherwise* **239**   *The Perils of the True Duotone* **242**   *From Start to Finish* **245**   *The Final Curves* **248**

Flexing the Muscles of Photoshop 3 253

Four Major Improvements **254**   *Preparing a Layer Options Merge* **254**   *Creating a Density Mask* **257**   *Selective Color to the Rescue* **259**   *Where Is the Focus?* **262**   *The Lighting Effects Filter* **264**   *Layers Make Alterations Easier* **266**   *Professional Color with Photoshop* **268**

Glossary   271

Notes and Credits   281

Index   287

ACKNOWLEDGMENTS

The publication of this book coincides with the twentieth anniversary of my becoming a graphic arts professional. During all of that time, I have been managing computerized production systems. (The graphic arts was one of the very first industries to computerize.) Although digital color correction as a serious craft is only a few years old, a lot of the techniques are just throwbacks to the days when computers weren't as powerful as they are today.

Along the way, I have been fortunate in having worked for companies that specialized in different things: a color separator, a newspaper, printers, a type house, prepress facilities, all of them committed to high-quality work. This has given me a view of color from several different angles, and I think has made this a much better book. However, I have naturally accumulated many debts along with this knowledge.

During this time, technology was changing rapidly, just as it is today. That I was permitted to change with it is largely due to my having bosses who were committed to keeping pace and who were willing to share their very considerable technical knowledge with me. I have been extremely lucky to have had bosses the likes of Bert DePamphilis, Val DiGiacinto, Dave Perskie, Mario Rampone, Gary Samuels, Herb Sorkin, Bill Wilcox, and Tom Worley.

Knowledge flows uphill as well as down. The best graphic arts technicians are the ones who are willing both to learn and share their skills with others. Much of what I know has been taught by the people who have worked for me. I have supervised well over a hundred people in my career but certain individuals stand out for their desire to find the most effective way to do things and their unwillingness to settle for second quality. I particularly wish to thank Bill Carberry, David Dayton, Crawford Hart, Franklyn Higgs, Baruch Gorkin, Dave Joseph, John Schroeder, Rose Smith, Vinny Truchsess, Zep Volpato, and Sheila Zodel. Working with these individuals was both pleasurable and professionally enriching, and without them, this book would not have been possible.

Many of the chapters in this book are based on my columns in *Computer Artist* magazine. The enthusiastic response from readers by e-mail, fax, carrier pigeon, and what have you is what prompted my editor at *Computer Artist* to demand more coverage of color correction, and what convinced John Wiley & Sons that there was a market for this book. It is clearly correct to say that without those who took the time to express their approval, this book would never have happened.

Tom McMillan is the editor who did the above-mentioned demanding. The idea of a regular column on production issues was his. His suggestions and editing have been consistently on target.

Paul Farrell, my editor at Wiley, believed in the concept enough to push through the plan to publish the book in this form, expensive to produce as it was. He provided valuable insight in his reading of the manuscript, particularly in pointing out areas that the average reader might find difficult to follow.

Many improvements in design and text were suggested by Micheline Frederick of Wiley, who was a pleasure to work with throughout.

I thank my present employer, Cardinal Communications Group in New York, for graciously allowing me time off to work on the manuscript.

Adobe Systems, Inc. kindly provided prerelease copies of Photoshop 3.0 software for use in preparing this book.

The digital photography in this book was done by Andy Darlow. He and John Timem provided technical support for my imperfect understanding of this process.

My understanding of the Kodak Photo CD technology was helped immeasurably by Matthew Vere.

Speaking of Kodak, I think the world both of the company and especially its personnel. Anyone who gets a contrary reading from my digs at calibrationism is mistaken. Kodak has contributed probably more than any other company to quality color reproduction. Especially, I would like to salute Kodak Electronic Publishing Systems of Billerica, MA. Many dedicated, knowledgeable, and helpful color professionals work there.

Several vendors of stock-photo CDs gave permission to use their products. Their names, together with information about them, are found in the Notes and Credits section.

Sharon Kaufman offered valuable assistance and encouragement in getting the project off the ground.

Ralph Viola, who is color-blind, showed considerable courage, in my view, when he volunteered to take training in color correction. His success is documented at the end of Chapter 4.

Cathy Panagoulias gave a careful initial edit to the manuscript before I submitted it to the publisher. She is also my wife. I thank her for her patience during the writing period, and dedicate this book to her.

I thank the members of my family not just for their support, but because they took many of the original photographs shown here.

It is customary in closing one of these sections to stress that any remaining errors are solely and exclusively the fault of the author. As most of the people mentioned above can testify, confessing to errors is not one of the strong areas in my professional life. But I refrain for a different reason. Color is an unusual area in its paucity of provably correct answers. You may think of techniques better than the ones I propose, or you may not agree with my assessments of which images look "better."

If upon full consideration, therefore, you find that you think I have made errors and misstatements, I am *not* sorry; I am delighted, actually, that you have developed enough confidence in your color judgment to think so.

The Two Worlds of Photoshop

Adobe Photoshop is really two programs. One produces startling and brilliant graphic effects: composites, mathematical filters, shimmering halos, multiple merges, and the like. The other handles the more straightforward, everyday business of making sure that a picture is as lifelike as possible on the printed page. This book is a guide to getting the most out of this second, but hardly secondary, program.

igital image processing has become a reality so rapidly, and the pace of technological change has been so ferocious, and the costs so unpredictable that most people who have anything to do with it are intimidated. Rightly so.

Adobe Photoshop, with its history of stability and aggressive addition of new capabilities, has led the way through this minefield and has captured a commanding market share, as well as a boisterous following among designers. Although its simpler features are easily understandable, it is one of the deepest and most complex of all applications. The person who fully grasps every Photoshop capability has not yet been born.

Photoshop's phenomenal growth, fueled by corresponding advances in affordable computing power, has masked one of the consequences of its complexity. The program has diverged into two separate disciplines.

The first world of Photoshop has gotten the most attention, because most find it more exciting. It consists of spectacular graphic effects that have not previously been possible. What I consider to be the best book on this Photoshop world contains guidelines on how to accomplish the following, among other things:

• Creating an artificial paper-texture background for photographs that start with a white background.

• Simulating motion in the objects in a photograph.

• Making images seem carved in stone.

• Creating the illusion that an object in the image is wet.

• Making part of an image seem to wrap around some three-dimensional object.

• Making a color photograph black and white, and then putting color back in so that it resembles an antique hand-tint.

Given somewhat shorter shrift than any of these intriguing topics is the second world of Photoshop. There are only two pages on "Image Enhancement." That is the second world. The second world is one of better and more lifelike color, increased detail, more contrast, more believability in our images.

Adobe's own documentation, outstanding as most observers concede it to be, is also heavily weighted toward spectacular special effects. Less than 10 percent of it addresses the second world, and that part is largely inaccurate.

Color Enough for All of Us

Novel artistic possibilities are exciting, but they miss the point of the desktop color revolution. We are using far more color than five years ago not so much because it is cheaper and easier to do so as because we believe that color communicates information more effectively.

And no wonder. Color is a powerful emotional stimulant. We say, for example, that red and orange are *warm* colors and blues are *cool.* These are not just technical designations: the presence of these colors literally makes our bodies feel colder or warmer. Stunningly, color seems to have the same effect on animals: experiments show that animals kept in a red room will start to pant at a lower temperature than those kept in a blue one.

It would seem to behoove us to try to harness this great power by making our images as sharp and lifelike as possible.

The second world of Photoshop has a more frustrated population than the first one, as color correction fluency is not picked up easily. The basic techniques are mature: electronic scanners, which color-correct in much the same way we do today, were introduced nearly 20 years ago. Throughout that time, those skilled at correcting color, whether by hand or on a sophisticated system, have been the highest-paid and most sought-after people in the industry—more so than photographers, strippers, typographers, designers, or art directors.

But the people who had this skill tended to be scanner operators, who would achieve their ends by twirling the dials of their behemoth machines, and by dot etchers, who would make color changes by hand in existing graphic arts film, using a combination of photographic techniques and a solution of potassium cyanide.

Although individuals who understood color well enough to enter one of these crafts were rare, the high-end prepress companies (and that is *my* world) found enough of them to make it possible for the color buyer to feel confident of good results. At a price, of course: the cost of getting a perfect scan five years ago was around a hundred times more than getting a fairly decent one today.

If you are not one of these professionals, but want to achieve professional results with your color images anyway, today you shoulder a heavy burden. Better desktop scanners, digital cameras, the Kodak CD process, and unlimited-use digital stock-photo resources give us color images for a fraction, a very small fraction, of what professional photographers and prepress houses might charge. The flip side is that the original images are not as good as they used to be, leaving it up to us to fix them.

Some Assumptions

This, then, is a book about how to make images jump off the page. The limitations of the discussion will be as follows.
•   The examples will be almost exclusively photographic images. These tend to present more quality issues than graphics that are largely generated by the artist.
•   The supposition will always be that these images are being prepared for conventional offset printing. This is a more demanding application than, say, preparing them for video or for reproduction on a composite color printer. You can, of course, extrapolate.
•   Only those skills normally associated with professional image management will be dealt with. This means color adjustment, local enhancement of pieces of the image, creating black-and-whites and duotones, correction of gross defects such as dust and scratches, extensions of backgrounds and shadows, silhouetting, and simple merges of two or more images. An ample literature on once-in-a-lifetime

special effects makes it unnecessary to devote space to them here.

The assumptions about you are even simpler:
•   You have some means of importing images into your computer, whether through CD, interface to a scanner, dealings with a service bureau, or whatever.
•   Your computer setup is technically adequate for what you intend to do. What exactly this means depends on what kind of work you propose to do in Photoshop. It also depends on what version of the program you are using: Photoshop 3 does not run particularly well on computers with only eight megabytes of RAM. Although sufficient RAM is important and generally speaking the more of it you have the better, often Photoshop performance can be improved more dramatically by having a fast, defragmented hard disk with considerable space available.
•   You have at least enough knowledge of Photoshop to be able to open files and find most commands; and at least a vague notion of how one goes about selecting a part of the image to work on. We will not, however, spend much time reiterating what the program documentation has to say. The concepts of color correction are simple enough that anyone can wade in, but the water can get very deep very fast.

The Use of Photoshop 3.0

This book was prepared using prerelease versions of Adobe Photoshop 3.0 and uses 3.0 terminology and screens throughout. However, I believe that it will be some time before earlier versions of the program will vanish. Largely, this is because the new version does not perform well on computers with limited RAM, and that is what most nonprofessional machines have. Also, it is not clear how quickly version 3.0 will become available on every platform.

As a compromise, therefore, when there is a major difference between how Photoshop 3 and earlier versions would handle specific problems, both methods are discussed. The only exception is in Chapter 14, which is specifically about kinds of work that are very difficult without version 3. In Chapter 9, an extended example (the correction of Old Faithful) intentionally uses a technique available in all versions, although a superior method exists in Photoshop 3.

Do not be overly concerned about version differences. Most color correction techniques in Photoshop are substantially the same as they have been since version 2.0, which was the first one to have real support for CMYK. Whether you run Photoshop on a Macintosh, as I do, under Windows, or on a Unix-based system, is irrelevant.

For that matter, if you are more comfortable with a different program, Photoshop itself is not even necessary. Unlike the first world, which requires an intimate knowledge of program features, color correction is not very application-specific. The same techniques would be used on a high-end retouching system or in any of Photoshop's desktop competitors.

Professional Photoshop™

*Color Correction, Retouching, and
Image Manipulation with
Adobe Photoshop*®

Figure 1.1 *The Grand Canyon, seen from Powell Point. This picture does not capture the canyon's majesty, its rich redness. No photograph could possibly do that. The question is, is this the best representation of reality, given our technical limitations? This professional photograph is digitized and offered for sale by a leading graphic arts vendor. Can it be improved? How would you do it?*

CHAPTER 1

Preflight: What Shall We Do with This Image?

Before tackling color correction, there needs to be a consensus on what we are trying to accomplish. Is the idea to portray a photograph as accurately as possible, or what a human viewer would have seen, had the viewer been the camera?

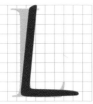 et there be light, the Lord said, and since then it's been nothing but headaches for those of us interested in quality color printing.

The big problem is not so much that the Lord created such a large visible spectrum, but that He also endowed us with an acutely sensitive and highly adjustable visual apparatus. The combination of these two factors makes it quite impossible to create digital images that have even remotely the clarity of real life.

Can a camera capture the majesty of the Grand Canyon? Anyone who has ever been there knows that it cannot. To generalize further: Photographs can never rival reality. Their tonal range is too small. Possibly more important, when the human eye is confronted with a preponderance of similar colors it adjusts unconsciously, gaining sensitivity to those colors at the expense of others. A camera lacks this flexibility; it faithfully records what it sees, even if the human eye would see something different. When we look closely at the Grand Canyon, with its rich redness, our eyes compensate to let us pick up a greater variety of reds. The camera sticks to its original settings.

Even if it could magically make itself more sensitive to reds, though, it could not record nearly the range of colors that the eye can see.

Defining "Quality"

We can probably agree that a color photograph is "worse" than the image would appear in real life. Similarly, an amateur photographer using a $12.50 disposable camera will surely produce a "worse" image of the Grand Canyon than a professional with a first-quality instrument.

If we convert the image recorded by either photographer to digital information, we will get a "worse" image still. Just as between real life and a photograph, between a photograph and a scanned photograph there is a decrease in the range of colors that can be portrayed and a loss of some detail.

Next in line of deteriorating quality comes the printed piece. Again, image quality and color space is lost, all to the detriment of realism.

There is yet another quality leap between color printing on reasonably good paper, such as is used in this book, and printing on poor stock, such as newsprint. A final indignity that can be imposed on an unfortunate photograph is to lose its color altogether, in those occasions when we must print it in black and white.

Now that I've trashed the entire printing process, it should be pointed out that the news is not all bad. If we can't achieve the quality of a photograph on the final page, well, neither can anyone else. The viewer, consciously or not, understands this and cuts us a break. The viewer judges the quality of a printed picture in comparison to other printed pictures, not against original photographs and certainly not against what the viewer might perceive in person.

The *really* good news (or, for the lazy, the really *bad* news) is that, even in our relatively low-quality world, skill means a lot. Just as there is a huge gap between the work of a professional photographer and someone who just points a camera and clicks the shutter, the difference between the work of a color technician and that of a dilettante will be obvious even to the most inattentive observer.

That analogy can be carried further. In photography, a number of crutches have emerged that enable the less-skilled to improve their pictures. Things like auto-focus and automatic exposure are a big help to people who don't know how to set these things manually, but the camera's judgment cannot ever be as good as a professional's. In our own field, there are similar crutches: better mathematical transforms, color "calibration" systems, automatic adjustment of color spaces, or Photoshop's **Image: Adjust>Variations** menu. These can be of help to the beginner—but not to us!

The similarity with photography breaks down in one important area, however. The objects that the photographer takes pictures of, whether outdoors or in the studio, are generally just as easy or as difficult to shoot as they were five years, or 50 years, ago. That is not true for us: technology has reduced the price of getting the base product that we work with, but it has also reduced its quality. We are dealing with lesser originals, so our job *is* harder than it was a couple of years ago. Of course, that means that we will have to be better.

The Goals in Color Manipulation

Before charging into color correction with both guns blazing, we'd better have some idea of what we're aiming at. This is a ticklish topic.

Leaving aside for a few chapters the cases where we want the printed piece to be at odds with the original photograph (as when the sky is overcast in the original but we want happier-looking weather) the standard instruction in the industry is "match the art." By this, we are supposed to understand that we are to produce something that reminds the viewer as much as possible of the original photograph, granting that we are smashing it into a grotesquely smaller range of colors.

Some color scientists interpret this to mean that the process should aim at an absolutely literal translation of the original, compressing all parts of its color range in an inflexibly egalitarian fashion.

That glib approach has its limitations. If the original photograph has a scratch or dust on it, nobody would question that "match the art" means take it out.

Next, there is general agreement that if the photograph is flat, it is the job of the computer artist to fix it. By "flat" we mean lacking contrast, which means lacking a good range, which means that either the whites are too dark or the blacks too light, or both.

In printing, our color range is so limited to begin with that we are not too willing to lessen it, even if it is literally correct to do so. So, to most professionals, "match the art" means, set the lightest white in the original to the value of the lightest white that we can print and still show detail, and set the darkest black in the original to the darkest combination of inks that we can conveniently accommodate. The results of this approach cause no end of astonishment to the uninitiated. Nobody thinks that a snapshot will reproduce as well as a high-quality transparency, but that is because the transparency has so much more of a dynamic range. Once we scan and correct the two, they'll each have the same range, and as long as the snapshot was as detailed as the transparency, it will print just about as well.

Should We Match the Art?

Another major issue, particularly in dealing with photos taken outdoors, where lighting conditions are unpredictable, is that when we compress the colors of the original into our colorspace, we sometimes exaggerate an existing color cast.

Color casts are—well, if you go back to Figure 1.1, that's a color cast. The whole image is way too yellow. Every color is affected. Casts are usually caused by suboptimal lighting conditions, but they can also be introduced or aggravated by lousy scanning. Casts come in every conceivable color and also vary in strength. This one is pretty awful. But even a relatively mild cast can damage an image, because casts play havoc with neutral colors. By neutral colors, we mean whites and grays. Neutral colors, as will be repeated over and over in these pages, are one of the chief torments of computer artists. They must be carefully balanced, or they won't stay neutral. The lighter the gray, the easier it is to mess up.

Annoyingly, there are many things in life that are of a neutral color, and if our image shows them otherwise people will think we don't know what we are doing. Paper, asphalt roads, elephants, shadows, packaging materials, porcelain; the list is endless. In Chapter 4 you will encounter a picture of a horse that your logic will tell you must be white, yet has a pink tinge in the photograph.

The question is, should we correct this, assuming that the horse is actually pink in the original photograph? After all, it's "match the art," isn't it?

The argument against correcting is simple. If we fool around with the color balance of the image we may change a lot of things besides the horse. Although a pink horse does prove that a color cast infects the original, perhaps the photographer or the final client *likes* the way it is affecting the other areas.

As against that, if we were looking at the horse ourselves, rather than at a photograph, we would see a white horse, not a pink one. Human eyes are highly efficient at rejecting color casts in ambient light. Cameras are not so good at it. Probably the lighting conditions at the time *were* slightly pink. Our eyes would have compensated. The camera didn't.

I find this to be a convincing argument. So do most professional color people. It is, however, not unanimous.

For the purposes of this book, war is hereby declared on color casts. When we identify them, we will reduce or eliminate them. If you agree that this is the right approach, read the next section carefully, because it is not obvious, yet it follows logically.

Matching the Meaning

Success in color correction depends very much on the imagination. We need to visualize the kinds of changes that are possible and the effects they may have.

Instead of showing you a picture of what I am starting to talk about, I would like you to imagine a couple of pictures. As we go along, there will be quite a few more of these hypothetical situations.

First, please imagine a picture of your backyard, taken at fifteen minutes before sunset on a day with pleasant weather.

Ready?

The first question is, did you imagine what your backyard looks like at that time of day, or how it would look in a *photograph?* There's a big difference. At that time of day, it is much darker than at, say, noon. Once again, though, our eyes would have compensated for this by becoming more sensitive to dark colors. Once again, the camera would not. Even if the lightest and darkest areas of the photograph are correct, overall the image will be darker than you remember.

This is exactly what occurs when we are in a relatively dark room with the lights out. We adjust to the environment and after a while it seems normal to us. If the lights get turned on suddenly, we are dazzled, and it takes time for us to start to discern obvious visual details.

When our vision adjusts to changed surroundings, it's not as if we can see more colors. We just evaluate them differently. If we increase the range of dark colors we see we have to decrease how many light colors we can perceive. If we are staring intensely at the incredible reds of the Grand Canyon, we lose the ability to see the normal range of greens.

As it happens, color correction by computer can work in exactly the same way. The question is, should we do it? In other words, Photoshop lets us do exactly what our eyes do at fifteen minutes before sunset: lose discrimination in lighter colors so as to be able to make finer distinctions among darker ones. Thus, we will see moderately dark tones as lighter than they are in the original photograph.

It seems to me that if we are going to correct a pink horse to agree with what our eyes would have seen, it must follow, as the night the day, that we must correct this sunset as well.

As you can see, the simple decision that color casts should be corrected leads to some unexpected logical consequences. Let us extend the concept further, with one final, more agreeable imaginary picture. Imagine, please, an attractive individual of whatever sex you prefer. This person is clothed in a bathing suit, drinking a piña colada, standing amid tropical foliage at a resort hotel somewhere in the Caribbean.

Relaxing, isn't it?

In deciding what to do with this image, as color technicians we need to know a little bit more. Imagine further, then, four different possibilities. Suppose that this is:

a. a picture of a family member, for personal use and enjoyment;

b. a posed picture to be used to sell bathing suits in a clothing catalog;

c. intended as a promotional piece for the hotel;

d. a shot for a horticultural magazine article discussing the flora of the island.

I put it to you that these four scenarios require four different corrections, even though the basic picture is the same. Part of the reason is just a matter of commercial priorities: in cases a, c, or d we will not care particularly whether the color of the person's bathing suit exactly matches the original, but in case b we will care very much indeed. Mostly, though, it is just a matter of placing ourselves in the position of an actual observer. We would be concentrating on whatever most interested us. If that happened to be the person, or the bathing suit, or the palm trees,

Viewing Conditions: Do Our Eyes Deceive Us?

That the human visual system changes its perception of colors, in reaction to both the surrounding light and to the colors of nearby objects, has been documented scientifically for nearly two centuries. This has two important implications for graphic artists. First, what the camera records is not necessarily what the human would have seen. Second, when we look at printed pages or color proofs, we had better be confident about lighting before we start drawing a lot of conclusions.

Color professionals view original artwork and proofs in small white booths illuminated by tungsten bulbs engineered to precise specifications. This lighting is roughly comparable to outdoor conditions on a sunny day, so if the weather is nice, you really don't need a viewing booth. If you have neither a viewing booth nor a sunny day, however, be aware that strange things can happen. A phenomenon called *metamerism*, for example, causes different colors to appear the same under certain lightings.

If you are concerned about color quality, yet don't have technically correct viewing conditions, a reasonable compromise is to view twice. In other words, if you have to look at it under office lighting, look at it once in your office and once in a location where you think the lighting conditions are different. If you draw the same conclusions about the color in both places, go ahead and trust your instincts.

that particular area would gain definition at the expense of things that were not as important to us. What the camera saw was accurate. But it was not real.

That, in short, is the case for aggressive color correction.

The Sources of the Images

We now embark on three hundred pages of image evaluation and enhancement. A few words on procedure first.

In this book, the bottom half of Figure 10.5 is a professional photograph that was scanned on a top-quality scanner. All other images contained herein are either amateur photos, digital camera shots, come from desktop scanning sources, or, most commonly, from CD-ROMs of stock photos. Several hundred of these disks are currently available. From the designer's point of view they are absolutely wonderful. For one-time fees of between $25 and $300, we get a hundred or more images for royalty-free use. Since, as you can see, most of them are perfectly usable, they are a huge bargain.

For those interested in acquiring these images or knowing where they came from, each one's source is identified in the Notes and Credits section of this book, as are some of the quotations and more oblique references made in the text. When there are before-and-after versions of such an image, the "before" version is, color-wise, exactly as it appears on the disk. When necessary, I have resampled down to a more appropriate resolution and/or sharpened the image. When the image was not in CMYK format to begin with, I converted it using the default Photoshop separation settings suggested in Chapter 2. Unless otherwise indicated, the "after" version is derived from the "before" version *after* the sharpening, resampling, and conversion. When some of the people working for me saw the first proofs of this book, they accused me of having applied extra unsharp masking to the "after" images. Not true. When color settings are good, images do tend to look better-focused than when they are not. All of the "before" pictures (except for Figure 1.1, which was to prove a point) have had the same overall sharpening applied as their "after" counterparts.

You Be the Judge

A book about color manipulation is not like other instructional books. There is much more room for disagreement. You do *not* have to agree that the corrected version looks better than the original.

Color means different things to different people. Varying interpretations of what is important in a picture are possible, as we saw in our imaginary trip to the Caribbean. And possibly most important, individuals do see color differently.

There is a widespread belief, quite untrue, that except for color-blind people, we all see more or less the same thing. This is disproven by the industry-standard color perception test, the Munsell test, in which one is asked to arrange in proper order a series of pegs that vary only slightly from one another in hue.

I have taken this test many times, and administered it to hundreds of people. I can categorically confirm something that will not surprise you, that people in their twenties on the whole have much better color perception than older folk. Furthermore, in my experience, young women usually do best of all.

It is not just a matter of deterioration: people develop patterns, and each individual will see different things. To get personal for a moment, now that I have turned 40, I appear to have become less sensitive to green. I don't know what you expect; I don't fit into the same pants I wore in 1975 either, among many other problems. When I was 25 I could get a perfect score on the Munsell test from a distance of 10 feet. Nowadays I miss parts of the green test no matter how close I get.

This has major ramifications. A person who sees color the way I did when I was 25 will not just be able to see detail in greens that I can't. If we are both looking at a red, for example, I may see it as a rosier color, less of a fire-engine sort of red. Or maybe I react to red a little differently anyway as a result of some unfavorable childhood experience. It has also been seriously suggested that blond individuals see color differently than do persons with darker hair. The point is that no two people will ever totally agree on what color represents. If you like the way a picture looks then its color is right for you regardless of what I think. The corrections here are my idea of good color. If you sometimes don't agree, it is perfectly normal and understandable.

The CMYK Standard

This is a professional color joke.

Q. How many color scientists does it take to change a light bulb?

A. None. The standard has just been changed to darkness.

People involved with color printing for a living tend not to be very tolerant of those who preach other standards than the one we all use, which is CMYK. Within about a hundred pages you will be a believer, if you are not already. For the time being I ask you merely to accept that CMYK is the system that all printers and virtually all prepress professionals employ, and the one that will be used almost exclusively here.

CMYK is the abbreviation for the four inks—cyan, magenta, yellow, and black—that are used in normal printing. These four are sometimes referred to as the *process colors. K* is the abbreviation for black because at one time it was shorthand to refer to cyan as *blue* and to magenta as *red,* so the letter *B* is ambiguous. In the pressroom, *blue* and *red* are still synonyms for cyan and magenta, which can lead to confusion, but in this book, we will use *blue* and *red* as they are commonly understood in everyday English.

Every color that the press can reproduce with these inks can be expressed in terms of percentages. 70C0M100Y means 70 percent of the maximum cyan plus the absolute maximum yellow, with no magenta. We leave off the black in cases where it is zero, which it frequently is.

The numbers just given describe a color known as Kelly green. If you are to become a decent color corrector you will have to understand this intuitively: you must know approximately what will result from any mixture of colors. Similarly, you must know the general impact of changing any of these numbers slightly. Suppose, for example, that we increase cyan. This will move us toward a color we might call forest green. If we remove cyan, on the other hand, we will tend toward chartreuse, and eventually, if enough cyan comes out, toward yellow.

Yellow cannot go higher, since it is

already maxed out, but if we reduce it we will start to see a purer, yet less intense, green. Magenta cannot go lower, since it is at zero now, but if we increase it some very interesting things will happen, and happen fast.

In a situation like this, where two of the three colors predominate, the odd man out (the magenta here) is called the *unwanted color*. This is somewhat of a misnomer. It is not unwanted at all by the intelligent artist: we want it a whole lot, because we can do more to add punch to the image by manipulating it than we can with the dominants.

The unwanted color controls how "clean" or "dirty" the dominating color appears. When working with green, the addition of magenta moves it toward brown. Magenta has such a powerful impact on green that if we can engineer detail into the magenta we are certain to see it in the green, even if the cyan and yellow plates have poor contrast. We will spend all of Chapter 9 discussing the many uses of the unwanted color.

To get an idea of how the four color plates interplay, have a look at Figure 1.2. This is a quiz. These are the four plates of an image. It is up to you to decide which is which, without the benefit of seeing the entire image in color.

Four Plates, One Objective

This test is not that easy, except for identifying the black. The purpose of black is to strengthen dark areas. It cannot be used in light areas at all. Consequently the black plate is invariably the lightest of the four process inks. That means it is Plate 1 in this example.

Untangling the other three is more dif-

ficult. Unfortunately, much of this image is neutral. The lighter areas of the bird's face, the ground beneath his feet, and his legs and underbelly, are examples. We know this because all three color plates are approximately of equal darkness in these places.

To identify which is which, we need places where the colors are not balanced. There are two areas that meet that description: the background behind the bird, and the bird's eyes. In the background, Plates 3 and 4 are strong and Plate 2 is weak. In the eyes, Plate 4 is very strong and the other two are very weak.

So, the bird has bright eyes. The eyes are either yellow, magenta, or cyan. The color of the background is purple or blue (if 3 and 4 are cyan and magenta), green (if they are cyan and yellow), or red or orange (if they are magenta and yellow).

You take it from there. Once you have yourself convinced, check Figure 1.3, which shows all six possible permutations of these colors, and see whether your choice appears to be the winner.

You should at this point be very clear on the circle of colors, especially in terms of the complementary colors that they damage so effectively. Magenta falls between red and blue. It kills green. Cyan falls between blue and green. It kills red. Yellow falls between green and red. It kills blue. And black kills everything.

You will also need to adopt professional terminology regarding color ranges. We call the lightest white areas of the image the *highlight*. In Figure 1.2, we can judge from studying the four plates that this area is located in the bird's face, since all colors are light there. Taking Plate 4 as an individual image, the highlight might be in the face but it also might be in the lightest areas of the feathers, which are darker in the other colors.

The darkest area of the image is called the *shadow.* This can be very confusing, since we often deal with literal shadows, like the shadow that is behind the bird to the right. But for graphic arts purposes, the *shadow* of this image is the pupils of the owl's eyes.

Quartertone, midtone, and *three-quartertone* are defined as the intermediate ranges of the picture. There is no set demarcation line between these areas. A value of 25 percent is plainly quartertone and 50 percent is midtone, but what about 35 percent?

This seeming ambiguity is not as bad as it sounds. Since nobody can guess color values with single-digit precision, we need more inclusive words. If you look at what you perceive to be Kelly green somewhere in an image, you cannot possibly (I don't think) tell whether it is 65C2M97Y or 71C4M93Y. You can, and should, think to yourself, cyan three-quartertone, magenta highlight, yellow shadow. That way, if you are planning some other correction in the image that would affect the cyan three-quartertone, you will realize that you may also have an impact on the Kelly green.

Though the exact numbers were unimportant there, here is one that you *do* have to wear next to your heart. 5C2M2Y is the magic number that defines the minimum highlight that most presses can carry and still show detail. Upwards of 80 percent of images have white areas somewhere. The lightest white almost always should be set to this value, or something very close. Our eyes are acutely sensitive to variation in light colors and consequently highlight value is crucial to the success of the overall image.

Figure 1.2 *These are, in random order, the cyan, magenta, yellow, and black plates from a certain image. Can you tell which one is which?*

The darkest shadow area is not nearly as important a number, because we lose a lot of color perception in dark areas. Also, this value varies a lot depending upon what kind of paper and press the job is being printed on. But, for now, assume 80C70M70Y70K is the darkest shadow that we can hold if we expect to see any detail. An image with no area that can legitimately be made into a shadow is very rare, although some do exist.

Obviously, we can get much higher and lower than these two endpoints. There is nothing in Photoshop to stop us from making areas 0C0M0Y, or for that matter 100C100M100Y100K, although trying that kind of a shadow is a good way to make a lifetime enemy of one's printer.

Recalling that our biggest disadvantage is that we don't have access to as big a

Figure 1.3 *Six color permutations of the owl image of Figure 1.2, showing what happens when the cyan, magenta, and yellow plates are shuffled around. The numbers in the bottom show which of the plates of Figure 1.2 are being used for what color here. Was your guess about which plate was which correct?*

range of colors as a photograph, why don't we make what range we have absolutely as large as possible, by pushing the envelope of the minimum and maximum values?

We can perhaps ascertain the wisdom of this by asking the owl we have been working on. In this image, the highlight is in the face and the shadow behind the legs, or possibly in the tailfeathers. All three of these areas ought to give us the impression of texture, either from the presence of feathers or of sand. If any part of the owl's face is zeroed out we will instead get an impression of white paper. If the shadow areas are too dark we will perceive a black blob. So, in this case anyway, we must stick with the recommended numbers for shadow and highlight.

Figure 1.4, however, which is about as simple a correction as can be imagined, demonstrates the perils of dogmatic adherence to numbers. Really it is not so much a color correction as a range correction. All it takes to recognize its effectiveness is a little common sense.

The sun is going to be the lightest area of the image. Orthodoxy suggests setting that value at 5C2M2Y. But what is the point? Do you see any detail there? The sun's defining characteristic is its brilliance. We have nothing to lose by zeroing it out, and by doing so we open up valuable real estate.

In just the same way, the danger of an excessively dark shadow is that it will lose detail and seem to be nothing but an area of solid black. In the camels, the drivers,

Figure 1.4 *Cost-free color correction. There is almost no detail in either the brightest or darkest areas of this image. This means that we can go beyond normal quality limits in portraying them (bottom), giving ourselves more contrast without losing anything of value.*

and the ground, that is exactly what we have already. So how can we hurt things by going beyond the usual limits? By increasing the range of the image, we get more contrast. Do you see it in the clouds?

If you agree that the second version of this image is palpably better than the first, it seems that you must also agree that before doing anything to a picture, a careful analysis of its strengths and weaknesses is the key to success.

The Power of Curves

Photoshop is one of the most terrifying applications around in terms of the number of capabilities, tools, and commands thrown at the user. Luckily, the professional can ignore most of them. A few techniques handle the bulk of corrections.

In the arsenal we will bring to bear against inadequate color in the coming chapters, the most useful weapon is also the most frightening.

Input-output curves (found under **Edit: Modify>Curves**) are by far the most important correction tool in Photoshop, or any other color manipulation program. They operate in close conjunction with the density readout provided in the Info palette (if not visible on the monitor, go to **Window: Palettes>Show Info**).

Curves can remap the entire image, or affect only a limited range of one color, or anything in between. Writing curves is numerical. If we leave a particular color's curve alone, we will get a straight line at a 45-degree angle. If we start adding points, we may get sections of the curve that are steeper or flatter than others. In the areas that are steeper, the image will show more contrast, and in flatter areas there will be less. When the curve is higher than the original 45-degree line, the image will be darker than it was at first, and in areas where the curve is lower, the image will be lighter.

We can apply curves strictly by numbers, or we can check Preview in the Curves dialog box to get an interactive feel as we manipulate. Either way, the density readout in the Info palette (Figure 1.5) will show both the present value and what will happen if the curve is implemented.

The power of curves is immense. They are by far our most effective correction tool, and we will come back to them over and over. If you understand how to

---

Image Manipulation: What the Terms Mean

Options in image manipulation with Photoshop are nearly unlimited. They do, however, fall into five major categories. These are the terms that will be in use.

•**Color Correction** is the intelligent massaging of data in the entire image to get a more reasonable color balance, more lifelike overall appearance, and so on.

•**Local Correction** is the removal of defects such as scratches, hairs, and dirt, plus color changes that are intended to affect isolated areas only.

•**Local Enhancement** is the use of Photoshop's tools to accentuate or suppress certain of the image's details. We may, for example, sharpen the features of a person's face, or play down parts of the image that compete with the areas that are important to us.

•**Retouching** is the outright elimination of elements that were part of the original image, or the addition of elements that were not. This technique can be as simple as removing a scar from a person's face or adding chocolate chips to a bowl of ice cream, but there is really no limit to how complex it can get.

•**Special Effects,** which get little attention in this book, are creative moves that are intended to make attractive images that the viewer will understand are not real. They can include complicated image filtering and patterning, surrealistic merges, and drastic color alterations.

apply curves you will get great color even if you never use any other feature or tool in Photoshop.

Figure 1.6 should give an idea of what they do. The improvement in the Grand Canyon image is entirely curve-based. The techniques are discussed using comparable images in Chapter 4.

Obviously, though, these other things have their uses. I will list the ones we will cover in a moment. First, however, now that we have defined the most underrated feature of the program, a word about the most overrated, the one that most often snags nonprofessionals into needless or even counterproductive correction cycles.

Photoshop makes it seductively easy to "select" areas of an image to be worked on in isolation, so that any changes will affect only the selected region and not the rest of the image. Human nature makes us want to fix things that are obviously broken. So, upon encountering a pink horse, the natural, understandable reaction of most Photoshop users is to select it and fool around with it until it becomes white.

This is not the best approach. If there is a pink horse in our image it may be our most blatant problem but it is not our only one. Whatever caused the horse to appear pink will also have an impact on the rest of the picture. It will be subtler, probably because we are seldom as sure about what colors are impossible as we are about pink horses. An overall correction of the picture is likely to make *everything* look better, not just the horse.

There are certainly times when we have to select. Clearly, if we are silhouetting part of an image or extending a background, there is no way around making a selection first. When one important area

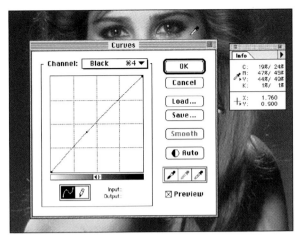

Figure 1.5 *When adjusting input-output curves (center), the Info palette (right) displays what the inking values will be before and after the curve is applied. The area being measured is defined by the cursor.*

of an image is horrendously defective and the rest is more or less OK, we also need to select. If we are trying to enhance some very small area with one of our retouching tools, it makes sense to isolate it from any surrounding areas that are much different in color or texture. And when we have made some sort of electronic intervention to cover up some problem and we wish now to cover up the fact that we did it, the selection tools can help hide our tracks.

To think like a professional, when the idea of selecting crosses your mind, take your hands off the mouse and sit on them. Make a selection only when you are sure there is no other sensible way to handle the problem you are trying to fix.

All the Tools You'll Ever Need

Although we will be covering a wide variety of color problems, the fraction of Photoshop's tools that we will use is rather small. All the rest are unnecessary unless we get involved in heavy special effects, and sometimes not even then.

So, without further ado, and from left to right on the monitor, here are the tools of our trade. There will be a brief explanation of each of these when they are first introduced, but if you are not familiar with them ahead of time and are a coward by nature, recourse to the manual may be an option.

Starting with the toolbox, at the top we will need (although not as much as you probably think) the *selection tools:* the lasso, the marquees, and the magic wand.

In conjunction with these, the various simple commands located under the **Select** heading in the menu bar.

Next, the *practical tools:* there is nothing elegant about cropping off part of a picture or rotating it, but in the real world we frequently have to do it for efficiency's sake. So we will need the crop tool, and the **Image: Rotate** command. Also helpful, though more obscure, are the Quick Mask feature in the toolbox, and the Foreground/Background color change box.

The *retouching tools* for our purposes consist of the cloning tool, the airbrush, the blur/sharpen tool, the dodge/burn/sponge tool, and, on rare occasions, the smudge tool.

On to the menu bar. We will frequently change settings in **File: Preferences>Separation Setup**, normally for GCR reasons stated in Chapter 8, occasionally for other nefarious purposes.

Our **Mode** is normally CMYK, but we will be considering Grayscale and Duotone images as well, plus sporadic forays into RGB and LAB.

Photoshop's mathematical **Filter** options give creative artists lots of exciting choices. Here is where one can find twirls, mosaics, and motion blurs, and here is where we will leave them. In our world, the only filters we need are Unsharp Mask

Figure 1.6 *Does image enhancement pay? Below, a simple correction of Figure 1.1 (repeated for convenience, facing page). Time to execute this correction: around two minutes.*

Quick & Dirty

THE PREFLIGHT ANALYSIS

✓ Despite the maturity of the prepress process, there is no general agreement on a very fundamental question. Should the color technician try to match the original photograph, or what human observers would have seen had they been in the position of the camera?

✓ Humans and cameras do not see things the same way. If you have decided to make your images match the meaning of the art rather than the art itself, several sorts of correction will become very familiar.

✓ Our color perception changes so that colors we know are white or gray appear that way to us, regardless of ambient lighting. The camera will see a color cast if there is one, and will incorporate it into the photograph.

✓ When we focus on a certain object we will see more detail in it and less in surrounding objects. The camera will treat them all equally. This means that some pictures must be corrected differently in different contexts, depending upon what the viewer is supposed to be concentrating on.

✓ When looking at an image with an obvious defect, such as a pink horse, do not go charging in to fix it. Corrections are generally best made to the image as a whole. The pink horse may be your biggest problem, but it won't be the only one.

✓ The overwhelming majority of professional-level color correction work is done through manipulation of input-output curves.

✓ The CMYK colorspace, being the one that will be in use on press, offers the most precise control of the whole process. With four variables rather than the three of most other colorspaces, more effective correction techniques are possible in CMYK.

✓ Photoshop has a dazzlingly complete suite of commands and tools, but there is no need to be intimidated. High-level image enhancement and color correction requires only a fraction of them.

✓ Unlike other fields of endeavor, in color correction and image enhancement there is usually no right answer. We all see color differently and react to it in different ways as well. If you like the style of correction used in this book, fine, but don't consider it gospel.

and its complement, Blur; Noise and its complement, Despeckle; and now and then Dust and Scratches, introduced in Photoshop 3.

The awesome capabilities of **Image: Adjust>Curves** overshadow other important options under the same menu bar item. With **Image: Image Size** we control resolution, and with **Image: Canvas Size** we can arrange to have two files at the same exact size, a prerequisite for compositing. **Image: Adjust>Selective Color**, new in Photoshop 3, lets us get at particular colors wherever they occur, without affecting the rest of the image.

Image: Duplicate lets us make a second version of an existing document, very important in correction. As shown in Figure 1.7, **Image: Calculations>Blend** allows us to crossbreed plates or files, and, for more complex merges, we use **Image: Calculations>Composite**.

Select: Feather is an important command that lets us achieve soft edges when we are silhouetting or are forced to make a locally selected correction. Used to an extreme degree, it can also be an effective fadeout tool. **Select: Color Ranges** (Photoshop 3 only) is a useful way to isolate individual colors.

Of the palettes accessible under the **Window** command, the ones we will be visiting constantly are the density monitor (a.k.a. the Info palette) and the toolbox. There will also be frequent side jaunts to the Brushes palette, occasionally to the Paths panel, and now and then to the Layers palette, new in Photoshop 3.

There you have it. With this small group of tools, the whole gamut of professional color is accessible. Provided, of course, that we bring along the most important tools of all: our eyes and good judgment.

Figure 1.7 *Mathematical blends of two different plates are a recurring theme in color correction. Here is an example from Chapter 4: the cyan plate of this image (left) is weak and lacking in detail. The magenta plate (center) is more desirable. To create a cyan that is more detailed yet still lighter than the magenta, Photoshop lets us average the two: the image at right is a 70–30 blend.*

SEEING IS NOT ALWAYS

BELIEVING

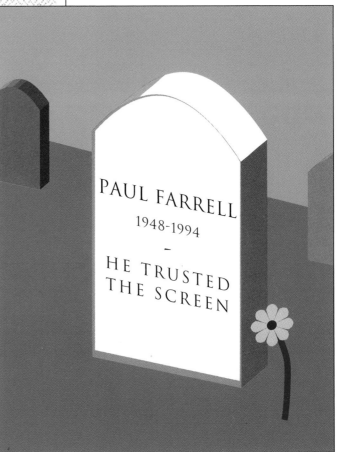

PAUL FARRELL

1948-1994

—

HE TRUSTED
THE SCREEN

Figure 2.1 *If you rely too heavily on the colors your monitor displays, it can be your funeral. At left, a screen grab showing what the monitor was displaying in preview mode (that is, what it was predicting the job would look like when printed). Below, how the file actually prints, believe it or not. Most cases are not quite this extreme, but the lesson is the same: go by what the numbers on Photoshop's Info palette reveal, not by what the screen is showing.*

Calibrationists and Buccaneers

In the prepress world, fortune favors the bold. There are so many unpredictable, uncontrollable factors that only an approach that treats each picture as an individual battle has any chance of success. Why press conditions vary, how to compensate for dot gain, why CMYK is cockeyed, plus considerable criticism of calibrationism.

he anguished cry rings out across the room as the artist examines the color proof. "No, no! That's not how it looks on the monitor! How can this have happened! I have no time to do this over! My boss will kill me!" etc., etc.

This scene is no less poignant the fiftieth time one sees it than the first. (Nevertheless, the prepress professionals watching it are the villains of the drama, for instead of being sympathetic, they are usually muttering under their breath, "What did you expect?")

This opens up an extensive line of inquiry as to how one predicts the way color will appear when it is printed. Though the topic is complicated, before we get into practical color correction we had better address it. Unfortunately, the discussion is made more difficult by those in the industry who try to make it seem simpler than it actually is. There are some dangerous people out there who say that all we need is "calibration" between all of our various devices and our worries will magically vanish.

That word, *calibration*, calls up such pleasant images of precision that coming out against it is rather like being in favor of cancer or against being polite to the elderly. The truth is that the concept has its uses, but it should not be used as a crutch.

The cruder calibrationist products do not work well in a professional setting, and cause more problems than they cure. These products may help people who do not know much about what they're doing, and for such individuals the gains of using them may outweigh the performance hit their computer system will take. Slower operation, frequent system crashes, and new and interesting possibilities for major error are other side effects.

There is a big difference between "calibration" and "repeatability." Nobody would deny that if we print from a certain file today, and then try again next week, we want the result to be exactly the same.

Yet, certain steps in the production process are inherently unpredictable. If we understand where these breakdowns can occur, we can insure repeatability without falling victim to the siren call of calibrationism.

An image manipulated in Photoshop can be intended for one or many different purposes. Most likely, we are planning to print it on a press, but there are several kinds of presses and each one has different color characteristics. All papers print differently. Worst of all, the same press model will behave differently depending upon age, materials being used, speed of the press run, and even the weather, among many other variables.

Perhaps we are going to video, which can produce many colors that are beyond the capabilities of a press but which cannot match the press's detailing, or possibly to a desktop composite printer. But, again, there are many species of color printers

and each one has a different color gamut. We will concentrate on printing presses here, not just because that is where most of you will be going with your images, but because prepress is the most difficult case. If you master it you should breeze right through any other color problem.

By now you may be thinking, though, how can this system possibly work? If there are many different types of presses, and printing conditions vary from plant to plant and day to day, how can we get the repeatability that we want?

This quandary scares a lot of people away from Photoshop, but there is nothing new about it. Printing was unpredictable long before color got to the desktop. So it is not surprising that a system evolved that took care of most of the problems. The system still works.

Printing Basics

Printing presses come in many shapes, sizes, configurations, and prices. However, there is one unifying thread among all commercial presses, and this feature solves many of the calibration and repeatability problems.

This happy feature is that the press operator has a great deal of control over how the colors will appear, regardless of what may have been done to the digital files previously. Granted, he does not have the monstrous range of color correction abilities that we do in Photoshop. Most adjustments on press are relatively minor, though, and the pressman has a good set of tools to make them, either in localized areas or on the job as a whole.

If we make final film for a job and present it, saying, print this to your normal house standards, to Printer A who uses

Press X, and also to Printer B who uses Press Y, it is hereby guaranteed that the two will produce different-looking results. This is very bad, and printers quite rightly prevent us from doing business this way.

If, instead, we have Printer A print the job first, and then show what he did to Printer B, Printer B will have no difficulty whatsoever in coming up with something that looks identical, all by twiddling little dials that control the ink fountains on the press. Although B's press conditions and normal ink settings vary from A's, one offset press still behaves basically like another, and it is easy enough to juggle things to match what the client wants. All the printer needs is to have something to look at to match.

Plainly, the best thing to try to match is a sample that has been printed elsewhere from the same film. This is called a *press proof,* and if this were an ideal world we would have one for every job we print. However, an initial press proof costs several hundred dollars extra.

The less-expensive substitute that we need, however, has to have the characteristics (and the limitations) of a printed piece. Imagine, for instance, telling a pressman to try to match the color of a sample of the picture pulled from a dye-sublimation desktop color printer.

That would never work, because a color printer and a printing press don't behave in the same way. For one thing, color printers tend to be able to print brighter colors, especially blues and greens, than can be had on press with CMYK inks. A pressman cannot match the unmatchable. For another thing, presses are capable of much more subtlety than color printers are. They are also subject to the phenom-enon of dot gain, which we will get to in a moment, while color printers are not, at least not to the same extent. Because of these factors, lighter colors tend to seem purer and brighter on the color printer than on press, and there is nothing the pressman can do to compensate.

Contract Proofs

Accordingly, printing companies refuse to accept work under these circumstances. They insist on a proof that is designed as much as possible to emulate the conditions on press. Normally this is a combined, laminated color proof that has been pulled from the final film, using a process that tries to compensate for dot gain. These proofs are frequently referred to offhandedly as matchprints, but were I to use this term so generically my publisher would shortly be hearing from lawyers for the 3M Company, Inc., whose trademark it is. MatchPrint, then, and DuPont's competitor, Cromalin, are the leading brands of such "contract proofs," which take around half an hour apiece to make and tend to cost around $100 for a standard page, more for larger sizes.

Such contract proofs are now almost universally accepted as a substitute for press proofs. Most printers will also accept digital contract proofs, in which fields the names of Iris, Kodak, and 3M are the most prominent.

To summarize the typical production scenario: we create attractive color pictures using Photoshop. If we are professionals, we do not trust the colors on the monitor as much as the numbers that the Info palette is reporting. If the numbers say 50C45M45Y15K that is a gray even if the monitor displays it as chartreuse.

We then, in all probability, import our Photoshop result into a page makeup file, likely into QuarkXPress or Aldus Page-Maker. To make sure all of our position-ings and croppings are correct, we send a copy to a laser printer or a composite color printer. Once satisfied that positioning is OK, we go to our imagesetter (or to a ser-vice bureau, if we don't have the resources to buy an imagesetter) and get film.

From the film, we generate a Match-Print or similar contract proof. If we like it, off it goes to the printer with the film, and if not, back to Photoshop to correct color some more.

That was a pretty hasty summary. Now, let's take the scenic route through the whole process, paying special attention to what can be profitably subjected to calibration or other color management techniques.

Black and White Printing

Black and white is the simplest form of printing, and to start the tour, we'll sim-plify it further by limiting the discussion to pages containing type only, no pictures.

In the old days of hot-metal typesetting and letterpress printing, proofreaders were paid a great deal of money because they had a unique skill. They had to be able to read type *backwards*. Since the metal type set in the Linotype machines of those days was actually mounted on press, and this type was what made direct contact with the printed sheet, it had to be the mirror image of what the desired final product was. As we say in the graphic arts, it had to be wrong-reading.

Nowadays, proofreaders read type the way normal people do, but the concept of right-reading and wrong-reading still is important. At virtually every stage of the process, the orientation of the job flips. Why is it that proofreaders now have an easy job compared to their predecessors?

In the letterpress days, the type became part of the printing plate. Today, the plate is made by photographic contact with the final film of the job. This final film may or may not be made by contact from some type of preliminary film. This, in turn, may or may not be a successor to a lot of smaller pieces of film that were stripped together by hand. The type that is respon-sible for the whole mess may have been output either on film or on paper, in which case it was photographed onto film.

You may now do some mental gym-nastics and reach the conclusion that since the final page must be right-reading, the plate has to be wrong-reading. That means that the film that makes the plate has to be right-reading, and the prelimi-nary film that makes the film that makes the plate must be wrong-reading, and so on down the pecking order.

That analysis is clever, but it doesn't work. In offset printing, the plate never hits the paper. Instead, the plate, which is made of anodized aluminum, is wrapped around a press cylinder that spins at high speeds. It is continuously drenched with a combination of black ink from one direc-tion and water from another. The dark areas of the plate, which represent the type, tend to attract the ink more than the water and the light areas do the opposite. As it rotates, the plate cylinder makes con-tact with a second cylinder of the same size. The second cylinder is covered by a layer of rubber known as a *blanket*. It is the second cylinder, the blanket cylinder, that actually contacts the paper.

Naturally, as the plate cylinder turns, a mirror copy of its contents is deposited (or *offset*, get it?) onto the rubber blanket. The blanket must be wrong-reading because it is the final thing that contacts the paper, so the plate, contrary to our previous analysis, must be right-reading, so the final film must be wrong-reading, so the intermediate film must be right-reading.

Generally, therefore, printers ask for film to be wrong-reading, except for those printers who use some intermediate process between film and plate (for example, making several copies of the film for simultaneous printing), and need it right-reading.

To take a concrete example: the printer of this book wants me to supply wrong-reading film. In the next chapter, Figures 3.8, illustrating poor imagesetting, and 3.5, which shows different screen rulings on the same page, require stripping some

Specifying the Color We Want: The Pantone Matching System

If we are lucky enough to be able to afford printing with additional inks besides CMYK, we need a way to be able to communicate to the printer exactly what we want the additional color to be. "Very light green with a pinch of an aqua feeling" may sound precise to you, but to a printer, it's, well, kind of gray.

The industry-standard way of coping with this confusion is the Pantone Matching System, a numbered grouping, with accompanying sample swatches (below right) of around a thousand colors. Several of them might answer the description of our aqua-ish green. All we need do is look at our swatch book, call up the printer, say "PMS 3258" or whatever, and hang up the phone. Although the printer won't have such a weird color on the pressroom shelf, Pantone issues instructions on how to mix it from combinations of other, more common Pantone inks. Simple and effective for printer and client.

One common source of misunderstanding arises when one specifies a PMS color and then attempts to construct it out of CMYK inks, rather than having the printer mix a separate ink for use as a fifth printing color. Photoshop, like most other desktop publishing applications, lets us do this. We can select PMS 3258 directly from the color picker. If we place that color anywhere in a CMYK file, Photoshop will insert the values that Pantone says will give the closest match—in this case 60C34Y.

The problem arises if you have seen a swatch of real PMS 3258 somewhere and suppose that 60C34Y is exactly the same color. It's not. The real thing will be far more intense, since it's a solid color, not two screened applications of pale inks on white paper. Because the cyan ink used in printing is so poor, matching blue, green, or purple PMS inks with CMYK is impossible. One can get something of the flavor of the color, nothing more.

In the swatch book at right two versions of each color appear side by side. One shows the specially-mixed ink, one the closest CMYK equivalent. Be sure you know which one you're asking for.

existing film into the final product. On these pages only, therefore, what I generate from my computer will be intermediate, not final, film. I will therefore specify right-reading film on these two and use it to construct a wrong-reading final page. On the remaining pages of the book, I will output wrong-reading pages.

This terminology gets iffy when dealing with film, which unlike paper, metal type, an aluminum plate, or a rubber blanket, can be read when it is upside-down. A wrong-reading piece of film becomes right-reading by the simple expedient of turning it over. When a professional calls a negative *wrong-reading*, other professionals assume that this means with the business side of the film facing the viewer. The business side, or emulsion, is where the imagesetter does its work; the other side is called the base. The emulsion side gives better results for duplication, so when we make one set of film from another by photographic contacting, their emulsions should face one another (we call this *E to E* contacting) and the orientation reverses.

If, in handling a negative, you have any doubts as to which is the emulsion side, it is normally the side that looks duller, but the infallible way of telling is to take a razor blade and scratch the film in a nonprinting area. On the emulsion side, the scratch will remove the black coating, but on the base side, it will not.

Professionals indulge in a lot of technically loose talk among themselves, such as calling cyan *blue* or magenta *red,* and using the ambiguous term *wrong-reading* to describe the type of negative most printers want. A better term is *down negative* (meaning, it reads correctly with the emulsion down, as opposed to an *up* negative). Best of all is the designation that is completely unambiguous, if somewhat lengthy: RRED, for Right Reading, Emulsion Down. I strongly suggest that when you designate film specification, you use the terms RRED and RREU.

Screens

Type is usually easy for the printer, since it prints in solid black. Photographs, which need a larger range of tones, are a complication. We want grays, but have no gray ink to work with: only black ink and white paper.

This problem has been around for a long time and the solution always has taken pretty much the same form. If you examine the likeness of George Washington on a dollar bill, you can see an old but workable technique. We sense depth and realism in Washington's face because we perceive several levels of gray in it. Upon closer inspection, this perception is provoked by black lines of variable thickness, small enough that we do not notice without looking for them.

Nowadays we tend to use a predefined pattern of dots of various sizes rather than lines. We could use something else, randomly spaced tiny black frogs if we wanted, but the principle is always the same. If the black objects are small enough, viewers can be fooled into thinking they are seeing gray.

There is a lot of technical progress being made in this area. We will talk more about it in the next chapter. For the time being, assume that we use a conventional *screening* method: a pattern of black dots that vary in size but are a uniform distance apart. The technically correct way of referring to this would be in terms of the number of dots per inch, but for obscure reasons, most people say *lines* per inch. The numbers that have traditionally been used in printing are 65, 85, 100, 120, 133, 150, and 175. Since screening is done digitally today, there is nothing to stop us from using some other number, but there are good practical reasons not to.

Suppose for the moment that we are using 150. This means that each dot would be a maximum size of .0066 by .0066 inches, and in an area that the dots were actually this large, the ink would be solid, with no differentiation between dots. The opposite of this condition would be no dot at all, so that only the blank paper is visible. At these extremes, there will be no detail whatsoever, just pure white or black. Therefore, we almost never have any use for either of them.

The size of the dots we use is defined as a percentage of the largest possible, and can be read through the Info palette. A reading of 50 percent indicates that the final dot will fill half of the space that it would if we were printing solid black. Photoshop does not know, however, what that space is going to be, as the screening value is determined in the next step.

From Photoshop or some other application, we will now arrange to have an imagesetter set our dots. It is at this point that we specify screen ruling, and it is now that serious calibration must begin.

The Info palette told us that our dot was 50 percent. The 50 percent will carry through as an instruction to the imagesetter. Digital information doesn't deteriorate, so the file will also say 50 percent tomorrow.

Imagesetters, however, are fractious

beasts. The laser beams with which they write are subject to voltage fluctuations and change over time. The processors that develop their film must be maintained carefully. Variations in age and temperature of chemicals and in processing speed affect the density of the image.

Similarly, if film stripping or duplication is involved, a lot of things can go wrong. The duplication takes place in a vacuum frame, where final film is exposed through a high-intensity light source shining through the intermediate film. Once again, changes in light intensity, vacuum, length of exposure, and processing conditions will annihilate any hope of getting the same result the next day.

For these reasons, imagesetting and stripping companies go to great lengths to keep tabs on and control these factors. By and large they succeed in making their product repeatable and predictable.

From here on, however, chaos reigns. Even though we are still talking about black and white, we have reached the point where there is going to be enormous variation no matter what.

Paper and Dot Gain

Next to the question of whether the pressman is in a surly mood that day or is feeling mellow, the biggest variable is the paper that the image will be printed on. To get an idea of how big a deal this is, consider printing an image on newsprint, which is the worst paper in common use, versus printing it on the chemically coated stock used in this book. Figure 2.2 makes the comparison graphically.

There is a much smaller range of colors to work with. Newsprint is yellowish-gray, so whites cannot be as crisp as we would like. Nor, perhaps surprisingly, can blacks be as black: newsprint is porous, and the ink seeps into it. The book paper's coating resists this intrusion. We see more ink, and thus a richer black.

Much the same thing happens every morning when I go through my normal routine of spilling part of my cup of coffee on a copy of the *New York Times.* Most of the coffee gets absorbed by the newsprint. If I spilled the same amount of coffee on a page of this book, less would be absorbed. More important, the stained area would look smaller: as the newspaper absorbs coffee, the stain appears to spread.

It works the same way with ink. In the case of the *Times,* 65 little cups of coffee per inch are being spilled wherever a picture appears. Coffee spreads. So does ink. When coffee spreads, we just see an ugly stain. When ink spreads, we see a darker gray than we ought to.

This phenomenon, *dot gain,* happens on every press and every paper. Obviously, though, it happens to a greater extent in poorer-quality papers. It is also influenced by the speed of the press, the brand and color of ink, how tightly the blankets are mounted on the cylinder, the type of imagesetter that produced the final film, how heavily the pressman is running the ink, and how humid a day it is, among other things.

If you are thinking that it is impossible to predict with any precision how much dot gain there is going to be, you are exactly right. Certainly, images prepared for use on book paper would be grossly unacceptable if we tried to print them in a newspaper, but there are huge differences even among newspapers. *USA Today* has greater dot gain than the *Times,* which in turn has more than the *Wall Street Journal.* Your local paper is probably drastically different from any of the three.

Color Printing

Thanks largely to Photoshop, newspapers as well as the rest of the printed world are moving rapidly toward more color. Of course, adding color compounds the difficulties of predictability.

Just as black and white printing takes place without any gray ink, color printing does not employ a tutti-frutti technology that can magically produce any hue. Instead, images are reproduced using four separate hits of ink on four different units of the press. There is complete agreement throughout the graphic arts industry that the four colors should be cyan, magenta, yellow, and black. There is no agreement as to what order to print the inks in, and, as you might expect, the order makes a difference. Some printers think black should go down first, because there is less of it, so the sheet will not be as wet and tacky as it goes into the second unit. Others feel that the first, second, and third inks will inevitably work their way into the subsequent units, contaminating those inks. They therefore favor yellow first and black last.

Last, but certainly not least, of the many reasons that it is not possible to make generalized calibrations at the printing stage, *it is entirely normal, appropriate and correct for different units of the same press to have slightly different dot gains.* Generally, black ink has the highest dot gain and yellow the lowest, but press conditions can skew these even more.

Now that it has been established that presswork is very much a give-'em-what-

Figure 2.2 *Newspaper printing gives much flatter reproduction because of less of a color range (simulation below, left). Special handling of the image is necessary to compensate for newspaper dot gain. The same Photoshop file that yields the top image on coated paper will look approximately like the image at bottom right if printed in a newspaper.*

The Colorspace Conundrum

Throughout this book we will be dropping in and out of various colorspaces. This can be a confusing experience, to say the least, especially since Photoshop can express and alter its images in four different colorspaces, each of which may be the best one for certain circumstances.

A *colorspace* is a theoretical model that lets us designate a broad range of colors by manipulating various values or channels. The range is not necessarily all-inclusive: CMYK, which we use most of the time, has no way to define a bright blue, and why should it? That is not a color that can be reproduced on press, so CMYK has no use for it. RGB and HSB accommodate bright blue, but not fluorescent orange, metallics, or anything else that might be brighter than ambient light. LAB can handle those, but it is not clear what good that does us in Photoshop, since our monitor (being RGB) can't display them, nor can we print them.

Of more immediate use, a serious user has to be able to display and manipulate the individual channels in each space, but they all use radically different models. CMYK makes the most sense, in that when we make a channel darker it makes the overall image darker. In RGB, the overall image gets *lighter*. In LAB and HSB, one of the three channels would make the image darker, but the other two have variable effects.

CMYK is the easiest and best format for color correction, but local retouching is more efficient, if not superior, in one of the three-variable colorspaces. HSB and LAB contain a lightness channel that can be used as a kind of super black. Photoshop 3's sponge tool is a refugee from HSB's S channel, but it can be used to advantage in CMYK work. Even the mathematically difficult opponent-color scheme of LAB, described in Chapter 10, has color correction uses.

Although CMYK is the colorspace of printing, and therefore the one that we will be using most of the time, throwing images into a more favorable colorspace is— and has to be, given the disadvantages we labor under—part of our standard repertory.

we've-got-and-hope-for-the-best kind of process, the question becomes one of getting the printer something that can be matched. That does not mean an exact prediction of press conditions. As we have seen, that is impossible. What it does mean is that contract proofs have to be somewhere in the neighborhood of what the press can print.

To start with, if the contract proof is on a paper that is much whiter than the stock that will actually be used, forget about a match. A match is also impossible if there is a radical difference in dot gain from the contract proof to the press.

Accordingly, the manufacturers of contract proofs generally have six or more different methods: they can produce proofs that emulate low, medium, or heavy dot gain, and they can be made on white stock for commercial work, or slightly off-white to predict publication results.

In CMYK, the C Is for Cockeyed

The calibrationist buzzword of the day is *device-independent color*. The lofty goal is to create a system whereby a single digital file generates, within reason, color that looks exactly the same on monitor, conventional press, waterless press, color copier, ink-jet printer, and every other conceivable device. Such systems are always based on some color scheme other than CMYK, and LAB is currently fashionable for this purpose. Frequently, this is coupled with some sort of color management system that is supposed to guarantee accurate reproduction in scanning. Since this presupposes that one would want to *keep* color casts, flat-looking photos, etc., not all calibrationists accept that scan control is a good idea.

Excessive reliance on calibration is not limited to deranged color scientists, although they are the ones who carry it to extremes. Many professional scanner operators indulge in it, too, by scanning a stepped black and white test image along with the real art. They manipulate the scanner controls to ensure that the black and white piece does not take on any color cast, thinking that this will give them greater accuracy in the live art.

This method guarantees that if the original art itself has some kind of cast, the scanner will not correct it. And, if you agree with the general idea stated in the last chapter—don't match the art but rather the *meaning* of the art— this is the wrong way to scan. Whether an image that is objectively gray scans as gray is irrelevant. What is important is that the areas in the live image that the viewer would see as gray turn out that way.

When we digitize a photograph for printing, we smash it into a much smaller range of colors. Calibrationists tend to make the dubious assumption that we should swing the sledgehammer the same way at each image, in the name of precision and accuracy.

Unless we are lucky enough to have access to a high-end scanner, most images will be presented to us in RGB format. An unbelievable quantity of sweat has been lavished on the question of how best to take the file into CMYK. Photoshop's conversion algorithm is much maligned in calibrationist circles.

As an intellectual proposition, it is extremely difficult, to put it as mildly as

SWOP: Setting the Standards

Variable press and film conditions are a particular problem in magazine printing, where the contents of advertisements come from many sources and little adjusting can be done on press. Expansion of color advertising in the mid-1970s caused no end of anguish for magazine printers. In response, the graphic arts community more or less spontaneously formed a committee to define the standards that should be required of advertiser, prepress supplier, and printer.

The 1975 resulting recommendations, formally known as the Specifications for Web Offset Publications, were universally adopted within a few years. SWOP has been modified and reissued every few years to take account of changing technology, most recently in 1993. With industry backing, a nonprofit corporation, SWOP, Inc., now is in place to distribute the standards and keep them up to date. Professionals frequently refer to SWOP standards even when preparing color jobs for purposes other than magazines.

SWOP 1993 comprises forty pages of tightly packed technical information on such matters as how to measure dot gains, specific inking requirements, what types of proofs are acceptable, and so on. A number of cautions to designers who try to do impossible things with type are included. The most significant limitation it imposes on the Photoshop user is in shadow areas. SWOP mandates that the sum of the values of all four colors cannot be higher than 300 (adjusted by many magazines down to 280) and that no more than one color can print at 100 percent.

These restrictions do not necessarily apply to commercial printing, but they do have important ramifications in our choice of Photoshop Separation Setup, as discussed in Chapter 8.

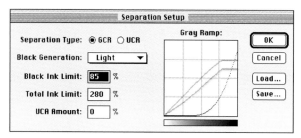

Figure 2.3 *Later color correction will be easier all around with this set of Separation Preferences.*

possible, in reconciling a conceptually perfect colorspace like RGB with CMYK, which is cockeyed and riddled with holes. The big problem in CMYK is that printing technology has not yet provided us with a reasonable cyan ink.

The cyan weakness explains why whenever we want to portray a neutral gray, we have to use more cyan ink than magenta or yellow. It accounts for why we need to have black ink available, to deepen shadows. Most importantly, it means that there is really no way of producing a decent blue on press. With today's process inks, we can attain quite a respectable orange, and there is nothing much wrong with our reds. But greens are second-rate and blues are a disaster area. If you doubt it, just thumb through the pages of this book and see how many brilliant blues you find. Or look at Figure 2.4 for one company's view of how few blues we can reproduce. When we mix magenta and yellow, we should, and we do, get red; when we mix yellow and cyan we should, and we do, get green, but when we mix magenta and cyan, it is an unequal struggle, and we wind up with a pallid purple instead of the desired blue.

Thus, forcing an image into CMYK inflicts grievous injury. It cannot be avoided, but we *can* fight back.

In color correction, we are engaged in battle against overwhelming odds. Our slim chance of success rests upon making the best use of our meager resources each and every time. To seize a strategic advantage we must exploit every possible way of attaining contrast, even if we have to sacrifice certain of our assets. We must be buccaneers, desperados.

This exploitationist position is anathema to the calibrationists, because it means that the "best" way to convert from other color spaces to CMYK is inconsequential. The opportunist will take a different approach to each image. In keeping with the philosophy of marshaling all available weapons, the opportunist also typically depends heavily upon one unavailable in RGB: the black plate. The mention of black in color correction arouses terror in the hearts and minds of calibrationists.

How, then, do we compensate for the bad blue when we make the conversion? One possible answer, and a serious one, is to pretend the problem does not exist. The gain of this approach is that all natural contrast is retained. The disadvantage is that richer blues will tend to go purple and cyans may appear too dirty. If blues and cyans are critical to the image, we can take the opposite tack in converting the image, muting the magenta and yellow to give the desired colors whatever strength we can.

Obviously, we can imagine pictures where either of the extreme approaches would be the right one. More likely, we will want to take some kind of compromise route, but exactly what we do will depend on the character of the image. If we are working with a good scanner operator and

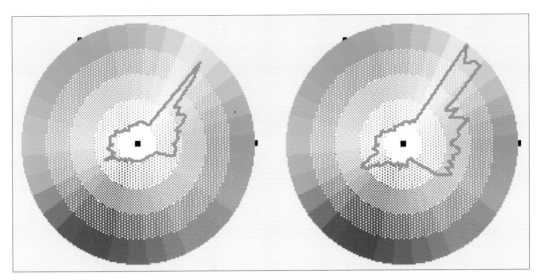

Figure 2.4 The areas outlined in red represent the views of a leading calibrationist company as to what parts of the RGB gamut can actually be printed under SWOP-standard conditions (left) and on a major brand of office composite color printer (right). In both, note the massive inability to print adequate blues and violets.

a high-end scanner, the CMYK images we get may not need much color correction. But if we start with RGB, some adjustment will help in almost every case. This is why Photoshop's conversion algorithm, for all the criticism it gets from the calibrationists, will do just fine for us.

Several user-definable variables alter the way the conversion takes place. The most important of these is shown in Figure 2.3. The functioning of this box will be discussed in Chapter 8, but for now let me strongly suggest that you adopt the values shown rather than Photoshop's default values. There are several reasons why these are better, of which the most important is that it is easier to manage the ensuing black when writing correction curves. But there will be times when we want something different. Before starting work, you should probably as a matter of course call up this dialog box (under **File: Preferences>Separation Setup**) to make

sure the desired values are still there.

In high-level color correction, there are times when it becomes necessary to convert a CMYK image to some other colorspace, usually LAB, in order to reconvert it back to CMYK using a different preferences setting. In some cases, it can even be right to separate the image in two different ways for a merge later.

Figure 2.5 demonstrates that we can get away with this sort of trickery. Well, once, maybe. Conversion between colorspaces is not an exact science. Every conversion decreases quality, slightly. Reconverting once is almost undetectable. At ten times, it is excruciatingly obvious.

Famous Last Words

When graphic arts professionals confront blown-out highlight areas like those of Figure 2.6, they shake their heads and smile knowingly, for the explanation is almost always the same.

Figure 2.5 *Some quality loss must be expected whenever an image changes color-space. Right, the original image. Bottom left, after conversion to RGB and then back to CMYK, the image is nearly identical. Bottom right, the image has been converted from CMYK to RGB and back again 10 times, and it is beginning to look the worse for wear.*

This type of color error strongly suggests that the operator believed the computer monitor rather than putting faith in the Info tool, where it properly belongs.

Once again, we find ourselves firing broadsides at the calibrationists. At least in the case of RGB-to-CMYK conversions, we could have sympathy for the bewildered professors who reject the swashbuckling approach to color in favor of wooden standards and certainties. When it comes to "calibrating" a screen to a printed sheet, however, science itself is against the scientists.

Like many Photoshoppers, I spent more for my monitor and its video card than my computer or my disk drives, so it isn't like I am overjoyed to say that it can't be trusted. But that's life; that's optics.

A screen that shines light into our eyes is simply too different from a piece of paper that reflects it. The most glaring — in both senses of the word — problem is in bright whites. The light of a monitor dazzles the viewer enough so that it is extremely difficult to tell the absolute white that yields the unacceptable zero highlight of the top of Figure 2.6 from the optimal 5C2M2Y of the bottom. There is no substitute, therefore, for sweeping the Info tool over the entire area to see if any of it is getting zeroed out.

The popular knock against color monitors is that they are RGB devices (if you don't believe it, look at one closely, and you'll see the red, green, and blue phosphors) trying to live in a CMYK world. This

Figure 2.6 *Monitors have difficulty differentiating very light colors, so it is not surprising to learn that these two versions look almost identical on screen—but there is quite a difference when ink hits paper.*

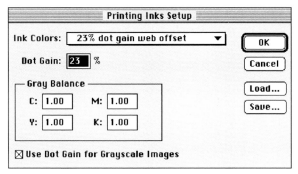

Figure 2.7 *Photoshop's compensation for dot gain. Altering these values will not affect output, but they change the way the monitor shows color, and will alter the results when Photoshop converts into CMYK from other colorspaces.*

The technology falls flat, however, in light or dark areas, where it is impossible to tell whether the value is acceptable for printing. It falls even flatter, along the lines of a pancake that has been run over by a steamroller, in portraying neutral grays.

This last problem is not going to go away. As previously discussed, our visual systems tend to reject color casts and to see what we expect to be gray *as* gray, regardless of ambient lighting conditions. This statement is not idle speculation based on personal experience, but proven science of such authority and long standing that in stating it I almost feel like I could come out for calibration. Scientists do not know exactly why and how this effect takes place. Either the eyes physically adjust to the lighting conditions, or the

is not actually so horrible. Today's monitors do quite a good job in emulating most colors, and if you are reasonably careful you can trust your screen about the greens of plants, the reds of autumn, and so forth.

Dot Gain: The Numbers, the Newspapers

Compensating for dot gain is haphazard at best, in view of all the possible things that can happen in the pressroom. It is compounded by a measurement system that is not exactly easy to understand.

The industry-standard way of referring to dot gain, which Photoshop joins in, is in terms of a percentage. Remarkably, it is not a percentage at all, but an almost meaningless number. Twenty percent dot gain means that if you send over an area that is defined as 50 percent, by the time it is printed it will look to the viewer like 70 percent (50 plus 20) would look, if this were a perfect world. Clear? In this system, 15 percent dot gain is nearly impossibly good and 35 percent unthinkably high. It does explain, though, why values higher than 80 percent in commercial printing and 70 percent in newspapers are apt to appear solid.

Photoshop does try to compensate for the fact that not all colors of ink are believed to have the same dot gains. A bigger problem, however, is that since dot gain is always measured at 50 percent, there is no way of taking into account situations where it is much greater at lower values. This is particularly true of newspaper printing, where apparent gain is greatest in the lighter ranges. Many newspapers are faced with the double whammy of high dot gain in highlights and a high minimum dot value (frequently 5 percent is the smallest that can be held). Under the circumstances, the use of zero ink coverage can be permitted much more than it is in other work. A value of zero is acceptable in almost all bright whites. And in creating bright, cheerful colors, such as blue skies, allowing the unwanted color, yellow, to drop out altogether is standard practice. Otherwise, the blue will appear muddier than Photoshop's display will indicate, due to the unexpectedly high gain in lighter values.

brain filters the data to satisfy its preconceived notion of what is gray. Or perhaps the two work in tandem. One way or another, the phenomenon is known as *chromatic adaptation.* It is extremely well documented. The first scientific papers on it date back to the 1850s.

What this means is, before laying out a small fortune on some system that purports to make your monitor a precise predictor of what will happen on press, ask yourself whether all that expensive subtlety is really necessary, considering it is incontrovertible that when you stare at a monitor, your color perception changes. If you stare at a screen that is showing approximately gray, it will become absolutely gray for you very shortly.

Relying on a monitor, however expensive, for sensitive color judgments is strictly for the squirrels. It is possible to make professional-level color corrections in Photoshop on a black and white monitor; give it a try sometime, or check out the last few pages of Chapter 4 if you'd rather. Meanwhile, if you want a screen that is *reasonably* accurate, the best way is to obtain a contract proof of some Photoshop file that is resident in your computer and has a broad gamut of colors. Every day, open up the file, compare it to the proof, and make adjustments if needed.

If there is a large variation, this can be adjusted using Photoshop's Gamma extension, or by adjusting the Monitor Setup and/or Printing Inks setup (which compensates for dot gain) shown in Figure 2.7. Once you have gotten reasonably close, close the file, sit up very straight in your chair, open your mouth wide, and say, "I will never make color judgments based on what I think I see on my monitor."

Why Not an RGB Press?

One of the more puzzling questions for the graphic arts student is, given the apparent superiority of the RGB colorspace, and given that the human eye is believed to perceive red, green, and blue as the primary colors, why don't printers use RGB (or even RGBK) inks rather than CMYK?

Well, mainly, if you only have red, green, and blue inks on your press, how are you going to print a yellow? An orange?

Red, green, and blue light is what our eyes react to. The ink on paper is merely used to manipulate it. We use magenta, for example, because it governs the amount of green light that reflects from the page. The more magenta, the less green light. Meanwhile, magenta has little to no impact on red or blue light, reflecting substantially all of it back to our eyes.

Thus, each process color is used to control one of the primaries. The problem with using red as an ink is that it controls *two.* Red ink would block out both blue and green light. Using such inks would make it impossible to reproduce colors that are formed when only one flavor of light is absent. One perceives yellow when red and green light reflects from the printed page. If all of our inks blocked two of the three colors, we would be out of business.

In short, we use CMY inks because they can be used to form R, G, or B, whereas R,G, and B would not be able to form C, M, or Y.

This technique is a surefire preventive against the kind of neutral-color problem shown in Figure 2.6.

The Eye Is the Arbiter

In many ways color science is a precise field. The spectrophotometers and other instruments that are used to measure color are outstandingly accurate, and

Quick & Dirty

CALIBRATIONISM VS. OPPORTUNISM

✓Calibration and repeatability are laudable goals, but we have to examine the entire process to see where they are appropriate. Certain parts can and should be made repeatable; certain other parts should, but cannot be; and certain others can be, but should not.

✓Professional users do not rely on screen representations of what color will look like. Rather, they trust the numbers reflected in Photoshop's Info palette.

✓It is theoretically nearly impossible to so calibrate a monitor that we would be able to judge whether colors intended to be neutral would actually print that way. Human color perception changes when staring into a light source, such as a monitor.

✓CMYK is a weirdly shaped colorspace because of the weakness of the cyan ink. Although reasonable oranges and reds are possible, blues are quite poor. It is difficult to reconcile this with a colorspace like RGB,which is conceptually perfect and which may contain brilliant blues. There cannot be one best method of converting from RGB to CMYK: it will depend on how prominent the blues are.

✓When conversion to CMYK may present a problem, turn on Photoshop's 3's gamut alarm. For areas that need to be toned down prior to conversion, consider use of the sponge tool.

✓There is great variation between printing characteristics of different presses or even units of the same press. Furthermore, print quality is influenced by weather conditions, when the inks were mixed, the mood of the pressmen, and many other extrinsic factors.

✓Because of the unpredictability of the process, printers adjust their presses on each job to try to match a high-quality client-supplied proof. There is no such thing as just running a file. They generally will not accept a job without such a contract proof, which should be approximately accurate for dot gain and for whiteness of stock.

✓The Pantone Matching System is the industry-standard method of specifying spot colors. However, if you are using the CMYK inks to emulate a PMS color, be aware that there can be a considerable difference.

there are several well-proven, mathematically sensible models that can portray nearly any color.

It must be quite a blow to spend so much energy studying a subject and then come to realize that anarchy reigns. It's bad enough that presswork is so unpredictable, but what must really gall the calibrationists is the idea that ad hoc decisions are the best way in scanning and in RGB-CMYK conversions, when there apparently exist reliable, repeatable, scientifically accurate methods of matching the art.

And yet, here is a concession of defeat from the leading academic authority on color:

"Always remember that nobody accepts or rejects for color because of numbers: it is the way it looks that counts.…Properly applied, the instrument can extend the usefulness of the eye. The eye is the final arbiter; the instrument, the aid…no one can deny that it is the visual appearance that counts at the bottom line."

You betcha. And, by visual appearance, we usually mean, those qualities that make the viewer say, "Ah! Lifelike!"

So, in summary, what we need to do is make the image look more like what a human observer would see and less like camerawork. At the risk of being repetitive, we need not match the art, but match the art's meaning.

The major areas for consideration are:
• In dark environments, the human visual system adjusts and sees everything as lighter, but the camera does not.
• If ambient lighting conditions favor one color, humans won't notice, but the camera will.
• If similar colors are in close proximity, human beings will see more difference in the colors than is actually there, but the camera will lump everything together.
• The human visual apparatus sharply reduces the perceived intensity of reflected flashes of light, but the camera puts in catchlights wherever it sees them.
• When humans concentrate on a single object, that object gains contrast and everything else loses it, but the camera is egalitarian.

Altering images to accord with the realities of human perception is possible, but not by any calibration algorithm. We must look at each picture as the individual opponent that it is, and we must take cutlass in hand, if necessary, to seize it and bend it to our will.

Figure 3.1 *The amount of detail that a top-quality scanner can pull out of a 35mm slide is astounding. The large picture is a little grainy, which is what you might expect for a scan done at nearly 10,000 samples per inch.*

CHAPTER 3

Scanning, Screening, Resolution

Today's Photoshop practitioner gets digital images from many sources, and at many prices and quality levels. Once they're in the system, though, a baffling series of numerical guidelines come into play. Here's the spots per inch lowdown, for scanning, monitors, imagesetting, and printing.

Before entering the exciting world of color correction, it helps to have something to correct. This chapter discusses the various means of acquiring an image and making sure it is in the form best suited for reproduction.

This is also a chapter about dots per inch or spots per inch or samples per inch or lines per inch, which mean the same things to some of us but not to others, and what the appropriate measurements should be for monitor, scan, screen, and imagesetting. After that, we will briefly hit the controversial topics of screening technologies and moiré avoidance techniques.

Photoshop has the happy capability of being able to read nearly any graphic format (except for RIFF, the native format of its competitor, ColorStudio). Once Photoshop has the data in one format, it can convert it freely into most others.

There are several common formats for graphic images, and we will cover their pros and cons briefly before exploring the many ways of obtaining the images and converting them into digital form.

• **Tagged Image File Format**, or TIFF, comes in several different flavors and is the most common format for printing and information interchange. TIFFs can be grayscale, RGB, CMYK, or bitmap. In Photoshop, we can save TIFFs in either Mac or PC format regardless of what type of computer we use, and we can also save disk space by compressing them with an industry-standard stuffing algorithm known as LZW. This takes time and renders the files unprintable until they are decompressed.

The TIFF format is stable in Photoshop use, but there have been some isolated problems involving other programs. One of the most notorious involves dropping TIFF images that are either silhouetted or have light edges into the page-layout program QuarkXPress, hereinafter QXP. Quark uses a picture box for placing such an image, and the color, or lack thereof, of the box's background ought to make no difference. Regrettably, if the QXP user selects "none" as the background color, the silhouetted TIFF will become unacceptably ragged around the edges. The solution is to use a box with either a "white" or a "0% black" background, or, if that is not possible, to convert the TIFF into:

• **Encapsulated PostScript**, or EPS, the standard method of exchanging illustrations and photographs between applications. In principle, Photoshop can read EPS line graphics as well as photographs. In practice, the files had better emanate from its sister application, Adobe Illustrator, and even then it had best not contain a blend. Fortunately, most illustration programs export their product in a form that Illustrator can read, and if Illustrator can

open and save the file, Photoshop will be able to read it.

• There is an EPS variant known as **Desktop Color Separation**, or DCS, a.k.a. five-file EPS. This format was originally proposed by Quark as a means of speeding up imaging of files, which it does. The image is in fact broken into five pieces: the four printing colors, plus a smaller placeholder file that other applications use for positioning. At the moment, only QXP and its competitor, Aldus PageMaker, are very happy about dealing with this format. Importing it into anything else, such as Illustrator, will cause no end of trouble.

Standard or composite, EPS files are even more stable than TIFFs, but they also take up more disk space. For peace of mind, I have always used composite EPS as my prime file format. When I signed the contract for this book, however, I found it necessary to purchase a 2.5 gigabyte hard drive, which I stupidly imagined would be sufficient for the project. Midway through, I became a sudden convert to TIFF.

• Native **Photoshop** format has become an industry interchange standard that most competing applications can read. Photoshop 2.0 format is slightly faster than 3.0 but takes up more space. The advantage of either format is that Photoshop opens and saves it more quickly than the others. Also, Photoshop 3 can compress mask channels colossally. If you are in the habit of making masks and saving them as channels within a Photoshop document, you should consider saving them as separate Photoshop 3.0 files. They will take up almost no space (as opposed to TIFF, for example, which would be just as large on disk as any other channel.) Photoshop 3.0 format files *can,* incidentally, be opened in Photoshop 2.5, unless they have active layers, which 2.5 does not support.

Other programs cannot print Photoshop-format files, but that is a blessing in disguise for organization purposes. For this chapter, for example, I have on my computer about a dozen different versions of the shot of London's Tower Bridge, because I wanted to save certain intermediate versions that are not supposed to appear here. And they *will* not, either; since it is easy to pick up the wrong version of similar images by mistake, I have made it impossible for myself to do so by the simple expedient of saving the non-printing images in Photoshop format and the others as TIFFs.

Other File Formats

If all you are concerned with is printing, you will never need to save a file in any format other than the ones named above. You should most emphatically not use the antiquated and error-prone PICT format, which is the normal format for simple bitmap images on the Macintosh. The pictures of the various Photoshop menus in this book, for example, were PICT files in RGB mode when I captured them from my monitor. Since I am printing out of QXP, which cannot place PICT files accurately, I was obliged to take all the files and convert them to CMYK, then save them as TIFFs in Photoshop.

If disk space is at a real premium, you may wish to save files in the format of the Joint Photographic Experts Group, which compresses them drastically. Unlike the LZW compression available for TIFFs, which when decompressed gives exactly the same image as the original, JPEG, in trying to conserve as much space as possible, actually discards information it hopes will not make a difference to overall quality. When decompressed, therefore, the image will not be quite the same. The higher the original compression, the worse the final quality.

If you like to exchange low-resolution images in on-line services, you may find a use for CompuServe's Graphic Interchange Format, or GIF. It has no real purpose in professional imaging.

Some formats, such as Scitex CT, are useful only in exchanging with products of a specific vendor. Others, of which the best-known example is TWAIN, have technical advantages that may make them more prominent in coming years. TWAIN, incidentally, stands for Technology Without An Interesting Name. This is an example of programmer humor.

One format that we will certainly be seeing a lot of is Kodak Photo CD, which is rapidly becoming a standard. Photoshop can open images in this format, but must save them as something else. There is also a separate utility available from Kodak that may be somewhat more efficient. Photoshop's method requires a fair amount of random access memory, especially at the highest of Kodak's five resolutions. Computers with limited RAM can take up to half an hour to open one high-resolution PCD image, if they can do it at all. Full discussion of the format is in Chapter 10.

Image Sources

The images we work with come into one of these formats from many different sources. Easiest for us are images that are already digitized: if we purchase a CD full of stock photos, all we have to do is open them and live happily ever after. Adobe gives us a couple of free images to play with as part of the Photoshop package, and it is also possible to obtain digitized images from a previous user.

If we have access to a digital camera, we can click the shutter and deposit images directly into our computer. Less expensive models, such as Apple's Quick-Take, don't really give us enough resolu-tion for print work, but higher-end digital cameras emphatically do, as demon-strated in Chapter 10.

With one of many video-capture add-on products, we can grab video images, even directly from a television broadcast, but there will not be enough resolution for quality printing, and there will also be copyright-infringement issues to consider.

But in the majority of cases, we will have some photo that was taken by a camera that uses good old film, and now we have to digitize it. Some-times we will get a color print, sometimes a negative, some-times a positive transparency.

In the latter two scenarios, we have the option of taking the film to our local Kodak CD shop and having them put the image on disk for us. This is a very inexpensive and reason-ably high-quality process.

If we choose to scan using more conventional technology, there are several quality levels to choose from. At the top of the line are an elite group of scanners that mount their im-ages on a rapidly spinning drum. The technology is vin-tage 1975 and largely analog, but boy, is it good. Light shin-ing through, or bouncing off, the original artwork hits a de-vice called a photomultiplier

Figure 3.2 *This print was yellowed with age, as accurately captured by a desktop scanner (top), but a high-end scanner can discard even such severe color casts.*

that emits an electric current whose intensity depends on what it saw.

The skills of this device's operator are crucial. In addition to being able to impose general input-output curves in the same way we do, such scanners have selective color-correction somewhat better than Photoshop 3 and considerably superior to that of previous versions. They also outperform Photoshop in unsharp masking, where they make a separate scan for additional accuracy, and in the generation of an accurate black plate through gray component replacement. Although the scan is in RGB mode at first, an onboard computer converts it to CMYK, and that is what we get as final output. All of them are capable of scanning at extremely high resolutions, as you may have gathered from Figure 3.1.

The three leading manufacturers of these impressive machines form a veritable United Nations. Dainippon Screen, or DS, is Japanese. The German company of Dr. Rudolf Hell Ing. is now affiliated with the traditional typesetting firm, Linotype, which is also headquartered in Germany. And Crosfield Electronics, which is English, is now owned by DuPont.

High-End Scanning

In the right hands, these scanners have an overwhelming quality advantage over any competition. They can, however, cost close to $100,000, not exactly chump change for the desktop artist. If you have

Figure 3.3 *Properly handled, a good scanner finds color and detail in the most awful originals. This snapshot came from a disposable camera, and the lighting conditions and subject matter are quite difficult. The desktop scan, (top), matches the print.*

to buy such scans from an outside vendor, be prepared to dig deep into the wallet.

More than that, there is a shortage of good operators. As prepress has become more decentralized, and more fringe companies have become involved, the secrets of making a good scan have largely been forgotten. As they are exactly the same manipulation techniques described in the remainder of this book, if you understand them you will not only be good at color correction in Photoshop but you will be a better high-end scanner operator than 90 percent of those currently so employed. It is not difficult to learn to mount art on the drum, get it in focus, set resolution, and hit the start button. If your scanner operator doesn't take quality control much further than this, you will still get a reasonable image because of the device's outstanding optics, but it is a heartrending waste of a good machine.

At the lower end of the quality spectrum are desktop and hand-held scanners. Upwards of a dozen vendors market these and prices start in three figures. In recent years quality has greatly improved and prices have come down, a trend that can be expected to continue.

All of these flatbed machines scan with light-sensitive semiconductor arrays known as Charge-Coupled Devices (CCDs). All can handle prints and other flat art, and some have add-ons to allow scanning of transparencies.

Such scanners generally cannot be adjusted for individual colors, and are incapable of unsharp masking. These corrections become our responsibility with Photoshop. Also, they all suffer from a major weakness: for technical reasons, CCDs have a lot of difficulty with darker tones. When an image has important detail in shadow areas, CCD scanning is a poor choice.

Paradoxically, the worse the original image, the more we may need the help of a good scanner. Figures 3.2 and 3.3 show how a high-end scanner can compensate for really poor originals. Both shots were scanned from prints. In the case of the castle in Spain, the photograph had yellowed badly with age, as accurately portrayed in the desktop scan. The high-end scanner laughed this off. The image of Badlands National Park in South Dakota was taken, ugh, with a disposable camera, and the print was about as flat and amateurish as could possibly be. Again, the desktop scan is a better representation of the miserable state of the original art, and again intelligent drum scanner settings saved the day.

Figure 3.4 gives an even better representation of the strengths and weaknesses of CCD-based technology. This image comes not from a desktop scanner but from a digital camera. The box of chocolates was photographed in studio conditions. On the whole it is an impressively detailed image (the color balance is perfect, and look at the texture in the golden package) but there are some problems. The pieces of chocolate at top left and upper right are very dark, and the CCD camera, displaying its weakness in shadow areas, has lost most of the detail. With considerable effort, we can isolate these areas and fix them up, and we will in Chapter 10. But a photomultiplier scanner would not have gotten us into this mess in the first place.

There exists a growing third class of scanners: stripped-down drum scanners

Figure 3.4 *This photograph was taken by a digital camera that dumped data directly into a computer, without film or conventional scanning. In spite of the impressive overall look, it displays the typical problem that CCD-based devices have in dark areas. The chocolates at top left and upper right have lost almost all detail.*

using photomultiplier technology, but without all of the sharpening and color correction tools of the behemoths. These midrange scanners cost less than $50,000. In about 90 percent of all cases, in my opinion, they produce scans that are every bit as good as those of their more expensive relatives. There is often a limitation on the size of the original, however.

Resolution Defined

According to my search-and-replace utility, I have thus far used the word *resolution* eight times in this chapter, without ever bothering to define it. Since much of the rest of this chapter is devoted to exploding the myth that resolution equals

quality, an overview of the topic is now necessary.

Before we geek types get our hands on it, a conventional photograph is *continuous-tone*. The film that the photographers use is coated with light-sensitive molecules of silver halides. When exposed to light, some of these molecules will change color and others not, but, with molecules being as small as they are, we cannot perceive this. We see one smooth range of tone, not a bunch of dots.

Once converted for use in the digital age, however, the image is truncated in several ways. We cannot address a space even remotely as small as a molecule. We describe the limitations of our work under the general heading of resolution, which at some stages we can adjust and at other stages not. In the United States, resolution is expressed in the number of spots, samples, dots, pixels, or whatnots per inch, whereas in most of the rest of the world the standard is whatnots per millimeter.

When a scanner goes to work, its opinion of an image will be governed by small samples. A desktop scanner may look at 300 tiny samples per inch of original picture. For each, it records the color it sees and eventually gives that information to Photoshop. Each sample, for Photoshop's purposes, is a pixel: if you blow up the image as much as possible on the monitor, the square shapes of these individual color samples become clearly visible.

Most people sloppily refer to this as a 300-dpi scan, meaning dots per inch, although pixels, samples, or spots would be less ambiguous. Nevertheless, I will reluctantly accede to the general custom and call it 300 dpi henceforth.

The figure of 300 is usually adjustable at the time of the scan, sometimes to extremely high numbers, as in Figure 3.1. It is also adjustable in Photoshop using **Image: Image Size**, but it is dangerous to do so unless you know what you are doing.

Confusingly, there are other resolutions that will affect how the image is handled. First, the computer monitor has its own resolution: its phosphors fire at a fixed frequency of, usually, 72 spots per inch. This means that when it is displaying an image that is at, say, 300 dpi, it has to average out much of the picture to fit its own technical limitations. So, one cannot tell by looking at a same-size monitor rendition whether an image is grainy, or has dirt or scratches on it; these things may

have been temporarily interpolated away, but they will reappear in print. We therefore have to blow each picture up on screen to compensate for the lack of resolution. Often this will result in an image that is much bigger than the screen, so that we have to scroll around to examine every part of it.

Upon hitting the print key, the resolution of the imagesetter becomes a factor. Laser printers tend to have a resolution of 300 dpi as well, although this is thankfully getting higher. In other words, the printer can put down spots of black toner $\frac{1}{300}$ by $\frac{1}{300}$ of an inch, or it can leave the spots blank. Its big brothers, graphic arts imagesetters, work in the same way, but at much higher resolutions, and using photographic paper or film, which is vastly more accurate than plain paper and toner.

Most imagesetters today have at least two resolution choices. The device upon which this book is imaged, being European, offers resolutions of 100, 200, or 300 spots per millimeter (1270, 2540, or 3810 dpi). Intermediate values are not possible.

Which scanning and imagesetting resolution to use depends heavily on the final type of dpi in the process: how many dots per inch will be laid down on press.

Resolution and File Size

Keeping resolutions within reason is important. The big gain is in productivity, but, contrary to what most graphic neophytes seem to believe, excessive resolution actually hurts quality in many cases.

Three hundred seems like such a small number that we don't realize how rapidly it adds up. Consider an 8×10 inch image, sampled at a resolution of 300 dpi and brought into Photoshop.

Each of the individual samples, or pixels, now portrays one of 256 values. The number 256 is of considerable importance, since it is the maximum number of color steps that the PostScript language can support. When we reproduce a black and white image, we want to be able to portray a smooth range of grays. PostScript confines us to 256 flavors, but that is plenty for convincing colors.

There are, after all, four different channels in a CMYK document. Each one has 256 conceivable values. That translates to 4,294,967,296 possible combinations. Because most of these colors theoretically duplicate one another, as we will see in our discussion of GCR in Chapter 8, we should probably round the figure down to a couple of hundred million. This is a lot more colors than human beings can actually perceive.

The number 256 is chosen as opposed to 314, 177.5, or the square root of 19 because 256, being 2 to the eighth power, is very conveniently handled by binary devices such as computers. If you have an array of eight bits that can either be zeroes or ones, there are 256 possible combinations. The eight-bit combination has so many applications in computing that it merits a special name: eight bits is a *byte*. We need one byte for each of our samples.

Doesn't sound like much, but watch it add up. Since we are working with four colors, we have four channels in our image, and each one needs a byte to define which one of the 256 possible levels of magenta or whatever it is trying to depict. So, we are up to four bytes per sample.

300 dpi means 300 samples in *each* direction. For one square inch, that's 300 samples across and 300 down, a total of 90,000 samples. Multiplying this by the four colors makes 360K bytes per square inch of image. An 8×10 image has 80 square inches. That makes approximately 30 *million* bytes, or slightly more than 28 megabytes on disk. If you want to know how much information that is, if you open up your word processor and proceed to type the complete works of Shakespeare, you will have only about 5 megabytes when you are done.

Ouch.

Even in today's world of cheap storage, 28 megs clogs our hard disk, slows down Photoshop and lays a big performance hit on our imagesetter. Thankfully, small reductions in resolution can have big effects in relieving systemic bloat.

For example, if resolution is cut by 10 percent, to 270 samples per inch, one might think this would reduce file size by 10 percent as well. Actually, it cuts it by around twice that. There will be 72,900 samples per square inch, not 90,000; the final file size will be 22.7 megs, not 28.2. If we could cut resolution to 250, the file size would be 19.5 megs; at 200, it would be only 12.5.

What Is the Right Resolution?

Obviously, it pays to reduce resolution. The question must be what the impact will be on image quality. Shockingly, cutting resolution often *increases* it.

Start with the press. There is a widespread belief that the higher the screen ruling, the better. Let us give this issue a little airing.

The point of screening is to fool the viewer into imagining grays where there is really only black ink and white paper. To the extent the viewer perceives dots, the ruse is not successful. Therefore, the dots should be as unobtrusive as possible.

That seems clear enough, but it doesn't mean we should go out and start printing everything with a 200-line screen, the way a lot of knuckleheads do. Trouble is, the smaller the dots, the harder they are to print. If the dots are on the cusp of what the process can tolerate, the following unpleasant things start to happen.

• Darker areas tend to plug up, resulting in a perceived lower maximum shadow.

• The minimum acceptable highlight dot goes up; at some point a dot simply becomes too tiny for the plate and the blanket to hold. Overall, the highlight will become inconsistent.

• The image will begin to appear soft as transition areas become less distinct.

• Dot gain will appear to increase.

Now, at what point does all this nastiness start to kick in? In newspaper printing, as a rule it happens at about 100, so most newspapers print with an 85-line screen and 65-line is not uncommon. Some, however, do use a 100-line screen and I know of at least one that has successfully used 120 lines.

As paper starts to get a little better and as we migrate to commercial presses, the tolerance goes up. Reasonable uncoated papers can easily hold a 120-line screen and there can be some success with 133.

Magazines that use coated paper generally use 133, but some try 150, and most will accept ads with a 150-line screen.

High-quality commercial printing, such as annual reports, uses more expensive coated papers and usually is done at 175, sometimes even 200. And waterless offset, a relatively new approach, appears to make it much easier to hold small dots.

There have been successful uses of a 300-line screen with this technology.

The sad truth is that many printers overstate their own capabilities. A large part of my career has involved preparing color ads for reproduction in national magazines. The screen ruling is almost always either 133 or 150, and most magazines will accept either. My observation is that overall the 133 group has had a considerable quality edge.

Granted that smaller dots can lead to printing problems, there is much more of a case for finer screens when printing black and white than color. First of all, there are four times as many dots to distract the viewer. More important, *the larger dots in color printing are not black,* but rather softer colors that are much harder to focus on. If you doubt the impact of this, turn to Chapter 12, where there are a number of color and B/W images side by side, and see if you don't think that the B/W screening is much more pronounced.

For these reasons, I suggest that you be conservative in specifying your screen ruling for color printing. The decision process we went through in the production of this book may serve as an example. 150 is more or less the industry standard for book work, but then again, most books are black and white, where the screening is more pronounced. The printer chosen for *Professional Photoshop* offered us either 133 or 150, and having been bitten in the behind once too often by printers who claim to be able to deal with 150, I held out for 133. (It would, of course, have been suicide for the printer to suggest to as valuable a client as John Wiley & Sons that 150 might be too difficult.)

Figure 3.5 *A finer screen ruling ought to look better, but not if the dots are so small that the press has difficulty holding them. Clockwise from upper left, the same image with a 85-line, 133-line, 150-line, and 200-line screen. For jobs like this book, industry standards suggest 133 or 150.*

On the other hand, I had been having some imagesetting problems at 133, so there was a case to be made for 150, but we finally decided to stick with 133. In Figure 3.5, you will find out whether we

Speaking the Scitex Language

If someone refers to an image being at *res 8,* you are hearing terminology of Scitex, Inc., the overwhelming market leader in large image management systems for professional prepress.

Being an Israeli company, Scitex employs metric designations, so its rulings are in spots per millimeter rather than per inch. Res 8 is, therefore, what we would call 232 dpi. Res 10 is 254 dpi and Res 12 is 305 dpi. Scitex files must be at exactly one of these resolutions to be imaged. This means that if your Photoshop files are going to be output through a Scitex system, it is a total waste of effort to work at very high resolutions, since the Scitex system will have to resample them. This resampling will almost invariably be downward, because Scitex does not believe in excessive resolution, recommending about 1.6 times the screen value.

Other Scitex terms that may cause confusion: they, stubbornly logical, abbreviate Black with a B, so their colorspace is *CMYB.* Their picture files are called *CT* (for continuous-tone); these are merged with *LW* (for linework) files, which contain type and similar graphics. PostScript page layout files enter a Scitex system through a conversion process known as a *Gateway.* Once converted, the type can no longer be edited, so if any changes are needed the whole process starts from scratch.

Scitex LW files, therefore, are useless to anyone without a Scitex system, but Photoshop can both read and write in Scitex CT format. Some Scitex users tend to refer to a Photoshop image in any format as *a CT,* which may be confusing, although it makes perfect sense.

were right. The images are screened at 85, 133, 150, and 200. The 85 and the 200 are ridiculous extremes; one is pointlessly coarse and the other, I am confident, will wind up an unholy mess.

So, why do you have to be the judge? Why can't I tell you whether the 133 or the 150 came out better? Simple. Contract proofs have no difficulty even with 200-line screens. On mine, the 200-liner looks like the best of the bunch.

Imagesetter and Scanner Resolution

Another danger in specifying too fine a screen is that it may overreach the capabilities of the imagesetter. A little arithmetic will tell whether this is the case.

PostScript, as we said, supports 256 different flavors of each color. If the imagesetter cannot produce at least that many, quality will suffer.

That means that for each area that may comprise a printing dot, the imagesetter should have at least 16 of its own spots available in each direction. If it does, there will be 16 times 16 possibilities for each dot, which is, neatly, 256.

If we are using a 133-line screen, therefore, imagesetter resolution should be at least 133 times 16, which is 2128. For 150 it should be 2400 and for 175 at least 2800. Having greater resolution does not hurt but neither does it help. It would therefore be foolish to image this book at 3600, since 2400 is sufficient. However, persons who cannot image at higher than 2400 should not be using 175-line screens. The imagesetter will *produce* a 175-line screen on request, mind you, but printed quality will be better with 150.

Last, we consider the resolution of the image, a highly controversial topic, and

Figure 3.6 *The perils of over-resolution show up in two more versions of London's Tower Bridge. At left, a high-quality scan at 250 dpi at the enlarged size. Top left: the same picture, the same scanner, the same dpi, different magnification. And at top right, the version on the left, down-sampled by BiCubic interpolation in Photoshop to match the resolution of the smaller shot. That is a better quality choice than outputting it at 25 percent of original size. Below left, the two smaller pictures upsized (Nearest Neighbor interpolation to retain the pixel characteristics) show why the image scanned to proper size is better than the one with four times the resolution. And at bottom right, the same 35mm image upsampled again, this time using BiCubic interpolation.*

one that the Photoshop user must be intimately familar with.

The industry consensus is that the appropriate resolution is between 1.5 and 2.0 times the eventual screen ruling, times the enlargement of the image. A few people hold out for more or for less, but they are a distinct minority. If you accept the general view, then for 150-line screen work, resolution should be between 225 and 300 dpi. More than that simply wastes disk space and imaging time.

Excessive resolution can also affect the quality of the image in ways that are not always agreeable. Since there are always more image samples than halftone dots, some kind of averaging process is going to take place. The greater the ratio of samples to dots, the more averaging. From this, it is no great leap to realize the point demonstrated clearly in Figure 3.6, that higher resolutions tend to result in a smoother, or, if you like, a softer look.

To see why, consider another imaginary image. Please conjure up an image of the face of a dark-haired man who has not shaved in 24 hours. Suppose we wish to accentuate his stubble. Should we scan at a relatively low resolution, or a high one?

You might think that a higher resolution would capture more detail. That would be correct. You might think it would follow that the higher resolution would show more beard. That would be false. Do you see why?

First of all, forget the idea of seeing individual whiskers. There is no chance whatever that objects so small could be shown with any accuracy on press. Instead, the image, if it is effective, will *suggest* stubble by portraying an irregular, black-speckled pattern in the face.

When the scanner passes over this face, it will see black if it happens to sample a whisker, and pink if it does not. So, individual pixels may be drastically different. But the more we average them, the closer they will become. Say we are printing with a 150-line screen, and scanning at 300 dpi. In this case, each halftone dot will be based on the average of four scanning samples. But if we scan at 600 dpi, it will be based on the average of 16. Each 16-sample element will be a lot closer to a uniform flesh tone than would be the case if there were only four samples. At the lower resolution, we will not be able to detect what is going on in the face, but we will see that *something* is going on, and we will read beard.

This analysis is confirmed by Figure 3.6. You will probably agree that the better of the two images at 35mm size is the one that was originally scanned for that purpose. The one with four times as much resolution looks too soft. Unsharp masking prior to the reduction in resolution, as discussed in Chapter 7, would have helped, but not enough.

The image was resampled down to the correct resolution using Photoshop's best-quality method, BiCubic interpolation (this method is established under **Edit: Preferences>General**). Changing back to the low-quality resampling method, Nearest Neighbor (which will hold the shape of the pixels as the file gets bigger), we can resample the two images back up and compare what is happening to them.

A good look at the pixel pattern makes it clear that while excessive resolution has certain problems, it also has some advantages. The diagonal lines of the outside of the structure are less jagged and more realistic in the image that was originally at the higher resolution. As against that, the interior seems to lack life. The lower resolution version is more irregular, suggesting action.

These findings suggest a selective approach to scan resolution. Stay with the 1.5 to 2.0 times screen ruling guideline, but be prepared to go up when it is important to achieve a smoother look. Examples of when this might be desirable:

• When doing advertising for furniture or for computers, where the featured objects tend to have diagonal lines that might turn out too harsh and jagged at lower resolution.

• When portraying skintones that we want to be as smooth as possible.

• When the image involves type.

• When there is a good chance that the image may have to be resized upward (it being a lot easier to cope with too much resolution than too little.)

One last word on setting the resolution and the size of the image in Photoshop. If you are interested in cutting down on imaging time, print the image at 100 percent of size. A picture being printed at 100 percent with a resolution of 300 dpi is in principle exactly the same as one printed at 200 percent with a resolution of 600, but it will actually print much faster. Adjusting the size of the picture is easily accomplished under **Image: Image Size.** As long as the "Constrain File Size" option is checked, Photoshop will automatically adjust the resolution to accommodate the new size, and the recalculation time will be zero. All one need do is resave the file.

If we have, deliberately or not, gotten an image that is more than double the resolution of the screen ruling, it will pay to

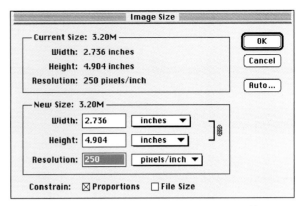

Figure 3.7 *This Photoshop menu allows resampling of an image (when "Constrain File Size" is not selected). Another valuable use is to save imaging time: if you are importing this image into another application but printing it at 90 percent of size, things will go smoother all around if you resize it in Photoshop so that the other application can use it at 100 percent of size. In this case, resampling is unnecessary. Just change one of the numbers in the dialog box, with "Constrain File Size" turned on, and the other two numbers will adjust automatically.*

downsample it, because Photoshop does a much more accurate job of this than do page layout programs. We again use the **Image: Image Size** menu, but this time, "Constrain File Size" is left unchecked (Figure 3.7).

Upsampling an image is correct only if the resolution is grossly too low, meaning less than the actual screen ruling. This might happen, for example, if we had no choice but to print from a video image. In such melancholy circumstances, Photoshop's BiCubic resampling will help. Rezzing the image up to the same value as the screen ruling or slightly higher will reduce the jaggedness of the image, though it still won't be terrific.

Olé, Have a Moiré

Figure 3.8 shows a PostScript dinosaur, a disagreeable patterning in the printed image, known technically as a *moiré.*

Figure 3.8 Moiré caused by faulty imagesetting, left. At right: a properly imaged version of the same piece.

Though advances in imagesetting technology have thankfully pushed classic moirés like this one to the edge of extinction, the phenomenon can still pop up from time to time.

Some type of interference effect is inevitable whenever two or more patterns intersect. In printing, there are four such patterns, one for each color. Since the pattern we use is so regular (one dot every ¹⁄₁₅₀ of an inch or whatever) we may find ourselves subject to such unpleasantness.

Fortunately, over the years the industry has managed to figure out good ways to minimize moiré, by proper control of the angling of the four screens with respect to one another. If the angle of each is 30 degrees away from any other, moiré is not eliminated, but it takes a more palatable form known as a *rosette*. If you take a magnifying glass to any of the pictures in this book you will be able to guess why.

There are only three 30-degree angles available (a 90-degree screen would be the same as a zero.) We need one more angle, and since yellow is the least pronounced of the process colors, that's the one normally chosen to be the odd man out. Yellow is therefore printed midway between two of the other colors, meaning only 15 degrees away from its nearest neighbors.

The problem is, imagesetters with fixed resolutions, and there aren't any other kind, have difficulty achieving very precise angles. In the mid-80s, when PostScript started becoming a market force, manufacturers figured that being in the vicinity of the correct angles would be good enough. They figured wrong.

The prevalence of moiré gave PostScript color a black eye and sent all the manufacturers back to the drawing board. Their new approaches by and large solved the problems. Sometimes the angles were slightly changed, sometimes there would be artificial bumps in the middle of the pattern, sometimes groups of dots would be combined into "supercells" that were themselves at slight angles to one another, and often there would be slight variations in the screen frequency, meaning that if we asked for a 133-line screen, the imagesetter might give us 133 in the cyan but

138 in the yellow. Usually a smoothing-out algorithm would take effect where dots were in the region of 50 percent; handled normally, there can seem to be a sudden change or banding. At 50 percent, dots will start to kiss each other whereas at lower percentages there will always be white space between dots. The apparent 50 percent jump is an optical illusion, but it is worth compensating for.

Each manufacturer trumpeted the advantages of its own sophisticated dodges over those of the opponents, but amid all these conflicting claims there are only two things to keep in mind.

First, they all work. Second, they *don't* work on each other's devices, so you *must* let each imagesetter handle its own screening.

Moiré unrelated to image content, therefore, is obsolete unless some human makes a mistake. In Figure 3.8, the mistake happened in imagesetting, but that is pretty rare because hardware vendors correctly make it hard for us to make disastrous changes. Photoshop is not so thoughtful.

Catastrophe beckons temptingly in Figure 3.9. When saving an EPS file, Photoshop allows the option of embedding angles and screen frequencies that will override whatever programming may be in the imagesetter. If you check the "Include Halftone Screens" box you will get, in addition to a probable moiré, a 53-line screen, Photoshop's default, unless you have been crazy enough to edit the angles yourself.

Not content with this mischief, Photoshop also gives us the opportunity in the same dialog box to override calibration settings that have no doubt been calcu-

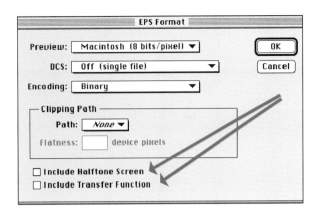

Figure 3.9 *The choice of any of the highlighted options in this box will cause printing nightmares.*

lated at great expense by the owner of the imagesetter. The transfer function should never be used in real life. Once in a blue moon it is conceivable that one might wish to alter the dot shape, though never the angle, of a halftone. If you ever do this, be aware that Photoshop leaves the "Use Halftone Screens" as a default for the next time you save something, the better to snare the unwary.

Orderly Chaos: The End of Moiré?

In 1992, manufacturers began to demonstrate an entirely novel method of screening: using the increased power of today's modern computers to create a "screen" that has no pattern at all. Instead of a relatively large 70 percent dot in a certain area, the imagesetter sprays random tiny dots that, taken together, comprise 70 percent of the possible coverage. The effect looks very much like applying Photoshop's **Filter: Noise>Add Noise** to an otherwise white area.

This method is called *stochastic* screening, from the Greek, meaning order in chaos. Its advantages are clear. First, since there are no patterns of dots, moiré is

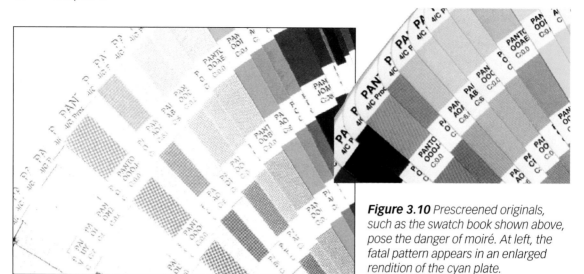

Figure 3.10 *Prescreened originals, such as the swatch book shown above, pose the danger of moiré. At left, the fatal pattern appears in an enlarged rendition of the cyan plate.*

impossible. Second, because the speckles of ink are so small as to be nearly undetectable, the technique gives the appearance of continuous-tone, almost like a photograph. And third, it solves in advance the problem we will face on the inevitable day when it becomes practical to print screened images with more than four inks. How to avoid moiré when five plates are in use is not well understood. If one or more of the plates gets a stochastic screen the problem goes away.

As against that, no one has enough experience with the process to be able to explain how images should be handled. Generalizing about the stochastic results I've seen so far, highlight areas have been poor, but there appears to be much more texture and detail in quarter- to midtones. The big problem seems to be transitions in dark areas. Ink coverage gets solid very quickly, which can result in posterization in shadow areas.

Whether there is a way around this, such as by developing a hybrid screening technique or by something we can do in Photoshop, or even whether my perception of the problem is correct, will be found out in the next few years. Already, however, developers are starting to experiment with semi-stochastic technologies. Esoteric methods such as a conventional screen interspersed with and printed at the same angle as a second screen comprised of much smaller dots, are also being tried.

These moves have merit, because even though imagesetting moiré is no longer a problem, the subject matter of certain images may contain a pattern strong enough to cause a moiré. The classic case is when one has to reproduce a printed original, such as a magazine page. Naturally, in order to print it, the original had to be screened. When we scan and output it, we impose a second screen. The result is guaranteed moiré.

A variation on this theme comes into play in Figure 3.10, in a blowup of an image that appeared in Chapter 2. This Pantone swatch book was photographed not conventionally, but by a digital camera that uses a sampling pattern in exactly the same way as a scanner.

Figure 3.11 *As part of the effort to strengthen a poor original (inset), we may wish to sharpen the black plate. This technique can lead to moirés (arrows) if it is not monitored carefully.*

A halftone screen is an obvious pattern, but the subjects of some images feature natural patterns that may cause moirés. This typically occurs in fabrics. Figure 3.11 demonstrates another sort of image-related moiré. We will see in Chapter 8 how sharpening or adding contrast to the black plate alone is frequently the way to add punch to the image. It can also, unfortunately, aggravate an existing pattern.

Moiré Control in Photoshop

The pattern in the swatches of Figure 3.10 is eliminated easily by repeatedly blurring the areas where it occurs. Usually, though, we are not so fortunate as to have an image with so few important details.

The traditional professional method of eliminating moiré in prescreened originals is to scan them slightly out of focus, then try to sharpen the resulting image. Sometimes rescanning with the art placed at a different angle will minimize the problem as well. If the pattern is not too severe, one or two applications of Photoshop's **Filter: Noise>Despeckle** or **Filter: Noise>Median** may suffice to remove it.

More promising, some developers have software that attempts to locate screening patterns and eliminate them. As this technique becomes more sophisticated, reproduction of prescreened originals may get easier. For the moment, fairly good is the best we can do, not just because of the inherent screening problem, but because, as noted in Chapter 2, printed pieces have far less dynamic range than photographs.

Subject-based moirés can frequently be overcome through blurring, local retouching, or scanning at a very high resolution and then downsampling. A better way, though, is to think back to the screening discussion. Just as stochastic methods kill moirés by wiping out the pattern inherent in conventional screening, the patterns in images can be blunted by adding randomness. Small quantities of **Filter: Noise>Add Noise** are highly effective. In Figure 3.11, the problem is in only one channel, but in full-color cases, this cheating will be less pronounced if we check the Monochrome option when adding the noise. This is a Photoshop 3 improvement; users of previous versions can obtain

Quick & Dirty
SCANNING, SCREENING & RESOLUTION

✓ Photoshop is able to exchange files, using standard industry formats, with most other applications.

✓ There are now many sources for digital images: high-end photomultiplier scanners; less expensive CCD scanners; digital cameras; Kodak Photo CDs; and a large number of stock photo and similar commercial CDs.

✓ With on-the-fly unsharp masking, selective color correction, great control of input-output curves, and flexibility in the size of input materials and output resolutions, high-end scanners clearly are the best quality choice—if you can afford them!

✓ In scanning, resolution does not equal quality. There is rarely any purpose in resolutions higher than double the eventual screen ruling (times the size of enlargement). Going significantly higher than this will actually reduce quality of final output by making the printed image too soft.

✓ As resolution increases, storage requirements go up very fast. A file at 300 dpi requires 2.25 times as much storage space as one at 200 dpi.

✓ There is general industry agreement that optimum scan resolution is anything between 1.5 and 2 times final screen ruling, times magnification. Satisfactory results are often possible with even less.

✓ On press, greater resolution does not necessarily equal quality either. It's great in principle to call for finer screens, but not if the printer has difficulty holding dots that small.

✓ When it is necessary to print from scans that are at too high a resolution, they should be downsampled in Photoshop, as this is more accurate than doing it on the imagesetter. Sharpening first will often help. Upsampling images that are at too low of a resolution will not help unless they are *grossly* low, as in the case of a video capture.

✓ Advances in screening technology have almost eliminated moiré in imagesetting. Progress is continuing in development of stochastic and semi-stochastic screening.

✓ Moirés due to patterns in the original image are still possible and must be watched for. Photoshop allows many countermeasures.

much the same effect in a more round-about way by converting the image from **Mode: CMYK** to **Mode: Lab Color,** adding noise to the L channel, and then returning to CMYK.

Before you get too worked up about moirés, I should reiterate that they don't happen that often. Unless you work with prescreened images, you may be lucky enough never to encounter an image-based moiré. Those caused by technical imagesetting difficulties are nearly extinct.

That goes as well for much of this chapter. Neophytes get intimidated by all the numbers, but there is actually quite a lot of leeway. We say that the minimum scan resolution should be 1.5 times the eventual screen ruling times the enlargement, but if you drop to 1.2 or so, the chances are that only experts will be able to tell the difference in most images.

It is fair to say that in these matters just about the only thing to fear is fear itself. Ten times as many reproduction problems are caused by people who equate higher scanning resolution with better quality than by those who take a chance with marginally low values. And a thousand times as many printing problems are the result of trying to force the square peg of a 175- or 200-line screen ruling into the round hole of a press that is not built to support it than by those who take the conservative approach and elect to plod along with a slightly coarser screen than what is currently fashionable.

Figure 4.1 *If you don't believe that successful color handling can be a matter of numbers only, without a "calibrated" monitor, yet think that the image below is a substantial improvement over the original, you will be in for a surprise at the end of this chapter.*

CHAPTER 4

By the Numbers: An Introduction to Curves

When looking at an image for the first time, we often see what we perceive to be many small problems. As often as not, these are all part of a bigger problem, which can be solved all at once with a single application of Photoshop's most powerful tool, input-output curves.

onkeying around with the color balance of photographic images is not a sport for the timid, or so goes the conventional wisdom. Believing this, people go through the most simian sorts of shenanigans trying to make their color look believable. They select this area, sharpen that one, call up histograms of the image, apply strange filters, and generally try to demonstrate that if an infinite number of art directors employ an infinite number of digital tweaks somebody somewhere may throw them a banana.

And yet, ninety percent of color correction could be handled by monkeys. That ninety percent, using a strict numerical approach with little room for artistic judgment, is what this chapter is all about. To console the creative, in the next chapter we will pick up the nine percent gained by intelligent image analysis. The final one percent comes only from practice and is beyond the purview of this book.

The rules for this ninety percent of color are so simple that they can be stated in one sentence.

Use the full range of available tones every time, and don't give the viewers any colors that they will know better than to believe.

This is nothing more than a restatement of the buccaneering philosophy developed in the first three chapters. We are backed into a corner, forced to accept a much smaller range of colors than we would really like. In response, we will stubbornly refuse to cede an inch more of our territory.

To see how this deceptively simple concept works in practice, here is an imaginary problem that may at first seem ridiculous. Figure 4.2 is the black and white image that graces my magazine column. The question is, supposing the unsupposable, that it were in color, how would the rules apply? What would be our major objectives in correcting it?

At this point you may say, how can we possibly know what a black and white image should look like in color, any more than we know how colors would look to us if we were Martians?

That attitude assumes that we know nothing about the colors of this image. Actually, we know quite a bit. True, we have no idea what color my tie should be, but what about my hair? As you can see, I don't use Grecian Formula. What color hair do you think I have, green? By all human experience, it has to be gray.

Similarly, we have no clue as to what color my jacket is, but men in business attire usually wear shirts that are either white or some distinct other color, not some muddy combination. Here, it appears to be a *white* shirt.

And, though my skin is dark, there are limits to the range of normal skin tones.

These considerations are very typical. The giveaways of problems in color reproduction are almost always fleshtones and neutral colors—grays and whites.

A General Approach to Correction

If we are to use the full range of available tones, we must find the whitest and darkest areas of the image, and make them as light and as dark as we can, given our paper and printing process. Many pictures are complex enough that we must mosey around quite a bit to find these endpoints. Here, though, the lightest point is evidently somewhere in my collar, and the darkest is in the stripes of my tie.

At this juncture, we make a decision as to how strictly we will adhere to our general guidelines on highlight and shadow.

Figure 4.2 *This image is in black and white, but we can make generalizations about how we would treat it if it were in color.*

This decision depends on how significant we believe the particular endpoints are to the overall picture. In the case at hand, I would say that preserving detail in the white shirt is important, so we should try to stick with a highlight of 5C2M2Y, but I am not particularly interested in holding detail in the stripes of the tie, so I would not go to excruciating lengths to stay within normal shadow range.

All that remains is to enforce our numerical decisions by means of curves. Since there are neutral colors in this picture (the hair and the shirt) and also fleshtones, we must check, before applying the curves, that these colors stick to certain standards.

The numerical rules are so very important that even though they appear elsewhere in the book, I will restate them here. These values are generally pretty good for commercial printing and they are the ones used in this book. For higher-quality printing the highlight and shadow numbers will be more extreme and for newspapers and other such lower-quality work they will be further away from zero and 100 percent.

• For the minimum significant highlight that is supposed to be roughly white, use a dot of 5C2M2Y. Cyan ink not being as effective as magenta or yellow, we have to use more of it to attain a neutral color. This highlight value is critical. Humans are quite sensitive to color in light areas, so a variation of two points in any ink could result in an unacceptable color cast.

• For the maximum significant shadow area, use 80C70M70Y70K. One or more of these numbers can be higher in a deep color; navy blue, for instance, might be 95C65M15Y50K. Many printing applica-

tions, however, require that the sum of all four numbers be no higher than 280, so where the shadow is to appear roughly black, stick to my suggested number, not worrying that it really adds up to 290. People don't have good color perception in areas this dark, so, if need be, we can take liberties with one or two of the ink values. Don't do this without a good reason, though. An unbalanced shadow often is a symptom of a color cast that may be subtly hurting other parts of the image.

• For an area that is supposed to appear white or any shade of gray, the magenta and yellow values should be equal and the cyan should be 3 to 5 percentage points higher. If there is a problem meeting this requirement, it is better to be too heavy in the cyan than either of the other colors, since bluish grays are much less noticeable than greenish or reddish ones.

• Caucasian fleshtones should have at least as much yellow as magenta, and up to 25 percent more. The cyan should be a fifth to a third as heavy as the magenta, depending upon how bronzed a person is. For a dark-skinned person like myself, 20C55M60Y will do; lighter-skinned people can go 10C40M40Y or even lower.

Writing Curves: A First Step

To start, we open up the color image and check the density values, using the Info palette, in the highlight and shadow areas, plus the areas of known colors—in this case, the shirt, the face, and the hair. It is helpful before doing this to hit the Shift Lock key. This changes the screen cursor to a crosshair icon that yields more accurate values.

The picture of me is simple enough that we can keep these numbers straight in our heads, but as images get more complex, writing down the density values and what we propose to do with them can be helpful. To the extent the image does not meet our target numbers, we apply curves to force it closer to them.

To do this, open **Image: Modify>Curves**. Ignore the default curve, which we almost never use because it affects all four channels at once. Go directly into the individual colors. To agree with professional practice and also with the examples in this book, please set shadows to the right and highlights to the left. This is done, if necessary, by clicking on the light-to-dark bar at the bottom of the curves panel.

The horizontal axis of the curve represents the original values of the image. The vertical axis represents the values you wish the image to take. The lines are at intervals of 25 percent.

The default curve is not a curve at all, but a straight line at a 45-degree angle. If we decide that we are going to change it (and we may well decide to leave it alone) we can keep it a straight line by changing one or both of the endpoints. This is not usually as effective as inserting one or more intermediate points with the mouse and adjusting them up and down. If we do this, Photoshop will turn the straight line into a curve.

If the entire new curve falls below the original 45-degree line, the corrected image will be lighter than the original. If it falls above the default, the new image will be darker. Most of the time, we will want to write curves that fit neither description, but that make some parts of the image darker and others lighter.

Parts of such a curve will wind up being steeper than 45 degrees, and, to compen-

sate, other parts will have to be flatter. When the curve is applied to the image, areas covered by the steep parts of the curve will gain contrast, and areas covered by the flatter parts will lose it.

In the imaginary color image of me, suppose that we measure the lightest area of the white shirt and discover that it is 12C10M18Y. Measurements of the stripes of the tie find 70C65M85Y50K.

We start by adding two points to each curve. In the case of cyan, we want what is now 12 percent to become 5 percent, since we are shooting for a highlight of 5C2M2Y. We will also insert a point that brings 70 percent up to 80. Similarly, we adjust each of the other colors so that we hit the targets for highlight and shadow.

Before clicking the OK button in the Curves dialog box, we run our selection tool across the neutral areas of the picture. The Info palette will now tell us both what the values are and what they will be, if the curve is applied. Ideally, the neutral areas will be truly neutral (i.e., equal magenta and yellow and slightly more cyan); if not, we will have to make further adjustments to the curves.

If a major amount of work went into construction of these curves, we should take advantage of the Save option in the Curves dialog box before doing anything else. If we do this, and then decide that a slight modification is necessary (or, heaven forfend, if we make some big mistake and are forced to **File: Revert** to the last saved version of the image) we can cancel the changes we made, then reopen the Curves dialog box and choose the Load option to reinstate the curves.

That is really all there is to color correction, and if you truly understand curves, you know how they can eliminate color casts, increase contrast, and make the image more lifelike, all at once, without any local correction, without using any esoteric program functions.

So much for theory. Let's roll up our sleeves and correct some color.

Many Birds with One Curve

In this chapter, we'll tackle four images that come from stock-photo CD-ROMs. They are, therefore, highly typical of the work we may be called upon to do in real life. We will start by analyzing Figure 4.3 in exactly the same manner as we did the

Figure 4.3 *Original (top right) and corrected versions of a stock photo. The curves (below) produce not only a greater range, but the illusion of a sharper picture.*

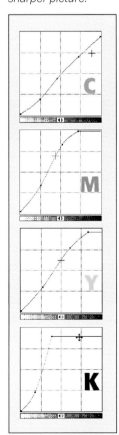

imaginary color picture of me, which is exactly the same way we will examine every image we henceforth encounter.

First question: Where are the highlight and shadow? First answer: Not as obvious as in our imaginary example. We will have to try a few possibilities. Second question: Are there any known colors? Answer: Not really. The building itself is white, sort of, but we don't know how close to neutral we have to come. (Yes, the trees must be green, but we have tremendous latitude as to *how* green.)

Here is what I learned from inspecting this image with the sampling tool. The lightest area of the image is the bench in front of the door, at 2C1M1Y. Parts of the sky measure 5C1M2Y, which is nearly a perfect highlight. The darkest area is a tie between a part of the door and some of the shadows in the trees to the right of the building, at 90C50M55Y30K. That's as much magenta as there is anywhere in the picture, but there is as much as 70 percent yellow in the green trees. Measuring the light areas of the building's exterior yields readings of around 25C0M3Y.

If this were the old days, now would be a good time to look for the scanner operator, with the objective of shoving this image down his throat. Regrettably, such remedial action is no longer possible. Fortunately, Photoshop lets us compensate for this inadequate art.

Incidentally, at this point, you can turn your monitor to grayscale if you like. It is all monkey work from here on in. Now that we have a general read of the picture, we can color-correct in black and white just as easily—and the screen refreshes ever so much faster.

Whether you are willing to take that particular plunge or not, here is what the measured numbers imply.

The highlight is acceptable as is, if we pretend that we did not notice the bench. Having zero magenta in the building proper is no good. The shadow value is very weak, but more than that, it confirms our worst suspicions about the picture as a whole. Why, would you guess, is the shadow cyan value 35 points heavier than any other color? Do you think that the building door is supposed to be a shade of blue? Is it not more likely that there is just plain too much cyan in this image? That's what I think, and I think it suggests strongly that our initial perception is correct, that the building has too much cyan as well.

Accordingly, the curves will be as follows. Cyan: keep the highlight value constant, dip at 25 percent to try to reduce the tint of the building, slight reduction everywhere else. Magenta: sharp increase everywhere, moving all points that are currently zero up to 3, and the maximum value, currently about 50, into the 80s. Yellow: slight increase everywhere, since we cannot increase too drastically without screwing up the greenery. Black: as drastic an increase as is possible without demolishing the image.

The result of these moves is to take the shadow from 90C50M55Y30K to 85C92M65Y55K and the color of the building from 25C0M3Y to 18C3M5Y. These numbers are not great but they are much better than they were before. The picture now has more pop and clarity. You would almost never know that the original was so awful.

Figure 4.4 Applying the curves below to the original (top right) results in the center image. Bottom, an alternate version that attempts to further subdue the blue cast by increasing the amount of blue-killing yellow in the image.

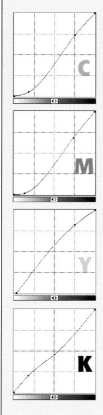

Fighting the Blues

The undesirable color cast in Figure 4.3 was somewhat subtle. In Figure 4.4, it's about as subtle as a 500-pound gorilla.

This time, the cast is not cyan but blue (i.e., cyan and magenta both), painfully evident to the naked eye, but here are the confirming numbers anyway.

Highlight: the roof of the back of the house, 9C8M4Y. Shadow: the peak of the house, 94C85M56Y75K. Known colors: snow is supposed to be white. Instead, the lighter areas are in the neighborhood of 18C15M5Y.

At this point, you may throw up your hands in disgust and ask why photographers never get it right. Actually, they do. The incredible human optical system is what causes problems.

Everybody knows that when we are in a darkened room, our eyes adjust to the environment and become more sensitive. When somebody turns the light on suddenly, it dazzles us.

Not everybody realizes that the same thing takes place in color perception. Our brains want to reference everything to a neutral environment, so when we are flooded with light of one color we compensate by making our eyes less sensitive to it—all unconsciously.

The supplier of this photo states that it was taken somewhere in the northern part of Russia. That would account for the harshness of the sunlight, and it is perfectly reasonable that all this ambient light could be very blue. The camera, precision instrument though it is, is to the human visual system as an Amiga is to a Cray. We tell it to record what it sees, and it sees the blinding blue that our own eyes are programmed to ignore.

In this image, the obvious move is also the correct one. The highlight is too dark, so I will try to bring it back down to 5C2M2Y. The shadow is dark enough, but it is no more balanced than the highlight was. The cyan and magenta, especially the cyan, are too heavy everywhere. The yellow is too light everywhere.

The blue cast is simply too great to eliminate totally, but the curves shown resulted in the center cut of Figure 4.4. We'll come back to this image in a minute, but right now we have Figure 4.5, and a new set of problems, to consider.

Skin Tones in the Studio

It shouldn't shock you that three out of four of the images in this chapter were photographed outdoors. That is where the big color casts show up. In studio shots like Figure 4.5, lighting is much better controlled, so the originals should generally be good—but that doesn't mean there is no room for improvement.

Our numerical analysis starts with the irksome news that there is no highlight to be found. The shadow is beneath the left ear. It measures 66C62M70Y45K. Known colors: skin tone. Samples around the face show 1C24M24Y, 0C26M29Y, 2C36M36Y, 5C47M42Y, and 11C46M40Y.

These numbers are a lot closer to what we would like than they were in the first two images. Since this is Caucasian skin, magenta and yellow are supposed to be roughly equal, and that seems to be the case. The cyan, however, is too low. Without it, the skin looks pinkish and unhealthy. Cyan is the suntan color: it pushes fleshtones toward a golden brown.

At last, we are out of the realm of monkey see, monkey do, since there is nothing

Figure 4.5 *This photograph was taken in the studio, so lighting conditions should be ideal. As the top right image demonstrates, however, there is still room for improvement. At right, the correction curves.*

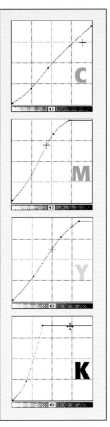

white in this picture that we can call a highlight. Do not make the mistake of looking at the gold earrings for help, for reasons I will explain in a moment.

Well, there is nothing for it but to go color by color. The cyan highlight we already know to be wrong. Five percent is supposed to be the minimum cyan dot, but there are places in the face with zero or one. The magenta highlight is not bad. In the lightest areas of the hair and right arm, where yellow predominates, the magenta is between 2 and 5 percent.

What about the yellow? If we had some nice light blue, we could measure what the minimum yellow is, but the photographer did not oblige us. Instead, we have logic. We know from the skin analysis that the yellow and magenta are properly balanced. We just found out that the magenta highlight is correct. By inference, so is the yellow.

The typical color-correcting chimpanzee would now think he knew how to fix this image. He would increase minimum cyan from 0 to 5, put a little bump in at about 10C to get extra cyan in the fleshtones, and increase the values of everything over 40 percent so as to get a heavier shadow. Not bad for a lower primate, but do you see why it won't work?

Well, if it weren't for those confounded earrings, it *would* work.

The ape would be foiled, however, by the presence of our first specular highlight.

As a rule, cyan, magenta, and yellow should never be zero. If they are, detail cannot be held and the image will look blown out, as was the case in Figure 2.6. The exception is when the most important detail is brilliance. The classical large example is Figure 5.6, an image of sparks being generated by a welder. More frequently, specular highlights are caused by reflections of flashes of light, as in silverware, a mirror, or, here, the earrings.

When adjusting the highlight, these must be ignored, which is why we could not have used the earrings here. Metal reflects light, so they are full of deceptive speculars and partial speculars that have a yellow dot only.

The ape approach would set the specular highlights in the earrings to 5C0M0Y. In the middle of golden jewelry, this is definitely no good.

In real life one might be inclined to select the entire image, deselect the earrings, and apply the chimp curves. Since the premise of this chapter is that artists spend too much time correcting locally when global corrections are feasible, this would not be politically correct. Another plan is needed.

Figure 4.6 *The pink horses below are clearly wrong, but they are merely the most obvious of many problems.*

Blending Plates for Contrast

My recourse was to make a new cyan plate, a mathematical blend of 85 percent of the old plate and 15 percent of the magenta. Then I applied curves that deepened everything in all colors over 40 percent, so as to take full advantage of the available tonal range. Big difference, no?

A mathematical blend is a dangerous proposition and should only be undertaken after careful study. In the above case, it would have been suicide to blend the cyan with the yellow, which has the same flesh values as the magenta. It would have killed the yellow hair and the earrings. Fortunately, the magenta plate is very similar to the cyan, except in the fleshtones.

The only other element to check is the

lips. Before correction, they average 2C61M57Y. The cyan is too light there anyway, since the minimum should be 5 percent, so the blending will help. The shadow-deepening curves will boost the magenta and yellow but not the cyan. After correction, the lips average 8C67M63Y, which is just fine.

By now you may be thinking, correctly, that if a composite plate can help eliminate the mild red cast of this picture, it would certainly help counter the huge blue cast of the preceding one. So, back to the snowy Russian scene of Figure 4.4.

Blends work best where there are no bright, clean colors, since the whole idea is to neutralize. That's why we could not have used the technique in Figure 4.2, which was largely bright green. Figure 4.4 doesn't have this problem. It appears so blue because it is grossly short of the yellow that would neutralize it. The initial curves helped a lot but this technique will only go so far.

I therefore made a third version of the image, shown at the bottom of Figure 4.4, by blending 40 percent of the cyan plate

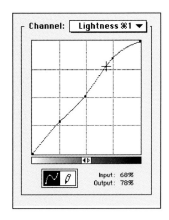

Figure 4.7 *The combination of LAB curve (top right) and CMYK correction (bottom left) neutralizes the horses and gives a much more lifelike image.*

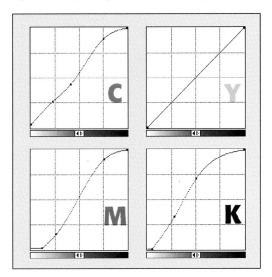

into the yellow. To avoid too much contamination of the sky, I then applied a curve that brought down the yellow quartertone. It would also have been reasonable to have isolated the house and inverted the selection before blending, so that the house might stay as blue as it was.

Behold a Paler Horse

If you have never seen a purple cow, nor ever hope to see one, you should probably find another field of endeavor. For a final variation on the same old theme, we'll do battle with a purple horse.

In Figure 4.6, we begin by rounding up the usual suspects. Highlight: the forehead of the near horse, 2C2M2Y. Shadow: blinder of the far horse, 71C57M71Y30K. Known colors: the horses obviously should be white, but the readings are 7C26M7Y, 10C31M16Y, 15C32M18Y. Also,

in the background is a Canadian flag that reads 10C70M75Y2K, although I happen to know it should have more magenta than yellow. And several of the flags should have neutral white areas as well.

Fixing the color balance here is straightforward. The cyan is slightly too low throughout. We know this because we have measured three nicely neutral areas—the highlight, the shadow, and the horses—and in all three cases the cyan was roughly equal to the yellow, whereas it is supposed to be a few points higher. Since there is no specular highlight in this image we can start our correction curve by making zero cyan move to 3 percent and keeping all other values correspondingly higher.

The yellow is OK as is. It starts at a perfect 2 and ends at around 75, which is slightly low, but acceptable.

Figure 4.8 The Grand Canyon again, this time from Encantadora Point, in a stock photo sold in CD form.

The magenta behaves peculiarly. It is correct in the highlight, too heavy in the quartertone, and too light thereafter. That sounds more difficult to fix than it actually is. We construct a curve that gives a minimum value of 2M and is completely flat for a while, meaning that anything that was 9M or lower will now stabilize at 2M. It starts its climb slowly, so that 30M becomes 15M, and then skyrockets so that the midtones will in fact increase.

The wrench in our monkeyworks is going to be the motheaten excuse for a shadow value. All three of the images we have worked with so far have had rotten shadows, but this is the worst. The black would have to more than double to make it acceptable. That's tough to do with curves.

This is one of those rare cases where CMYK is not the best colorspace. Before applying the planned curves, I converted to LAB, to take advantage of its brightness channel. There, using an S-shaped curve for a stone (Figure 4.7), I went after two birds.

There are two bumps in this curve. The top one serves to darken the shadow areas. The bottom one is what one might call a counter-correction. The magenta curve we are planning to impose will kill the color cast, all right, but

Figure 4.9 *Here, as in the bottom image of Figure 4.1, is a version that was color-corrected by Ralph Viola, a person with no previous experience with Photoshop or color work, among certain other disadvantages. Right, the curves he wrote to accomplish the changes.*

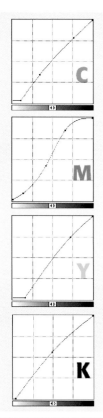

at a price. Flattening the range will hurt contrast in the magenta. The detail in the horses' coats will suffer. By steepening the brightness curve in the highlights, I am trying to pump contrast back in.

All that remains is to reconvert to CMYK and zap the image with the correction curves discussed above, plus whatever black move is needed to get full value in the shadow.

Of Values and Judgments

In the corrections to these four images, we made almost no "artistic" judgments. It was all numbers, numbers, numbers. There was no need even to use a color monitor.

And every single change was made to the image as a whole.

In short, once he got the hang of curves, there is absolutely no reason that an orangutan could not get these results. Years of retouching experience, artistic talent, and mathematical aptitude wouldn't hurt him, but they are not really needed.

Notice how these numerical adjustments have the habit of helping areas of the image that we never even thought about. Things like the flags behind the horses, the model's hair, the snow shooting into the sky.

Artists who worry their images to death tend to see such short-

Figure 4.10 *The image shown in Figure 4.8 was part of a color-correction test. Here's the author's version, done well in advance of the one shown in Figure 4.9. At left, his curves. Which rendition do you prefer?*

comings immediately and plunge happily and vigorously into a morass of individual moves. They isolate the horses and work on them; they fix up the flags one by one; they tediously darken the harnesses, and after eight hours they have something nearly as good as what the orangutan would have gotten in 35 seconds. That may be the most persuasive kind of number there is.

Neutralizing our artistic judgment along with the color casts gave us four images that came out much better than the originals—yet not as good as they might have been.

Determining that the horses are more important than the building, or that the model's face is more important than her arms, are the kinds of logical decisions that are too difficult for either apes or calibrationists. In the next chapter, we will exploit our superior intellect, and with a combination of good numbers and curves that improve contrast in the critical areas of the image, we'll get the color correction monkey off our backs forever.

Can You Top This?

At a recent trade show, I was greeted with many raised eyebrows and quizzical expressions when I suggested that it was possible to color-correct on a black and white monitor.

Of course, this was mostly bluster; I truly believe that a color monitor helps in color correction, if you don't take it too seriously, and that dedicated professionals would always get better results than baboons. But there is a grain of truth there, too. If it is not literally possible to train a monkey, there are certain art directors whom I would place in the same league.

The very idea that anyone would dream of correcting color based on anything less than the finest available screen was taken as great sacrilege, for there are lots of people in the industry who swear by expensive monitor-calibration methods, usually involving fancy software and suction cups. Not just the people who sell them, either. Here, with the vehemence typical of this group, is what a trade magazine writer had to say in 1992: "It's ludicrous to fix a photo's contrast on an uncalibrated monitor, since you have little idea how the resulting tonal range corresponds to the final print."

At Cardinal Communications Group in New York, where I work, I looked around for someone without much color experience and no knowledge of Photoshop, to see just how ludicrous a strictly numerically-based approach would be. I needed a color neophyte, and Ralph Viola, a supervisor, offered to be the guinea pig. He read a draft of this chapter, and I spent two hours with him one day where together we wrote curves to correct the same images shown thus far.

After that, I gave him four raw images to correct alone. Two of these appear in Figures 4.1 and 4.8, next to Ralph's results. The exercise was witnessed by several skeptics, who will attest that, other than by hitting the save key at the end, I offered no assistance, and that neither I nor any other professional was even present when he took his measurements and wrote his curves. The skeptics will also confirm that, for the very best of reasons, Ralph has specialized in typography and has had no significant experience with color.

Granted these limitations, Ralph's work is fairly impressive. Obviously, I chose

Quick & Dirty

COLOR CORRECTION BY THE NUMBERS

✓For 90 percent of the correction work we face, the rules can be stated in one sentence: Use the full range of available tones every time, and don't give the viewers any colors that they will know better than to believe.

✓In each uncorrected image, we must find the highlight—the lightest white—if there is one. Also, we must find the darkest area, or shadow. We will use curves to move these areas to the minimum and maximum values we expect to be able to hold detail with on press. Absent specific information to use different numbers, use 5C2M2Y for highlight and 80C70M70Y70K for shadow.

✓Specular highlights, meaning areas that are reflecting light, should not be used in setting the image highlight. Speculars may print all zeroes if you wish. Similarly, dark areas where detail is totally unimportant can print at heavier than the recommended shadow values.

✓Most pictures have some colors that are known to the viewer. Whatever correction curves are used cannot make these unbelievable. The known colors are generally either Caucasian fleshtones or areas that must logically be neutral grays or whites.

✓Neutral colors, of which there are plenty in nature, should have equal amounts of magenta and yellow, and slightly more cyan. The amount of black, if any, is irrelevant. As a bluish gray is less offensive than a reddish or greenish one, if you must depart from this, use more cyan.

✓In Caucasian skin, magenta and yellow should be roughly equal. Yellow can be up to 25 percent higher. Cyan should be between a third and a fifth of the magenta value, depending upon how dark the individual's flesh is.

✓When it is impossible to write global curves that will fulfill the requirements of the known colors, as where a face completely lacks cyan, resort to Photoshop 3's Selective Color Correction controls. Another alternative is mathematical blending of stronger plates into weaker ones.

✓Do not be seduced into a local selection of an area where the color is obviously wrong. Whatever is causing the undesirable color is also doing it in the rest of the picture, but it may not be apparent. Applying correction globally will cause overall improvements that you might not anticipate.

these two because they were his best efforts out of the four, but he made improvements in the other two as well. For the sake of comparison, he was correcting images that had also been corrected by me, independently and several weeks in advance of this demonstration. My versions are shown in Figures 4.10 and 4.11. Feet of clay! I think Ralph has me beat in one of them. Do you agree?

This exercise shows how far a little effort will take us. You may or may not do as well as Ralph Viola, although it is my hope and belief that you will be able to do sig-

nificantly better after reading this book.

If you are about to say, he wasn't using numbers, he was relying on the screen, it is doubtful that this would have done him any good. Ralph is color-blind. He can perceive blues to a limited extent, but is not able to distinguish reds from greens at all. In Figure 4.8, he was basically looking at a monochrome image (I think). Maybe that's why he did the best on this one.

My biggest regret is that, in looking at Figure 4.9, Ralph is probably unable to appreciate how effective his by-the-numbers corrections really were.

Figure 4.11 *The author's correction of the top half of Figure 4.1, again done independently and in advance of Ralph Viola's correction of the image.*

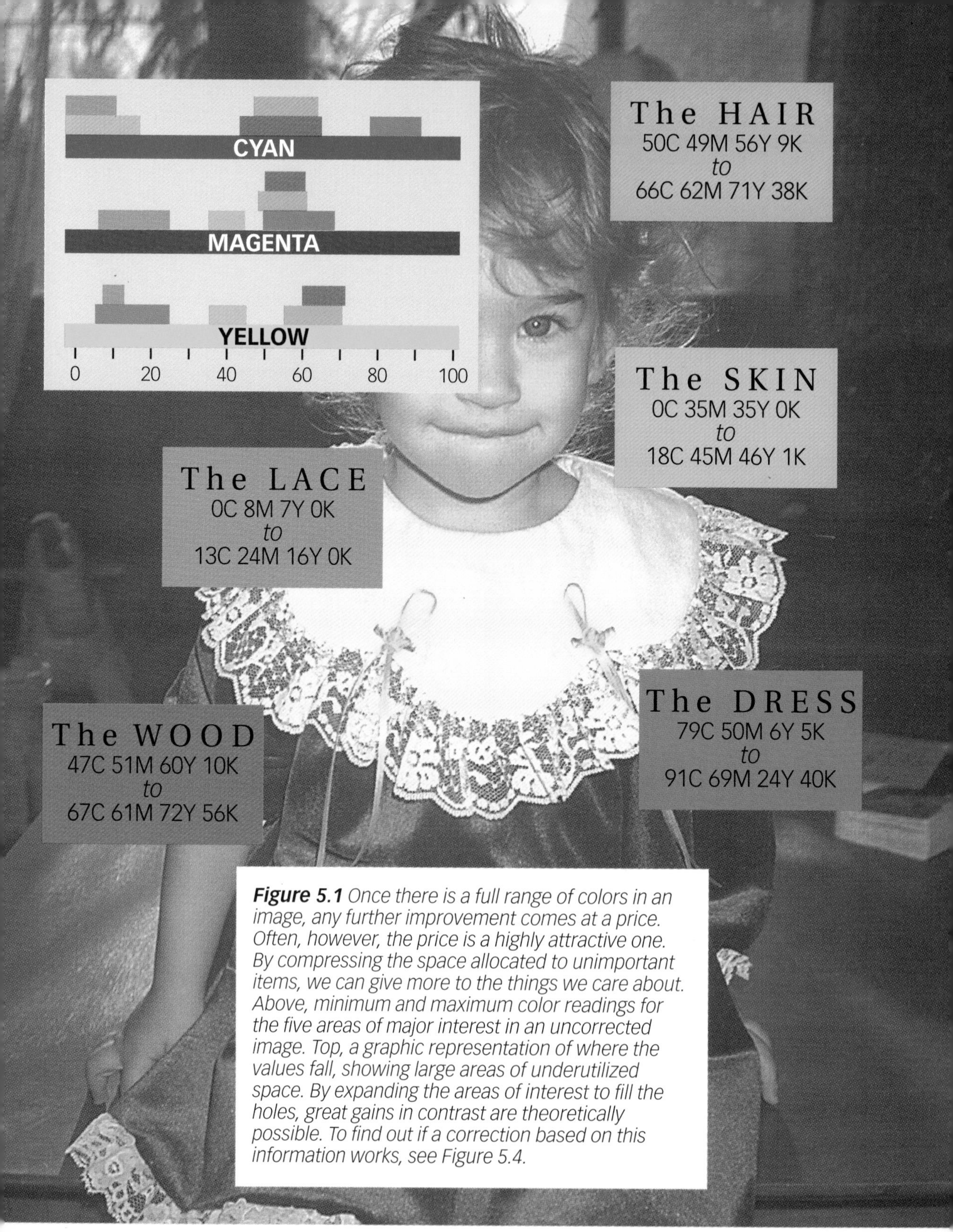

CYAN

MAGENTA

YELLOW

| 0 | 20 | 40 | 60 | 80 | 100 |

The HAIR
50C 49M 56Y 9K
to
66C 62M 71Y 38K

The SKIN
0C 35M 35Y 0K
to
18C 45M 46Y 1K

The LACE
0C 8M 7Y 0K
to
13C 24M 16Y 0K

The DRESS
79C 50M 6Y 5K
to
91C 69M 24Y 40K

The WOOD
47C 51M 60Y 10K
to
67C 61M 72Y 56K

Figure 5.1 *Once there is a full range of colors in an image, any further improvement comes at a price. Often, however, the price is a highly attractive one. By compressing the space allocated to unimportant items, we can give more to the things we care about. Above, minimum and maximum color readings for the five areas of major interest in an uncorrected image. Top, a graphic representation of where the values fall, showing large areas of underutilized space. By expanding the areas of interest to fill the holes, great gains in contrast are theoretically possible. To find out if a correction based on this information works, see Figure 5.4.*

Color Correction As Horsetrading

Once an image uses the entire available colorspace, there can be no gain in one area without sacrifices in another. Every improvement has a price. Fortunately, there are some real bargains out there.

Color correction is like life. We are forever having to make decisions involving allocation of scarce resources. I have eight hours free during which I would like to improve my skills; should I spend it making sure I understand every feature of a program I already know pretty well, or should I learn a new one? I have a couple thousand dollars available to spend on hardware: should I buy a disk drive, more RAM, a better video card, or a new CPU?

Tough calls like this are what put the fun in color correction and distinguish the successful artist from the calibrationist.

As we saw in the last chapter, there *are* some free lunches available. There, we avoided being shortchanged by making sure we used the full available tonal space, every time. And we adjusted curves so that colors that were supposed to be neutral got that way.

Those moves were unconditionally positive. They improved things at no cost to any aspect of the image. Best of all, very little judgment was called for.

Once there is a full range in an image, however, we pay a price for any further moves. Sometimes the price is too high, but it is sometimes astonishingly cheap. To be an adequate color technician one need only grasp numbers. To be good at it you have to be a bargain hunter.

To illustrate, we will use the same rules as last time. In correcting, local selection is not permitted. Neither is the use of any local retouching tool. All moves must affect the image as a whole. And, except where specifically noted, all corrections will be accomplished by means of curves.

How Green Is My Image

The top of Figure 5.2 is an image that, by the numerical standards espoused in Chapter 4, is good. The highlight, at 5C2M2Y, is perfect, and the shadow value is only slightly light. There is no neutral area that we need to worry about keeping gray, no fleshtone that could trip us up.

Although in principle all the available tones are already in use, we can make an improvement by being smarter in how we use them.

Consider a black and white image in which the highlight value is correct but the darkest value is only 60 percent, whereas our press could probably hold a dot of 85 percent without difficulty.

In such a case, a correction curve should be automatic and will almost invariably create a staggering improvement. The simplest approach is to have a curve that leaves the 0 and 100 percent endpoints alone and moves 60 percent up to 85. That will not just darken the picture: it will profoundly hike contrast throughout. Every detail will become more pronounced because there are now around a third more tones available and the curve will force everything further apart. That is,

any two dots anywhere in the picture will have more variation between them than before the correction, and this is what gives an image snap.

This by-the-numbers method is a great start, but it is somewhat wooden. As we saw, it can even be mastered by a color-blind individual. Without such a handicap, the intelligent artist can do better.

Curvewriting boils down to this: in areas where the curve is steeper than the default of 45 degrees, contrast will improve, and in areas where it is flatter than 45 degrees it will get worse.

In our hypothetical example the curve was steeper between 0 and 60 percent—and much flatter between 60 and 100. We don't think about that part, because nothing in the image falls in that range. So, the correction is very obvious, as there is nothing to lose by doing it. The curve damages an area of the picture that does not exist.

If you accept that, it is only logical to damage areas that *do* exist, but are not important. Every time we flatten a curve in one area it gets steeper somewhere else. It is thus possible to trade quality in unimportant parts of the picture for extra mustard in the parts we care about.

In Figure 5.2 everything we care about is green. The CMYK translation of this is, all areas of interest have 60 to 90 percent yellow and 50 to 85 percent cyan. Although darker areas have a lot of magenta, most greens have 2 to 30 percent.

That is not to say that there is nothing in the picture with less cyan and yellow. But those parts are few and far between. If hurting them is the price for extra contrast in the greens, that is a huge bargain and we should jump at it.

Figure 5.2 *The curve-based correction of the top image emulates what the human eye does when confronted with an excess of one color. Note the additional detail that begins to appear in the leaves at bottom.*

Having thus defined the interest areas, we proceed to design curves that will be steeper there. This is done, as shown in Figure 5.3, by bringing down the midrange values for yellow and cyan, and increasing the quartertone values for magenta.

Note, in addition to the extra detail in the leaves, that the insect has become browner in the corrected version. That happens to be what the human visual system does when confronted by a surplus of one color. This hopper would seem brown to us when sitting on a bright green leaf, but green in a different environment.

This interesting phenomenon of human vision, that we perceive colors differently depending on what surrounds them, is called *simultaneous contrast*.

Taking Inventory

An almost entirely green image is easy to fix in this fashion, but usually there are some complicating factors. If there were a face or hand in the image somewhere, or a blue sky, these curves wouldn't work.

As images get more complex, seat-of-the-pants responses have to give way to more careful analysis. Often, horrors, we actually have to take out a piece of paper and start writing down some readings, in a manner similar to Figure 5.1, but the extra time is worth it, because usually we can find some color ranges that are not being put to full use, and when we do, we will mercilessly compress them.

As always, the first order of business is to find the highlight, which is 0C6M6Y in the white collar of the little girl's dress, and the shadow, which is 73C57M68Y61K at the left of the background. Also, we note for future reference that the collar appears to be a neutral color, to wit, white, and

that there are fleshtones in the picture.

The second order of business is to decide what parts of the image we think are especially important. In Figure 5.1, there are five such areas, to my way of thinking: the girl's face; her hair; the white lace collar of her outfit; the blue dress; and the wooden table she is sitting on. We should be prepared to take some hits in the remainder of the picture if we can improve these things.

The cyan plate offers the most clearcut example of the finding-wasted-space

Figure 5.3 *The correction curves for (left) the grasshopper image of Figure 5.2 and (right) the picture of the little girl in Figure 5.4.*

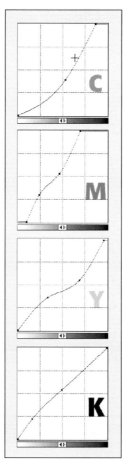
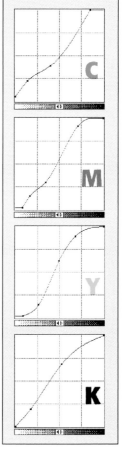

 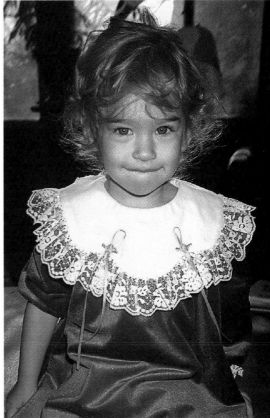

Figure 5.4 *All interest areas in this original (left) are either very light or at least moderately dark. As the values shown in Figure 5.1 demonstrate, there is nothing of importance in the quartertone range. This makes it possible to compress the quartertones and give more apparent contrast (right).*

approach. In cyan, both the lace and the skin are light, ranging from zero to about 18 percent. In the wood and the hair, values begin in the high 40s and continue into the 70s. The dress, being very blue, never has less than 70 percent cyan.

It seems, therefore, that in cyan, the area between 15 and 45 percent is currently useless. I intend to steal some of this valuable colorspace and use it to extend the range of the five important items highlighted in Figure 5.1.

In the other two colors, the specifics vary, but the principle, and the result, is the same. In yellow, it is not the lace and

the skin that are light, but the lace and the dress. Again, the hair, the skin, and the wood are heavy, and again, there is a large unused area between around 10 and 40 percent.

In magenta, the lace is the only important area that is light. The other four are darker, but there is nothing *really* dark in the entire plate. The unused space is smaller in the quartertones, but there is now another vacant lot in the shadows.

In short, although there is some variation in each of the three, there is basically nothing of significance going on between 15 and 40 percent in any of the plates.

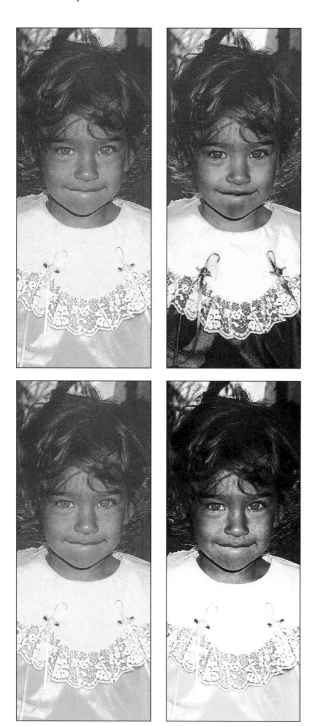

Figure 5.5 *If you are curious as to why the right-hand image of Figure 5.4 has so much more snap, compare the magenta (top) and yellow plates of the two images.*

The correction curves will therefore be steep at first, to get more contrast in the collar, then flatten in the no-man's-land of the quartertone, becoming steeper again to accommodate the face and the dress. Thus, the darkest areas of the dress get darker still; the lightest areas of the face get lighter. Overall, the range is the same as before, but it is allocated differently. Do you think it helps?

These particular curves violate general rules about shadow balance. After correction, the new shadow is 82C72M84Y69K. That is unbalanced, a greenish shadow.

If we were talking about highlights, this would not be an option. Humans are highly sensitive to variations in light colors. We cannot permit the white collar to take on a green cast. When the color is dark, however, no one will be able to detect the cast. The only reason for concern is that it is likely that if the shadows are unbalanced the rest of the picture will be as well. We can depart from the general rule if we find just and sufficient cause.

Here, my reason for not having a technically correct shadow is fear of two probable consequences: that the face may get too magenta, and that the dress may turn purple. Remember, cyan is a much weaker ink than magenta. When they mix in equal quantities, color theory says we should get blue—but we don't.

The individual plates of Figure 5.5 show clearly where the contrast was picked up. This, as you may have guessed, was an amateur photograph, taken under adverse lighting conditions with less than optimal equipment. The Kodak CD scan cost about a dollar. For all these disadvantages, the right side of Figure 5.4 is, in my view, professional color.

Figure 5.6 *Curves (below) that exaggerate contrast in heavy cyans, moderate magentas, and light yellows bring out the detail in the welder's jacket in the bottom image.*

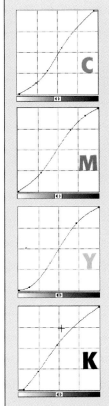

Figure 5.7 *A by-the-numbers correction of the top image using the techniques developed in Chapter 4 results in a greatly improved image, but not quite as good as the ones opposite.*

These first two examples were relatively easy because there was really no way we could have made the colors unbelievable. When we apply curves as radical as these, hues can change. The dress, for example, changed color during the correction.

If this were a clothing catalog and the dress were a featured item, changing its color would not be acceptable. As matters stand, though, it is purely an artistic call: do we want an exact color match to the dress, or are contrast and detail more important to us? I certainly vote for the corrected version.

Let the Sparks Fly

The welder picture (Figure 5.6) appears at first glance easier to correct than the one of the little girl. Even without measuring actual dot values the general approach is clear. We would like to emphasize detailing in the man's shirt. It's a blue shirt, which means heavily cyan and secondarily magenta, with small amounts of yellow. The brilliant sparks from the torch are specular highlights; they have to be as light as possible, meaning no dot at all. No additional contrast will be possible there.

Consequently, we will be steepening the part of the cyan curve that interests us, by reducing the value of whatever the minimum cyan in the shirt is. This will be at the expense of other areas in the picture that have less cyan than the shirt. If it is possible to increase the maximum cyan we will do it as well. The magenta curve will behave similarly: in lighter areas of the shirt we will have less magenta than before correction, and in the darker areas more. The yellow will steepen in a different way. Since the lightest yellow area in the shirt is probably around 2 percent, we can't go lighter, and will resort to making the rest of the plate heavier.

This strategy absolutely will make for a better shirt, but have you caught the danger?

Metallics, such as the welder's mask, have to be neutral. This means equal amounts of magenta and yellow, and slightly more cyan. It is OK to have a heavy hand with the cyan, as a cyan-tinted gray is still believable. If the cyan is high the magenta can be slightly high as well, giving us a blue-tinted gray.

But a metal mask that tends toward some other color is no good, and that is what we risk with the proposed move. Before correction, the mask is neutral, but the curve I just suggested will add yellow to it. Unless the curve also adds magenta, the mask will become green.

Neutrality problems are finessed easily enough—provided we take the time to identify them before applying the fatal curves.

Its Fleece Was White As Snow

The gains of using all available tones are striking, and it may be interesting to see how much is just a matter of setting proper highlights and shadows, and how much extra we get from stealing all the internal space we can from unimportant areas. The first three images were not all that horrible before we began, illustrating the power of this correction technique. But for present purposes we need a really bad original, and the one at the top of Figure 5.7 qualifies most emphatically.

What we have to work with here is so abysmal that I refuse to show the correction curves, for fear some reader might think that moves this drastic should be tried on more common varieties of image. The problem, of course, is that everything is flat. Even the lightest snow is a dull gray, and the animal's eyes and nose are not as dark as they should be.

The routine, by-the-numbers method is to find the lightest part of the image, somewhere in the snow, and set it to 5C2M2Y. Similarly, the darkest part, somewhere in the eyes or nose, will go to 80C70M70Y70K.

This dogmatic correction results in the bottom image of Figure 5.7. It is far better than the one above it, no doubt, but we are not done. Between the eyes/nose and

Figure 5.8 *The curves used to create the top image exaggerate contrast in all areas of the seal. In doing so, undesirable amounts of yellow and blue appeared; they are neutralized in the bottom image.*

the second darkest area of the image is an enormous gulf of unused space. Naturally, if we compress this, we will have more with which to depict the white seal.

The top image of Figure 5.8 reflects this kind of correction. Note how much more pronounced the animal is against the background, and the additional detail in the fur. This is a remarkable improvement over the dreary original, but when the move is this drastic, supplementary correction is occasionally necessary.

Here, some colors became too obtrusive. The seal's rear legs have a distinct yellow tinge, and the process of accentu-ating the animal made this color area too vivid. Likewise, the bluish background areas became too pronounced. Since there are no other important blue or yel-low areas in the image, I used Photoshop 3's **Image: Adjust>Selective Color** to reduce the intensity of these two colors.

This technique only affects areas that the program sees as predominantly blue or yellow, leaving the rest of the image alone. Here is one of the few times that such an adjustment will work better than curves: normally if a picture is too heavy in a yellow area it is too heavy in yellow ink throughout the image. Owing to the violence of our initial correction, that was not the case here.

As Red As a Lobster

Food shots are a prime candidate for con-trast-building treatment, so we'll end this chapter with one. Extra color range puts what we refer to as "life" into a picture. Not surprisingly, this translates to foods that look fresher and, hence, more appe-tizing.

Personally, I salivate at the thought of lobster even when the image portraying it is as bland as in Figure 5.9. Nevertheless, if it has to be used in advertising, the origi-nal is very far from being satisfactory.

Like the previous example, we have to correct the overall range, but when writing curves, we will seize the opportunity to extend range in the lobsters and the greens in front of them.

Analysis of the image yields the follow-ing grim statistics. Highlight, in the ice, is 1C4M8Y. Shadow, in several places, is around 53C66M97Y50K. So, the image has a yellow cast. This is confirmed by

several measurements throughout the ice. The cyan and magenta are always roughly equal and the yellow is 5 or 6 points higher. As you are well aware by now, if the cyan and yellow numbers were re-versed, that would be correct.

The lobsters themselves yield the fol-lowing kinds of numbers: 0C38M65Y; 6C45M78Y; 11C53M; 15C75M98Y3K. The greens appear flat because they are: four measurements came out almost identical, at around 70C30M85Y15K.

Our correction curves should clearly reduce yellow, slightly boost magenta, and greatly increase cyan and black. We will, of course, fine-tune the highlight and shadow values by watching the Info palette carefully as we adjust the curves.

Individual colors, though, will behave differently. The yellow will nosedive at the upper end of its range, because there is nothing of importance that has only mod-erate yellow. The magenta will get ham-mered in its midsection, to emphasize the areas that were between 20 and 30 per-cent (the greens) and 50 and 75 percent (the lobsters). And the cyan curve will build contrast in highlights (for the lob-sters) and three-quartertone (for the greens).

This successful move is an appropriate way to end our discussion of global cor-rection by curves. It may have struck you, when you saw the original image, that the cooked lobsters were the wrong color. Was there a time when you would have been tempted to make a local selection of only the lobsters so as to redden them?

The problem of the lobsters' color sim-ply went away by itself. We paid no atten-tion to it at all during correction. We just set the numbers to what we knew to be correct and everything fell neatly into place. It often does—when you consider the image as a whole and not as a bunch of pieces.

Old Myths and New Realities

Several challenges to conventional wisdom are suggested by this two-chapter series of color corrections. First, there really is a place for the thinking artist. No calibrationist system can hope to equal the work of someone who can make intelligent judgments as to what areas of an image need emphasis and which can be sacrificed.

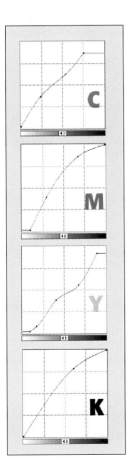

Figure 5.9 *Identifying and extending the range of the colors in the lobsters makes for a more appetizing bottom image. The correction curves that accomplished this are shown at right.*

Quick & Dirty

COLOR CORRECTION AS HORSETRADING

✓ If the full range of colors is in use, there will be a price for any further improvement in the image. We should therefore always be alive to the possibility of a favorable tradeoff, where detail in an unimportant area can be exchanged for contrast in a more vital one.

✓ A fact of human vision: when we look closely at a certain object, it gains detail, while everything else in our field of vision loses out. The camera, on the other hand, is egalitarian. We are fully justified, therefore, in emphasizing the details that we would like the viewer to focus on, at the expense of those we consider unimportant.

✓ When writing curves, areas of the curve that are steeper than before will gain contrast, but areas that are flatter will pay the price.

✓ Applying contrast-intensifying curves globally is both easier and more realistic than selecting parts of the image and working on them locally.

✓ Before beginning, take an inventory. List all the ranges in each color that fall in important areas. Use it as a guide not only to the areas that must be steepened but to those that can be sacrificed.

✓ Writing curves to increase contrast does not excuse us from the obligation to keep neutral colors neutral and to keep appropriate highlight and shadow values. Before applying the curves, check to make sure that none of these requirements are being violated.

✓ If the correction curves are extreme, the image must be carefully examined afterward at 1:1 resolution to make sure that it is not breaking up or posterizing.

✓ Contrast-enhancing curves often have favorable side effects. They may eliminate color casts. Also the techniques discussed in this chapter have the tendency to correct strange colors, as in the lobsters shown in Figure 5.9.

✓ The conventional wisdom in color correction is that everything depends on the quality of the original. That can become a self-fulfilling prophecy. With proper attention, decidedly mediocre originals can yield professional results.

Second, the desktop artist is now taking over the traditional work of the high-end scanner operator. That opposes the conventional wisdom that we are replacing the person sitting in front of a Scitex or similar system.

Actually, those folks don't know all that much about color correction, even though when they have to correct they do it in exactly the same way, with global CMYK curves. But they rarely have experience dealing with moves this drastic, because their original scans are so superior. On a quality scanner not only are the optics better, but one can apply curves or selective color corrections, and good operators know how to do both.

Having spent much of my career in supervising color production at high-end shops, I can tell you that on a day in which I was feeling charitable I would accept the original scan of the welder and, conceivably, that of the insect. Every other original in both this and the preceding chapter would have been bounced with great alacrity and more than a little profanity.

Certainly, first-quality scans would have given better results than all of our corrections, particularly in the seal and the lobsters. But the line must be drawn somewhere: if we want a nice picture of a baby seal, the best approach is to fly a photographer to Canada and arrange a shoot. Our budget may not allow for this (not to mention the hundred-dollar scan afterwards) considering that the alternative shown here cost about 50 cents to license the image plus less than five minutes to correct it.

The less-than-optimal scan is the wave of the future, like it or not. With so many stock photo CDs now available, as well as the success of the Kodak CD process and improvements in desktop scanner technology, color correction skill is essential for the modern artist.

Yet the conventional wisdom still is that the changes we have just seen are impossible. Here is a quotation from a book on halftone reproduction that was published in 1993.

"It cannot be emphasized too strongly that the quality of all photographs reproduced by the halftone process depends entirely on the quality of the original. No printing process, however refined, can compensate for a sloppy original. While a good process technician might well be able to enhance part of an image, it is usually at the expense of a tone elsewhere. For example, if lighter tones are heightened, the blacks could at the same time lose some of their density."

Right.

Such sanctimonious piffle gets disproven every day. Anybody would prefer to start with the best image possible, but life isn't like that. As we have seen, a lot can be saved from second-rate originals.

No question, when we make an improvement, "it is usually at the expense of a tone elsewhere." But the author of these remarks did not grasp that this expense can be quite reasonable, in the hands of a thinking artist. It is quite true that every change suggested in this chapter had a cost. Fortunately, a lot of the time, the price was right.

Figure 6.1 The purple hue of the sky in this image might prompt the designer to order a silhouette. This chapter discusses some of the many ways to go wrong in executing it.

CHAPTER 6

Selections and Silhouettes

Isolating and working on a single area of an image is not usually the best policy, but in some cases it can't be helped. Careful use of selection tools and masks allows smooth-looking silhouettes and composites.

iplomatic tactics are frequently necessary for success in color correction. Negotiation is always preferable to confrontation, because, just as people are not always of the same political view, they also see colors in different ways. And, as in politics, some of us get very violent in the views we espouse about an image.

In diplomacy, the global view is usually the best one. In handling color images, the same is true. When we see several small problems in an image, they are probably interrelated parts of a bigger problem. That was the whole point of the last two chapters, not to take local areas in isolation but to concentrate on the image as a whole.

The concept of *selection* is to limit the area in which changes can take place. If we select part of an image and then apply curves, the curves will only apply to the parts selected. As a general rule, we would like to avoid this practice, for the reasons demonstrated in Figure 4.6. There, we were presented with a pink horse that might have tempted us to reach for the selection tools. It would have been a big mistake, because although by selecting the horse we could easily have eliminated the color cast, operating on the entire picture improved many other areas that were not as clearly impossible as the horse was.

Nevertheless, there are some times when a selection can't be avoided. Here is a list of the major occasions.

• When *silhouetting,* which is to say, removing the background so that the foreground object stands alone, there is plainly no way around selecting the foreground object, inverting the selection so that the background is now the selected area, and hitting the delete key.

• When correcting color along the lines described in Chapter 5, if contrast-adding moves start to have adverse effects on the background. In such situations, it may become helpful to select the foreground object(s) and apply one last curve to them. This only helps in extreme cases; otherwise, the quality gain is not really worth the annoyance of making the selection.

• When making a drastic color change for artistic reasons as opposed to reproduction quality. In Chapter 10, for example, I tussle with a Kodak Photo CD image of a model posed against a background that is very close to being a flesh color itself. For one reason or another I could not tolerate this, and I could not write a curve that would change one but not the other. So I was reduced to selecting the background and changing it alone via curves.

• When trying to retouch in a certain area, to guard against accidentally affecting an area that is OK. Example: suppose we are working with a damaged original that has a large scratch across a critical and difficult area of the image. Fixing this will be tedious and may involve airbrushing, pixel painting, cloning, and whatnot. As all these tools are somewhat gross and hard to control, it makes sense to select

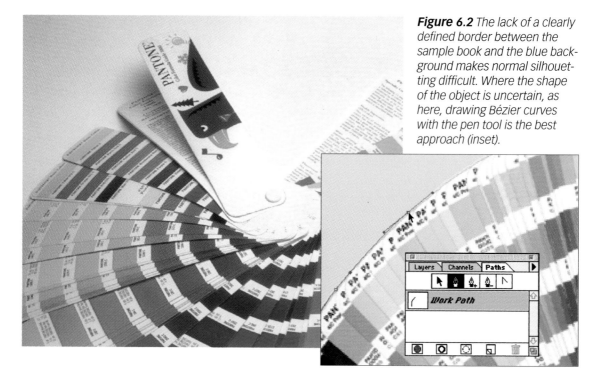

Figure 6.2 *The lack of a clearly defined border between the sample book and the blue background makes normal silhouetting difficult. Where the shape of the object is uncertain, as here, drawing Bézier curves with the pen tool is the best approach (inset).*

the scratch only, if that is possible, before starting our onslaught.

Importantly, selections can be made in any channel and the selection will hold when all channels are displayed. Conversely, a selection made in CMYK will hold even if we change the display to one color only. This lets us limit changes to a single color in a single area. Also, we can move the selection shape from one image to another, which is very helpful in complicated masking situations where we are dealing with more than one version of the same image. But I am getting a little ahead of myself.

Choosing a Selection Method

There are five selection methods in Photoshop, plus assorted commands to extend them. Once an area has been selected by any method, we can add to or subtract from it with the same tool or any other. We hold down the Shift key if adding to the selection; the Command key if subtracting. Selected areas do not have to be contiguous. If we are working on a person's face we can select both eyes without getting the nose.

First, one can select a rectangular or oval area using one of the marquee tools. This is chiefly useful in defining an area that will be ghosted out, or picked up as a block to go into another image.

The easiest and best way to select, when it happens to work, is the magic wand tool. We click where we want to select, and, if it is dissimilar enough from the area around it, the wand will find exactly what we want. The sensitivity of the wand can be adjusted by double-clicking on it in the toolbox. There are 256 levels of sensitivity, 32 being the default. It is better to

have it too low than too high: if it doesn't pick up enough image the first time, **Select: Grow** will add more.

• The lasso tool lets us draw the area we want to select, using the mouse. This is more accurate and predictable than the magic wand, but requires a steady hand.

• Using the lasso with the Option key depressed lets us draw a succession of straight lines by dragging the mouse and clicking on it. This is a fast and effective way of selecting areas that don't have complicated shapes.

• Most accurate, most flexible, and, you guessed it, most difficult, is the pen tool of the Paths palette. This allows us to draw Bézier curves like those found in most illustration programs. Bézier curves are a basic building block in PostScript graphics, but they take some getting used to. Their shape is governed by anchor points and control points that define the slope and angle of the curve. A full description of their use is, regrettably, outside the scope of this book. Unless you are exporting silhouetted objects to other programs using the Clipping Path feature, you can get along without Bézier curves. Those professionals who are comfortable with them, however, do most of their silhouetting this way. It yields lovely, smooth selections that can be edited easily, which is more than can be said for any of the other methods.

Figure 6.2 is ideal for the pen tool approach. There is almost no definition at the edge of the swatch book, so if we have to select the book, the magic wand will be hopeless. The designer can help out by placing the silhouetted image against a light background, so that the lack of an edge won't be so evident. That way, the

Option–lasso tool will be good enough. If, however, the book were going to go against a dark background, there would be no alternative to the pen tool, so that the rounded corners of the swatch pages would not look all ratty.

It is well worth the effort to learn how to compose and edit these curves, and mandatory if you are going to be using an art-creation program such as Adobe Illustrator. In the interest of simplicity, however, the exercises in this chapter will use the magic wand.

Avoiding the Cut-Out Look

At its simplest, silhouetting means complete removal of a background. To start things off in a somewhat more complex fashion, have a look at Figure 6.1. The foreground image is attractive, but the sky is the wrong color. It will be difficult to correct this by curves, since the sky color resembles that of the woman's skin. We can select the background only and apply curves to it, but suppose we have decided against that approach. Instead, we have chosen, or been told, to eliminate the sky and replace it with a uniform light blue, but to maintain the greenery at the bottom of the image.

To accomplish this, we will have to somehow select the background only, with the exception of the green area. This done, we will set our background color to a light blue and hit the delete key. All selected areas will vanish and be replaced by the background color, and all will live happily ever after.

There are several obstacles to get by in this process, so let's get the easy part over with. The background color is set by double-clicking on the background color icon

in the toolbox. Up will come a color definitions dialog box that permits entry of a CMYK specification. I used 15C3M3Y.

If we decide to silhouette with the lasso or the pen tool, we will outline, and thus select, the woman, the bicycle and the green background. The fact that this is not the area we need selected at the end means nothing. Once we are done, we **Select: Inverse** and the other half of the image gets selected instead.

Because **Select: Inverse** is such a snap to use, we always have the choice of trying to select either the foreground or the background. Here, the background seems more uniform and we will use it, but in Figure 6.7 the foreground would have been a better choice.

There is much more differentiation between foreground and background than there was in Figure 6.2, so the magic wand looks like a good way to avoid a tiresome session of drawing. There is plenty of variation within the background itself, though, so the wand will not be any walk in the park.

Figure 6.3 shows the progression of establishing the selection. The magic wand only works on adjacent areas, and the background here is broken into four pieces by the woman's arms and the bicycle. The area between the woman's right arm, her body, and the bike is the best place to start, because that is the section with the most contrast between background and foreground. The other choices have things like hair and wristwatches that might confuse the wand.

The tolerance setting for the wand is pretty much pot luck in a case like this and I left it at 32. When I touched the wand to the desired area, it was not wholly successful: some of the blue background was left unselected. I could now have gone back, increased the wand's tolerance and tried again, **Select: Grow**, which expands the current selection into adjoining similar colors, is easier. After three applications of this command, the entire blue area was successfully selected.

Rather than go through the same rigmarole with every other area of the image, the next step was **Select: Similar**. This command finds areas that have the same color value as the selection, regardless of their location. As the center image in Figure 6.3 shows, this scattershot method had some problems. It missed the lighter blues at the top of the image as well as parts of the darker blues. Also, pieces of the blue bicycle and some of the hair got picked up.

Selecting the light blue part of the background required no more than a Shift-click of the magic wand. Then, I moved into the lasso tool. Holding down Shift, I drew around all unselected areas of the background and, holding down Command, I drew around the parts of the foreground that were erroneously selected. Since all of the lassoed points were well away from the transition, no great skill with the mouse was required to do this, as opposed to the precision one would have needed to select the woman without using the magic wand.

Unkempt hair is a silhouetting problem no matter what approach we use, but it is especially bad with the wand. I left it alone here, but depending on quality requirements, I might have been more careful, or trimmed off some of the offending strands, or created a non-solid mask.

So, the entire background is selected, and we have a background color defined.

Figure 6.3 *At left, silhouetting begins by selecting the area beneath the woman's right arm. The "Similar" command picks up like colors in the rest of the image, but stray selections begin to appear in the bicycle and the hair (center). At right, the difficult contour of a person's hair is the biggest challenge for the "magic wand" method of selection.*

If we now press the Delete key the abomination of Figure 6.4 results.

Feathering and Saving Paths

In Figure 6.4 the biker looks as if she had been cut out with scissors and plunked down on the blue background. Since, in effect, that is exactly what we did, this should not be too surprising.

Photoshop's way of hiding these abrupt transitions is *feathering*, but before discussing that, another important omission on our part must be noted. We went to a lot of trouble making this selection, and it is rather presumptuous to think that we may never need to make it again. As actually happened, we may find that the selection was not completely accurate and we need to revise it. More likely, we will show our silhouette to our client, who will say, this was a terrible idea, go back to the original background but make it brighter.

In either case, we will need to remake our selection. To guard against extra effort, we should always save any selection path that requires more than a minute or two of work. This is done via the Paths palette. Once we have completed a selection, we click the arrow on the side of the palette and choose Make Path. When the path is completed we choose Save Path (Photoshop will now ask for a path name). If this is strictly a precautionary step, we Make Selection and go about our business, except that now, if disaster strikes and we need to reselect the background, we will be able to reload the saved path by clicking on it in the Paths palette. When the file is saved, the path will be saved with it for future use. The amount of disk space it takes up is negligible.

Back to feathering, which is an artificial blurring of the transition areas. We choose **Select: Feather** and specify a pixel radius, or, if reloading an existing path, there will be a prompt for a feathering value. For silhouetting work I find that 1.0 pixels is a good radius. The feathering works on both sides of the selection line, so that two pixels will actually be blurred.

The impressive effect of feathering is shown in Figure 6.5. At one pixel, the cutout effect of Figure 6.4 largely vanishes. A value of 10 pixels gives a blurry, antique kind of look.

Figure 6.4 *This silhouette is unsuccessful because of bad transition between the foreground and the new background. It looks cut out and pasted in.*

A major improvement, but there are still shortcomings. The selection was clearly not perfect, because pieces of the original background appear over the biker's right shoulder, and there are gouges in her left arm. The hair is also not too good. These things can easily be touched up if we are too lazy to go back and edit our path, but what about the abrupt transition from green to blue at the bottom of the image?

Fortunately, another easy selection technique can fix this. The two images of Figure 6.5 solve the problem together, if we can combine them. The 1-pixel version has the better biker, but the 10-pixel version has the acceptable transition from green to blue.

To have the best of both, we will go to the 10-pixel version and hand-draw, with the lasso, a selection of the transition area on each side. We will attempt to avoid getting any of the biker in the selection, but great precision is not really necessary. Now, we copy the selection into memory.

Image: Calculations>Copy allows passing a selection path from one image to another, provided the images are the

Figure 6.5 *The impact of feathering. The antique effect at right comes from a feather value of 10 pixels; a value of one pixel (left) suffices for a smooth transition.*

Figure 6.6 *By copying a selection to memory, then transferring the selection path to a different version of the image and copying back, the best halves of Figure 6.5 are brought together into a single picture.*

same size. Thus, an equivalent selection area gets defined in the 1-pixel image. When we paste from memory, the transition areas from the 10-pixel version fall neatly into the 1-pixel image. If we want to fool around some at this point, we can go into the Layers palette and save the pasted object as a temporary layer. Then, the Layer Options menu lets us change the opacity percentage of the object we just pasted in, so there can be an 80–20 split between the two images if we like. (Users of earlier Photoshop versions, which have no Layers palette, can do the same thing with **Edit: Composite Controls**, which no longer exists in Photoshop 3.)

Quick Masks and Quicker Blends

For our next assignment, turn back a few pages and recall the dramatic improvements we made in the horse image of Figure 4.6. Assume the following scenario.

We are graphics professionals. An art director takes the original photo to one of our competitors, a calibrationist competitor. There, she is presented with a contract proof of the insipid pink version of the horses, along with the explanation that this matches the art as precisely as science can; scanning conditions have been calibrated exactly to compensate for the type of film that is being used; this is the only means of staying faithful to the original; the method of conversion into CMYK has been endorsed by four RIT professors, three scanner manufacturers, two consulting firms, and a partridge in a pear tree; so you are quite wrong to be dissatisfied, as this is an empirically perfect reproduction, and on and on.

Dissatisfied nevertheless, she brings the digital data to us, along with the original art, thinking we will have to rescan it. Instead, we color-correct in routine buccaneering fashion, seeing our opportunities and taking 'em, winding up with a much more palatable version.

As clients are wont to do, however, this one now has a suggestion. She appreciates the incredible improvement we made in the horses, but not the similar move in the background. She concedes that the original background was too flat but asks that we find some intermediate background between the two versions.

I don't know about you, but I disagree with this interpretation of the image. As professionals, though, we will have to comply with the request. Happily, Photoshop makes it easy for us.

First order of business is to select the horses. The magic wand has no difficulty finding the white areas where the animals meet the background, and the interior can easily be rounded up with the lasso. The harnessing and carriage fixtures have to be traced.

As soon as the selection is complete, naturally, we save the path. Upon reinstating the selection, we choose a feather radius of one pixel.

Before splitting the difference between the two backgrounds, we need to create a third version of the image. This one will have the white horses from our version but the original background from the inferior one. Then, we close the original pink image, and combine the third version with our corrected version. With **Image: Calculations>Blend** we can specify any percentage of blend between two images. Since the horses are identical in the two images we are blending, only the background will change.

To get to this point, we will use Photoshop's Quick Mask feature. To use this, once an area is selected, click on the Quick Mask icon at the bottom right of the tools palette. This establishes a temporary fifth channel, and gives us a dis-

play of what areas the mask covers, as shown in Figure 6.7.

If the mask is satisfactory, the next step is **Image: Calculations>Composite**, where the composite image (Figure 6.8) will be the one we define as Source 1, except in areas covered by the mask, where it will remain what it is in the target image.

Masks have three significant differences from mere selections. Two of these are good and one bad. On the good side, we can edit masks exactly as other types of images, meaning we can use any tools we like. All we need to do is display the mask channel alone (with a Command–5, assuming there is only one mask in the file) and we can retouch it with the airbrush tool or anything else. This is certainly better than the lasso method of altering selections.

Figure 6.7 *Using the mask function, background from one image can be composited with foreground objects from another version.*

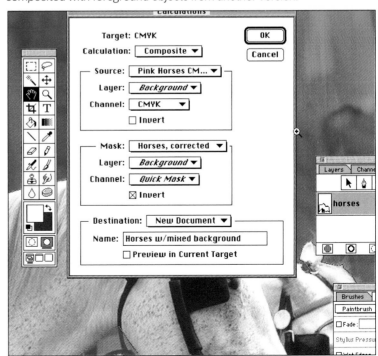

Quick & Dirty

SELECTIONS AND SILHOUETTES

✓Although color correction should generally be applied globally, there are times when a certain area must be isolated, either because it is going to be silhouetted, because there is no alternative to a local color correction, or because during a retouch we want to prevent accidental contamination.

✓Photoshop offers four major selection tools for irregular areas: the magic wand, the lasso, the option-lasso, and the Bézier pen tool found in the Paths palette. Once an area has been defined, it can be added to or subtracted from using any tool. Selections do not have to be contiguous.

✓The magic wand is easiest to use, but there are many types of selections for which it will not work. The pen tool is the most accurate and easiest to edit with if necessary, but it also requires the most skill.

✓Any time you have created a selection that involved more than a nominal amount of effort, save the selection as a path, using the Paths palette. This guards against having to recreate the selection from scratch later. The disk space used is negligible.

✓In silhouetting an image, it will not do to just isolate and delete the background. This will create a hard-edged transition that will look as though the foreground object was cut out with scissors. Instead, the selection must be feathered before it is deleted, to make a smoother transition.

✓Photoshop's Quick Mask feature is an easy and effective way of creating composite images. The mask is easily edited in case the first composite has quality problems. The Quick Mask is a temporary additional channel, although it can be made permanent.

✓Masks, unlike direct selections from paths, can have less than full intensity in any area, not just the feathered edge. They can also be edited freely using any Photoshop tool, including curves. These features make masking a prerequisite for complicated image merges, especially where one image has only a vague edge.

✓If you have created a mask that you may need again, save it as a separate document using Photoshop 3.0 format, rather than as a separate channel of the base file. This saves large amounts of disk space.

Figure 6.8 *The image on the right is a hybrid. Its background is 35 percent that of the left image, but 65 percent that of Figure 4.7.*

More important, unlike a selection, a mask can be partial. It need not be solid in all areas, and where the mask is defined as, say, 80 percent, when the composite is finally made it will have some of the attributes of both its parents.

Because of these advantages, masking would have been a better way to handle the hair problem in the biker image. We could have painted some of the stray hairs into our mask with a soft airbrush tool, allowing more of a natural look.

The disadvantage of masks is that they take up as much room as any color, so if we save a mask with an image our file size

goes up by 25 percent. In this image, we don't have to: since we have the selection path saved, we can always regenerate the mask easily if need be. But if we had retouched the mask extensively, we would have been well advised to save it.

In ordinary image work, this sort of thing is all one needs masks for, but, obviously, I have just scratched the surface of this tremendously powerful tool. Intelligent use of masking is the cornerstone of much dramatic special effects work in Photoshop. Anyone interested in this sort of creative work should give the study of masking careful attention.

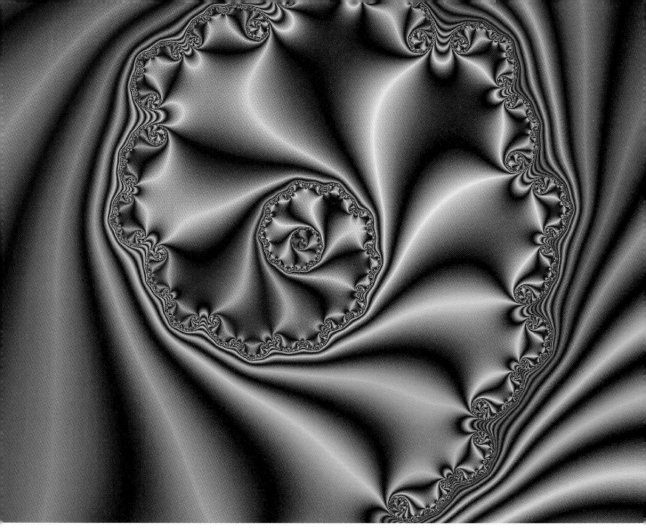

Figure 7.1 *What is a computer-generated graphic like this doing in a chapter on humdrum local enhancements? Surprisingly, it can be used as a correction tool.*

CHAPTER 7

Local Patchwork, Sharpening, And Enhancements

The best of originals have defects. The most artful subjects can sometimes be made even more fetching. Unsharp masking and other contrast-building techniques create the illusion of more depth.

When we say that an image is *good* we normally mean that it provokes some kind of pleasant emotional response the minute we look at it. As color technicians, we study all facets of the image intently before doing anything, but we must remember that the audience's reaction will be a much more cursory one. The viewer will absorb the image in less than a second, form an impression, and in that second we will have either won the battle or gone down in a blaze of swords and cannon fire.

For this reason, our focus has been improvement of the image as a whole, the big picture, if you like. It is easy to be penny wise, pound foolish about color correction.

There is, however, a nitty-gritty side of image enhancement, and that is the subject of this chapter. Much of this deals with fixing up outright defects, such as dust, hairs, and scratches. We also need to know how to add detail where none exists, as where an area is totally washed out, or where we need to create extra background.

In addition to knowing how to make the best of these bad situations, the color professional uses local correction tools in several clever ways to enhance areas of the image that are already good. We can accentuate details, make the image appear better-focused by judicious use of unsharp masking, and generally add some nice finishing touches.

Inspecting for Defects

Scanning pictures is far from being a clean process. Usually, the scan is of a piece of 35mm film, greatly magnified. Any dust, scratches, and other imperfections that happen to be on the film get magnified too, and often exaggerated. The scanner operator may contribute a hair or two. At high magnification the normal drum-scanning practice is to mount chromes in oil or gel, which minimizes the above-mentioned imperfections, but does not eliminate them. One must also, therefore, watch out for another kind of defect. If you have ever seen something in the mid-

dle of a scan that looked like a bubble, it probably was.

Fixing these problems is often easy enough, but you have to find them first. This means a careful examination of all parts of the image, with monitor display blown up to 1:1, meaning that one monitor pixel equals one image pixel. Assuming a monitor resolution of 72 and a scanned image in the vicinity of 250, the image will be almost four times as large on your screen as it is in reality. So it may not fit, and you may have to scroll around quite a bit, especially if your image is large. The whole inspection process may take five or 10 minutes that you would really rather not spare.

Nobody said the life of a graphic artist was an easy one. Ya gotta do it.

No matter the scanning source, there is no guarantee against this kind of defect. The highest-quality color separators occa-

Figure 7.2 The hair at left can easily be removed using the clone tool at full intensity. This image represents the easiest variety of defect correction.

sionally provide it, although they also go through the inspection process detailed above. The commercially available CDs that provide the majority of the images in this book have more than a few stray hairs in them, too.

Figure 7.2 features the everyday variety of annoying hair. It can be removed with what too many people consider to be the everyday touchup tool, the cloner.

Possibly because there are so many tools and suboptions in the

Photoshop toolbox, there is a strong tendency among beginners to use the easily understandable ones, but there is good reason to take a closer look.

All tools—the cloner, the smudger, the airbrush, the paintbrush, the dodge/burn/sponge, the blur/sharpen, and the pencil—have their attributes controlled by the brushes palette. All of them can be given different strengths (or opacities), and different widths of stroke. Except for the pencil tool, the stroke can also be feathered. What the tool does can be altered, too. There is a Normal setting, but this can be changed to lighten only or darken only, among several more esoteric possibilities. Photoshop 3 also has a **Filter: Noise>Dust & Scratches** that is of some utility in general cleaning.

In the case of Figure 7.2, none of this sophistication is necessary. The white is all the same and the orange is more or less uniform as well. So, the cloner, which picks up one area of the image and deposits it in another, will work well. Opacity should be set at 100 percent, as we don't want any of the hair to show through, and there is no need to be delicate here. We can set the brush width to any convenient size, and there is no need for feathering. Non-aligned is the best option for the cloning method.

There is one small nuance that you might have missed. Although we clone from an inside part of the orange letter, the correction takes place on the outside edge. If we are sloppy, we will spray orange pixels into the surrounding white area. One way to avoid this is to select the letter before working on it, but a classier way is to set the cloner tool to Lighten rather than Normal. That way, if we

Figure 7.3 *Because the hairs in this picture (enlarged here) cover a complex background, the cloning tool is not an effective way to remove them.*

should drop some orange onto white, nothing will happen, since orange is darker than white. The clone will affect only areas that are darker than the orange being duplicated.

Minimizing vs. Eliminating Problems

Defects are not always so considerate about where they fall. In the lower part of Figure 7.2, another hair falls in a textured area. Direct cloning won't work well there, since it will interrupt the pattern.

Remember that a screen display of 1:1 will display stray hairs somewhat more emphatically than the printed product. A reasonable approach, then, is to minimize the defect, rather than attempt to obliterate it.

It is frequently easier to eliminate hairs from individual plates than from the entire picture. When, as in Figure 7.3, a hair overprints greenery, chances are that it is prominent in the black and magenta plates, since those will otherwise be light. That means we can get at them easily in those channels with the clone tool. And if the magenta and black components of the hair are eliminated, leaving only the cyan

Figure 7.4 *Judicious placement of a couple of false trees covers up the defects of Figure 7.3.*

and yellow, which are heavy anyway, the hair may well not be noticeable.

Short of picking up the pencil tool and painstakingly reconstructing, pixel by pixel, what we think the underlying image looks like, the best depilatory treatment is the airbrush. Set width to a feathered one pixel, method to Lighten, and opacity to 85 percent. The objective is not to obliterate the hair but to blend it in naturally. If the area surrounding the hair is critical, select the hair itself before airbrushing it. As a rule, such difficult touchup is best done plate by plate. That way, colors that are receptive to the clone tool can be cloned, reserving the airbrush for where it is needed.

Figure 7.5 shows a less common defect, but one that illustrates that problems are

Figure 7.5 *The water stain at left is eliminated by placing a heavily feathered layer of similar texture on top of it.*

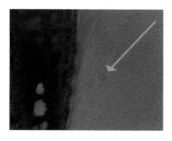

everywhere: the image came from a promotion for the quality of a company's images. The circular problem in the center of the image is a drop of water that dried out on the chrome. To avoid this, the operator is supposed to use film cleaner on the original before scanning it.

This blemish is not amenable to a direct clone because it is so large. A single hit of a feathered clone will be obvious, and repeated applications of cloning will damage texture. We could work in the four different plates to eliminate the spot, and then add some noise to each to cover our tracks. But a better way, since the skin appears to be the same tone and texture throughout, is to find a suitably large area nearby and simply drop it on top of the defect. To do this, select the area freehand with the lasso. It would be wrong to use any other method of selection, since straight lines and circles are much more obvious than irregular shapes.

Then, feather the selection area by a large amount, say 10 pixels. This will make sure there is no obvious edge when the final move is made. Now, place a copy of the selection on top of itself with Command–C, Command–V. The copy is now selected, and all we have to do is drag it over the blemish. (Had we not gone through the copying routine, when we dragged our selection over the defect the original selection area would have gone blank.)

As Dorothy found out with the Witch of the East, dropping something large on something unpleasant is often effective. Figure 7.4 demonstrates this as a method of correcting Figure 7.3. The hairs on the left side of that image can be toned down by normal methods, but the one on the right looks like it came off a goat. I dropped a couple of trees on it.

Extending a Background

Another important method of covering holes is *anamorphic* enlargement of critical areas. That's how we'll cover one of the largest holes imaginable in the next example.

Art directors and photographers are supposed to be on the same wavelength when it comes to design requirements. This is to avoid having one of them inform us that it is necessary to have an image of somewhat different dimensions than it is at the moment.

In the top half of Figure 7.6, the elimination of the yellow cast is by now routine for us, but what happens when we learn that the layout calls for half an inch more image at the top and that the art director refuses to countenance enlarging the picture?

To fill this order, after excising the yellow cast, we go to **Image: Canvas Size** and add half an inch to our height. We have to indicate that the existing image is to fall at bottom center of the new space, since Photoshop's default is to center it both ways. That would give us white space at both top and bottom instead of top only.

For reasons that will become clear, we now **Edit: Take Snapshot**. Once this is done, we can proceed to an anamorphic move in the sky.

An anamorphic reduction or

Figure 7.6 *Insufficient background is a common problem. In addition to poor color balance, the image at top is not vertical enough. Below, half an inch more sky and better color.*

Figure 7.7 *Building a larger background for this image starts with the freehand selection of as large a piece of sky as is reasonable, considering that the rock itself must be excluded.*

enlargement is an intentional distortion. It stretches out the image, much like a circus mirror, by pulling more in one direction than the other.

In Photoshop, one resizes anamorphically by unchecking Constrain File Proportions in the **Image: Image Size** dialog box and entering new values for height and width. There is not much use for this capability, because almost every image has elements that would seem obviously distorted, such as the trees here. If this image were a fiftieth instead of a half inch too short, for sure nobody would notice if we resized anamorphically, but it would still be better to resize the whole thing normally and just not tell the art director.

A sky, on the other hand, can be stretched quite a bit. If we select a section of it, we shuffle the anamorphic deck without affecting the rest of the picture.

The fact that as much as half an inch extra is needed puts pressure on us. If it were less, we might just select a rectangular area at the top of the existing sky and stretch it to fill. Stretching a piece to more than twice its original height, however, is not something we are likely to get away with. No, we need to steal more of the original sky, and we can't get a rectangular area of it, because the rock, which can't be part of the selection, will get in the way.

So, we draw a freehand lasso selection as shown in Figure 7.7, and feather it by 10

pixels or so. It is important to draw the selection by hand rather than make it out of straight lines, because once we start to stretch a nonrectangular area, things will get very ugly where the selection line meets the sky below. A straight line will be painfully visible and difficult to fix. We must make the shape irregular.

When the selection is complete, we go to **Image: Effects>Scale**. This will draw a sizing rectangle around the selection, and by moving the top control points to the blank top of our image, the selected area of the sky will stretch to fill. Here, we are not moving the control points horizontally at all, but it is possible to do both when resizing. Anamorphic is the default mode, but if you want a stretch-free reduction or enlargement, hold down the Shift key while moving the point.

Meanwhile, we are not out of trouble yet with this image. Stretching exaggerates irregularities. So, especially in the area directly above the rock, the stretch pulled the selection away from the rest of the image, leaving a hole.

Having taken the snapshot before stretching, we can fill this hole by setting the clone tool to From Snapshot, choosing a large feathered brush, high opacity, and running the tool through it. This may still leave some rough edges to fix, but that's a lot better than the two-square-inch hole we started with.

Focusing on the Unsharp

So much for damage control. Let us leave the tiresome but necessary drudgery of defect detection and correction for the more enjoyable meadows of local image enhancement.

Filter: Sharpen>Unsharp Masking, USM for short, is a potent method both on selections and on the image as a whole. Sharpening can also be applied through the blur/sharpen tool. We have no use for the other, cruder sharpening options.

The technical explanation of USM will come in a few moments, but all one really needs to know is that it is a sneaky way of making images appear to be in better focus. It works by exaggerating transition points. USM is generally necessary when an image comes down in resolution, for reasons alluded to in Chapter 3. If you turn back to Figure 3.6, you will recall that images that are at too high a resolution tend to appear soft. Their transition areas

Figure 7.8 *Below, two scans from the same high-end scanner: bottom left with USM completely disabled, bottom right with the scanner's normal sharpness setting. Top, Photoshop's sharpening algorithm is not effective in improving the bottom left image.*

seem weak. To see why, please imagine a picture of a lamp with a white shade in front of an off-white wall.

In real life or in a photograph, we perceive an abrupt transition between lampshade and wall, even though they are similar colors. Totally "accurate" printing of this would lose the edge between the two. Partly this is because the capabilities of our eyes exceed those of the camera. The visual phenomenon scientists call *simultaneous contrast* causes us to perceive greater differences in similar colors than are actually there.

The real-life line of demarcation is so fine that there is no hope of reproducing it on the printed page. If we try, it will look out of focus, no matter how sharp the photograph is. Our response must be to exaggerate that transition somehow, and that is what USM is about. If taken to extremes, USM will put a black line around the lampshade. Fortunately, the intensity of the sharpening is user-controlled.

Ideally, USM is taken care of during scanning. High-end drum scanners do it on the fly, and better than Photoshop, as indicated in Figure 7.8.

That does not mean that Photoshop's USM is unworkable. It had better not be, since we need to

Figure 7.9 *For the typical image, the difference between a high-end and a desktop scanner is better control of color balances, plus on-the-fly USM.*

sharpen almost every image that comes from a desktop scanner, digital camera, or Kodak Photo CD. Even a top-quality scan will need to be sharpened if it is to be printed at a much smaller size than originally planned.

Head-to-head competitions between an expensive scanner and lesser technologies are sprinkled throughout (Figures 3.2, 3.3, and 10.5), but these all have difficult originals that showcase the big scanners' capabilities. In those cases, we cannot bring the desktop images to within a thousand miles of the high-end scans.

Figure 7.9 is more typical. Although at first blush the desktop scan trails badly, the reason has nothing to do with the superior dynamic range of the drum scanner. There is no difficult detail in the shadow that one scanner is finding and the other losing. No, the difference is that 1) the operator applies color-correction curves to the drum scanner based on analyzing the individual image, and 2) the drum scanner has USM.

We can do both of those things in Photoshop.

Figure 7.10 is a sharpened, color-corrected version of the desktop version. It is not equivalent in quality to the high-end scan but considering the huge price differential one may think it close enough.

A Photoshop Makeover

Use of the unsharp masking filter on the image as a whole is merely one of many ways to offer the viewer a crisper image.

Figure 7.10 *In spite of the apparently daunting superiority of the top image opposite, Photoshop can bring the desktop product to a reasonably close quality match with a combination of curve-based corrections and unsharp masking.*

Some of the other common tricks are:
- **Better contrast.** When there is a bigger range of colors transitions become more pronounced. If you look at the exercises in Chapters 4 and 5, the corrected versions invariably appear sharper, even though no extra USM was applied.
- **Sharpening the black only.** The black plate is the one that emphasizes detail. Sharpening it can increase definition of the overall image without many of the nasty consequences of excessive USM.
- **Adding noise.** A slightly grainier image suggests more detail, but it is easy to go overboard. Photoshop 3's Monochrome noise option can help.

But Why Is It Unsharp? How Photoshop Brings Images into Focus

The traditional method of sharpening an image is, in fact, unsharp. In the old days of camera separations, the cameraman would shoot, in addition to the normal separation, an exposure that was deliberately out of focus. On a high-end scanner, the process is now automated, but the idea is the same. There are actually two scans: one in focus, one unsharp. Photoshop, of course, has only a single image to work with, but it makes a blurred version of it internally for USM purposes.

The sharp and unsharp versions are then compared, pixel by pixel. Where there is a difference between the two, it gets exaggerated. This increases the impact of transitions between colors.

To see how this works in practice, imagine a picture of a face against a darker background. The idea is to emphasize the transition where the face ends. In the original version, there will be a clear demarcation between light and dark. In the unsharp version, the transition line will be a gray blur. Therefore, when comparing the two, the unsharp will be darker at the extreme edge of the skin, but the original will be darker at the edge of the background. The USM algorithm calls for making the original image lighter still in areas where the unsharp version is darker, and for making it darker still where the unsharp version is lighter. In the imaginary picture, this finagling will result in a more dramatic transition. Instead of a simple light to dark, it will go light, lightest, darkest, dark. If we don't overdo it, the viewer will perceive the transition as being more in focus.

Photoshop gives us control of three variables in its USM filter. *Amount* defines how much exaggeration of the differences there will be. In our example, if an infinite amount of USM took place there would be a white line inside the edge of the face and a black one outside. Amount is stated in terms of a "percentage" ranging from zero to 500. 100 percent would, if you care about such trivia, tell the filter to double whatever difference it found between original and unsharp versions. I rarely use more than 100 percent at a time, but my originals may be better focused than yours.

Radius controls how badly blurred the unsharp version will be and, by inference, how wide the transition areas will be. This value is expressed in tenths of pixels. Nobody wants a halo around the image, so high values are dangerous. I normally use 1.0 pixels regardless of scan resolution.

Threshold gives us the option of ignoring transitions that are not pronounced. Expressed in Photoshop levels, ranging from 1 to 256, the threshold value is subtracted from any sharpening that takes place. Areas where sharpening would cause changes less than the threshold value will remain unchanged. The purpose of setting a threshold is to avoid sharpening subtle changes like the transitions in fleshtones while emphasizing real changes in contrast. Depending upon the original I use values between 2 and 6. Double-digit threshold values, unusual in professional practice, will confine sharpening to the grossest changes in contrast.

In small images, tweaking these three variables has almost no impact, so you can choose a default value that suits you (75, 1.0, 3 is mine) and fly with it. As image size gets larger, though, customizing the settings may help a lot. In these cases one should try a light application of USM, and if it works, cancel it and try progressively more intense settings until improvement ceases.

Because application of the USM filter to a full image can be quite time-consuming, these trial runs should take place using a smaller piece of the image. Photoshop 3 provides a small preview window in the USM dialog box, but it may not be informative enough. Selecting a small rectangular area in an important area of the image is still probably the best way.

• **Suggesting contrast by local correction**. By making certain areas lighter or darker, the viewer can be fooled into perceiving more of a range, even if the rest of the picture is not altered.

• **Boosting the black quartertone**. For the same reason that sharpening the black works. Transitions normally have a heavier black than their surroundings. Boosting contrast in the light blacks helps bring these out.

The biker image we worked on in Chapter 6 has a rather soft face. Let's use it to look at how some of these techniques work in practice.

The least costly way of adding some life is to add noise. Noise, or randomness, is one of our biggest allies in defect correction. Applied subtly, it can hide all manner of depredations. In difficult local corrections, it is common for lines to show where we have selected certain areas. This happened in our manipulation of Figure 7.6, for example. Throwing small amounts of noise at these problems covers them up considerably.

Noise is accessed under **Filter: Noise> Add Noise,** where we get to define a value that has no inherent meaning, except that the higher it is, the more variation in the tone of the random pixels that we are generating. When trying to hide local correcting, I usually use a value of 5. When looking for a slightly grainier effect, a setting of 10, as in the lower right of Figure 7.11, seems reasonable. In Figure 7.12, a noise value of 50 creates a weird variety of colored pixels.

A garish special effect like that is occasionally useful in disguising a really poor image, but more frequently, a heavy noise pattern should not have such a color vari-

Figure 7.11 *This soft-looking original, top left, is best treated with local enhancements (top right). Below, two other alternatives: unsharp masking (bottom left) and addition of modest amounts of noise (bottom right).*

ation. Photoshop 3 therefore gives us the option of monochrome noise. Figure 7.12 shows how this adds a pronounced effect, but a gray one, to the picture. Users of earlier versions would have to bring the image into LAB, add noise to the L channel, and reseparate to get the same effect.

Application of USM, as in the lower left of Figure 7.11, seems obvious enough when the face is as soft as this. The problem is that to bring out details we frequently have to accept a coarser look than we would really like. Here, a setting of 100 percent Amount seems to me to be affecting the woman's face unfavorably.

Figure 7.12 *Left, a noise value of 50 applied to the entire CMYK image. Right, a noise value of 10 with the Monochrome noise option selected.*

Also, USM, like many filters, is compute-intensive, especially if the image is large. This is a good argument for applying USM before going to CMYK, if the original is in a colorspace with only three channels.

If you have the time and the inclination, you can do better by a combination of little tweaks. I spent about five minutes on the upper right version of Figure 7.11 and it seems to me the best of the bunch. Here is what happened.

• Since I wanted sharpness in certain areas but not others, I activated the sharpness tool and chose a large feathered brush with an opacity of 50 percent. I brushed this over the woman's mouth, eyes, eyebrows, ears, and hair.

• To create the illusion of a greater color range, I decided to make lighter lights and darker darks. First, I hit the lightest spot of the hair with the magic wand, getting an irregular selection of light hair, which I feathered 10 pixels. This made a very soft transition when I applied curves to lighten the selected area. Then, I went to the burn tool, midtones method, 40 percent opacity, medium feathered brush, and traced

the dimples to darken them. I did the same to the shadow underneath the chin.

• It was now time to apply some makeup. With Photoshop, we can literally put bright red lipstick on this woman, but there is no need to run amok. Makeup experts know that very slight additions of color go a long way in making a face attractive. So, I selected the lips and applied a curve that forced both magenta and yellow up around five points.

• I then activated the airbrush, widest feathered brush, 20 percent opacity. Holding down the Option key, I clicked in the woman's shirt to define that pink as the foreground color. I then clicked once on each cheekbone, depositing a small amount of blusher.

• For eyeliner, I defined black as the foreground color, changed brush size to smallest and opacity to 50 percent, and I traced the lower eyelids with the airbrush.

• All this accomplished, I still felt that some overall USM was appropriate, but I only used 35 percent Amount. I also added five points of noise.

A more complete look at how this entire process improves a female face is in the example at the end of Chapter 10.

Photoshop on the Razor's Edge

To avoid charges of sexism, it should be pointed out that male faces have their own set of problems, especially if the male has dark hair. Limitations of the scanning process can create some really vicious five-o'clock shadows, and USM aggravates them.

The technically correct and most pristine method of reducing the beard is to take the pencil tool and repeatedly sample surrounding facial areas and drop them into individual whiskers. To me, this seems like an invitation to carpal tunnel syndrome, not to mention death from ennui. A more straightforward way is clearly necessary.

Our approach should be not to eliminate the whiskers so much as make them less noticeable. If there are easy ways to do this, we will go for them and leave the calibrationists to search for perfection.

The easiest place to find the whiskers will always be in the cyan and black plates, as Figure 7.14 suggests. The man at the left, whose facial hairs are finer, has nothing in the black, but the other man has plenty of beard there. Since a face normally has little to no black in it, these black whiskers are easily shaved off with the cloner or the airbrush. With the addition of some airbrushing of the cyan, we can give these gentlemen less of the scruffy look.

Using the Blur, Despeckle, or Median filters, which are more or less the opposites of adding noise and sharpening, will soften the whiskers, but also the face. They can therefore be used only in moderation.

The second and third versions of Figure 7.13 both have had the whiskers excised from the black plate. In the second version, I set the airbrush tool to Lighten, 75 percent opacity, wide brush, and opened the cyan channel. There, I found the darkest skin except for the whiskers themselves, and, by clicking on it with the Option key held down, selected it as the foreground color. Then I brushed over the area that needed a shave. This method reduces the darkness of the individual whiskers without doing anything to the rest of the face. The problem with eliminating too much cyan is that the whiskers will start to turn red. To counteract this, I ran the **Image: Noise>Despeckle** filter on the magenta channel only.

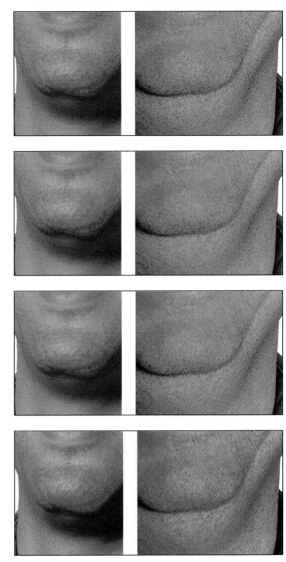

Figure 7.13 *Men's whiskers are often exaggerated during scanning and when unsharp masking is applied. The original image is at top; below are three alternate, relatively automatic ways of correcting.*

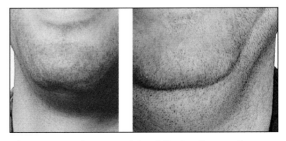

Figure 7.14 *The cyan plate of the top image above clearly shows where the whiskers are worst.*

The third sample uses blurring only. I ran the **Image: Noise>Median** filter, radius 1.0 pixel, on the cyan plate and the despeckle filter on the magenta. Then, I added five points of noise to each one.

The fourth sample employs a devious technique that will be more fully explored in the next chapter. It involves generating a heavier black plate by means of re-separating the picture, then killing the whiskers there.

A Fractal Facial

Figure 7.15 is a representative of those images that are just too attractive to throw away, yet contain a gross defect. Here, in spite of the beauty of the natural surroundings, the woman's forehead is completely blown out.

In the tropical context of the photograph, this should not come as a shock. Clearly, the sun is very strong. The camera, as we know, is much more sensitive to harsh reflections off a person's skin than a human observer would be.

If our gyrations with facial images have taught us anything, it is that texture is the main obstacle to success. Here, normal methods are doomed. We can't pick up other pieces of the face to clone, because there isn't any part of the face with an acceptable skin tone. We can't airbrush color in: it would be too uniform, and if we then add noise to it, the area is so large that the deception would be apparent. We can't apply correction curves because there isn't anything there for the curves to affect.

There are ways of handling this conventionally, but after all the drudgery of this chapter, I thought we'd have some fun and do it with a fractal.

Figure 7.15 The woman's face is almost completely blown out, unacceptable for quality printing, yet the overall composition is so attractive that we may be forced to do the best we can with it.

It seems unimaginable that anything as spectacular as the fractal that is Figure 7.1 could possibly have a use in mundane color correction, but, then again, fractals and their astounding properties were themselves unimaginable until about 10 years ago. Now they are the hottest thing in the image processing field, in addition to being a lot of fun to work with.

Fractals are not a part of Photoshop proper, but several programs are available that generate them, including a popular Photoshop plug-in, Kai's Power Tools. There is also no shortage of fractal images floating around on-line services, and libraries of them can be purchased on CDs.

Fractals defy an accurate brief summary, but they are mathematically generated images that are both chaotic and highly structured. They feature small random variations on an overall theme. Often the result is beautiful in a bizarre way, as Figure 7.1 is. The defining characteristic of fractals is an extreme plausibility. Although the artistic concept may be strange, the implementation is highly natural, and there are indeed scientists who suggest that fractals are the very cornerstone of nature.

To get down to brass tacks, a solid color with random noise is not a believable texture. A fractal is.

So, I used Figure 7.1's fractal to correct this image. Not directly, of course: first I applied curves to limit the fractal to a flesh color (Figure 7.16). Then, I copied a rectangle of it to memory, dropped it onto the image of the woman, and resized it using **Image: Effects>Scale** until it was slightly larger than her head (Figure 7.17).

With the selection still floating above the head, I now went to the Layers palette

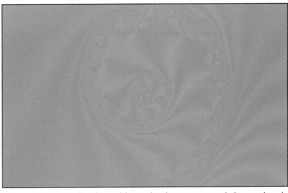

Figure 7.16 *The fractal gets hit with curves that bring it to the color of flesh...*

Figure 7.17 *...is placed into the base art and downsized until it just covers the face...*

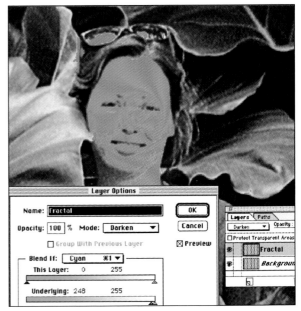

Figure 7.18 *...and Layer Options are used to restrict the alteration to the face itself.*

Quick & Dirty

PATCHWORK, SHARPENING, AND ENHANCEMENTS

✓Every digital image, regardless of how impeccable its source, must be carefully examined at 1:1 monitor resolution for dirt, scratches, hairs, and the like.

✓Simple defects on a simple background can be removed with the clone tool. If the background is complex and the defect large, it may have to be removed plate by plate, or by minimizing, rather than eliminating it. Another tactic is to pick up a large area of similar background, feather it, and drop it on top of the defect.

✓Anamorphic extension of existing areas is often the best approach when we need to create additional background. This will ordinarily require retouching at the edge of the selection that was used.

✓Unsharp masking is a Photoshop filter based on traditional prepress methods. The objective is to fool the viewer into thinking that the image is in better focus than it actually is. The technique is to exaggerate what the filter identifies as transition areas.

✓High-end drum scanners perform unsharp masking on the fly, so their images generally don't need further sharpening. Images from virtually all other sources do. One therefore needs a good understanding of the way the three-variable Photoshop filter works.

✓The unsharp masking filter takes so long to run that it is best to experiment with it on small areas of an image before applying it globally. When images are large, much can be gained by fine-tuning the USM process.

✓There are several well-known techniques for improving reproduction of faces, amounting to giving the person a digital makeover. Local sharpening, addition of noise, adding contrast, use of the dodge/burn/sponge tool, and special handling of the black are common tricks.

✓When there is a major hole in a critical area such as a face, and where there is no area that can conveniently be picked up and cloned to fill it, consider the use of a fractal. Though normally thought of as a special abstract effect, the defining characteristic of fractals is their believability. Provided their color variation is toned down to match the environment, they are suitable for such patchwork.

and saved it as a layer. This let me activate the Layer Options dialog box shown in Figure 7.18. This powerful tool allows one to define precisely what areas will be affected by the image merge. The definition can refer to values either in the overlay or the background image. In this case, I told Photoshop not to make the replacement unless there was virtually no cyan in the underlying picture. This excluded everything but the light areas of the face, since the hair, the eyes, and the green background all have significant amounts of cyan. I adjusted the sliders that alter the definition until I was sure that only the face was being affected. Then, I adjusted opacity until I felt the merge looked as realistic as it could, under the circum-

stances. This turned out to be a value of 75 percent. Figure 7.19 shows the final result.

(Users of earlier Photoshop versions, which do not support formal layers, could have done the same thing by using the command **Edit: Composite Controls**, which no longer exists in Photoshop 3.)

So ends our first and last foray into the remarkable science of fractals, which would usually be considered a part of the other world, the artistic world, of Photoshop. They do, however, hold a useful lesson for us.

This correction demonstrates that fractals can be more than attractive; they can be functional as well. Now, it is up to us to show that our kind of work can be functional *and* attractive.

Figure 7.19 *The fractal replacement of the inadequate facial tones is complete.*

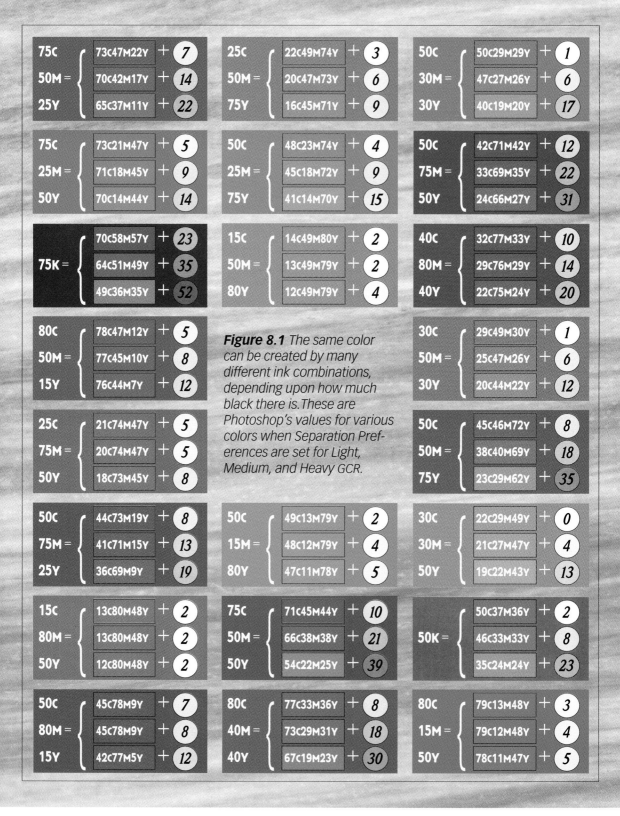

Figure 8.1 The same color can be created by many different ink combinations, depending upon how much black there is. These are Photoshop's values for various colors when Separation Preferences are set for Light, Medium, and Heavy GCR.

In Color Correction, The Key Is the K

Manipulation of the black plate is the most powerful tool in color correction. Gray component replacement, contrast-boosting curves,and other black magic can be used to engineer striking improvements. With four channels to adjust rather than three, a sensitive CMYK technician can get much better quality than in theoretically superior colorspaces.

six-year-old, a scientist, and an electronic retoucher were each given the same test in logic. They were asked, what do the following terms have in common: RGB, HSL, YCC, LAB, and HSB?

The six-year-old said, they all have three letters. The scientist said, each is a paradigmatic construct enabling expression of empirical visual data in the form of unique normative values of probative color equivalence. The retoucher said, each is a colorspace, but not CMYK, so to hell with 'em all.

That the six-year-old gave the most coherent and technically useful response is the theme of this chapter, in which we will discover how to make a weapon of the anomaly that sets CMYK apart from and above other color models: the presence of black ink.

The techniques discussed in this chapter are not possible in colorspaces, however attractive, that have only three variables. Taking full advantage of a four-letter colorspace can avoid a lot of four-letter words.

Black is not itself a color, but rather the total absence of color.

That need not deter us from using it in color correction. In fact, it should encourage us. Since black ink blots out everything, small changes in the black content of the image have a huge impact.

To emphasize black's power, we will make these corrections with the graphic equivalent of one hand tied behind us. Although these are four-color images, we will leave three of the colors alone and work on the black only, unless otherwise specified. As a further handicap, with the exception of one iteration of Figure 8.9, we will not permit the selection of any part of the image, but will rather apply all changes globally.

Let us begin the exploration of the glories of our four-letter colorspace by discussing two other three-letterers that are very poorly understood, GCR and UCR, and how to exploit them.

Until recently, artists looking for quality separations did not need to concern themselves with this topic. High-end scanners produced a CMYK file, exactly what we need to print with, and all this GCR/UCR stuff was taken care of by the time we got the files.

As the desktop revolution has progressed it has become more and more common to receive original scans that are not in CMYK. The particular format is unimportant. The point is that we will have to convert them into CMYK prior to printing and, when we do, we will need to have some plan regarding GCR.

The Role of Black

Almost everybody knows that the reason we use black ink in printing color pictures is that it adds depth and definition that the three process colors alone cannot.

Theoretically, we ought to be able to print with CMY only, but as Figure 8.2 shows, the actual inks are not quite up to the challenge. The colors that ought to be black have a slight reddish-brown tinge, due to the general inadequacy of cyan ink.

Note how CMY, just like the five other colorspaces referred to above, has three letters. As the six-year-old remarked, there is something special about the number three—uniqueness.

Take RGB. We can define any color in terms of its red, green, and blue components, but we cannot define it in more than one way. Any value is absolutely unique: the same color cannot be created by any other combination of R, G, and B.

HSB uses an entirely different model, but the result is the same. Rather than juggle the values of RGB light, it assigns a basic hue, then modifies it with a value for color saturation (purity) and another for luminance (brightness). Again, every conceivable color can be described using this technique, and again, each HSB color, except for pure grays, is unique.

And so on with the other color models, including CMY, which is an inverted version of RGB, and so it will be with any other theoretical system that may be developed in the future. Three variables are required in each, each color in the system has a unique value, and each model can describe any color.

It follows, then, that adding a fourth variable to any of these will create alternate ways to make colors that were already possible. If we are talking about inks, we also will expand the gamut of colors that can be produced on press. That the fourth variable happens to be black has nothing to do with it. If the fourth color were tangerine the considerations would be the same.

Figure 8.2 uses no black. Suppose that we had tangerine ink available to us instead. There is nothing tangerine in the picture, but that need not deter us. Tangerine could be used in any area that has a lot of yellow and at least a modicum of magenta. The likeliest areas answering this description are the children's red jackets, their faces, and their hair.

In other words, if our colorspace suddenly became CMTY, we could keep the jackets at approximately 5C90M75Y as they are now, or we might consider 5C75M70T25Y, which ought to yield about the same thing, or 5C85M10T65Y or any of a thousand other possibilities. We

would also expand the gamut of colors that could be printed. 50M100T100Y would be an orange more intense than could be gotten in CMYK.

A Hypothetical Colorspace

Although all these colors may be the same in theory, when ink actually hits paper there is a difference. If Photoshop would allow it, which it does not at the moment, we *would* use tangerine ink here—it would give us more detail, a less noticeable screening pattern, and more intense and lifelike colors. But whether to use a little or a lot of tangerine would be a controversial topic, and would doubtless depend on printing conditions as well as the character of the image.

Figure 8.2 *Below left, an image separated into C, M, and Y only, using Photoshop's None option for black generation. Note the lack of bite in the children's hair and other dark areas. Below right, a normal separation.*

If CMTY were really the color standard, many articles would be written on the proper ratio of tangerine to magenta and yellow in critical areas such as fleshtones. How odd it is, then, that so little attention is paid to control of black, which is a vastly more powerful ink than tangerine, yet can be analyzed in the same way.

This will be a lot easier if we revert to being theoretical. For the moment, then, let's forget about such annoying practicalities as dot gain, different printing conditions, the anemic nature of cyan ink and other obstacles to perfection.

In this best of all possible CMY worlds, mixing equal parts of the three colors, say 25C25M25Y, will result in a perfectly neutral gray. The same, in fact, as using 25K without any of the other three colors. These are the extremes, but we can also split the difference: 20C20M20Y5K or 15C15M15Y10K ought to work just as well.

Furthermore, this principle could be applied to any color that contains at least 25 percent C, M, and Y. So, 85C25M75Y, which is forest green, would be eligible: we could make it 70C10M60Y15K, among many other choices. Although forest green is not gray, it has a gray component, which we can partially replace with black ink, the amount of said substitution, if any, being very much up to us. Hence, gray component replacement, or GCR.

Back in the real world, dot gain and relative strengths of inks dictate numbers quite a bit different from our ideals (see Figure 8.1), but the principle is the same, and we need not worry about the mathematics because Photoshop does it for us, whenever we change from a three-letter colorspace into CMYK.

Each time we make this conversion, we have the option of generating a little black or a lot, or somewhere in the middle. Figure 8.3 shows the typical kinds of resulting black plates. The question must be, which is best? To which, happily, there is a clear and concise answer.

It depends.

GCR: When in Doubt, Do Without

The traditional method of creating a color separation yields a *skeleton* black, similar in weight to what is shown in the Light black generation example of Figure 8.3. In this method, black ink starts to appear when each of the three process colors is printing more than 25 percent and the sum of all three values is 100 or more. If the three colors get heavier the black gets much heavier, so that the darkest area of the picture will be in the neighborhood of 80C70M70Y70K.

Adobe, which usually boasts the best documentation of any software vendor, runs hopelessly aground in its discussion of GCR and its ideas of what to use for default settings. In fact, if you use their suggestions in preparing files for publication advertising, you will probably experience the ignominy of having a magazine reject your film.

Most magazines of circulation less than several hundred thousand adhere to the film standards known as SWOP, more fully discussed in Chapter 1. Among other things, SWOP dictates that total ink values in any area cannot exceed 300, which the majority of publications adjust downward to 280. This rule exists because, at the high speeds of a web press, greater volumes of ink can cause drying problems, especially where solid colors overprint, as in most traps. Worse, it can cause ink backup, which will contaminate the lighter inks and make the run inconsistent. Some titles, typically trades that print on lesser-quality paper, ask for an even lower maximum, like 260.

Enforcement of these standards is not uniform, but many magazines pay their stripping shops for a special SWOP ad inspection, and some magazine printers do the same before putting the job on press. If you are "in the neighborhood" of 280 you are no more likely to get stopped than if you go five miles an hour faster than the speed limit, but if the inspectors find 300 or higher your film will bounce, and that is a lot more serious than a speeding ticket, especially if it happens late enough in the production cycle.

As previously pointed out, a conventional separation may yield a shadow of 90C80M80Y70K, which sums to 320 and would therefore trash our magazine ad. This solves the problem of whether to use GCR; we *have* to use it in the dark areas, so that our value will change to the acceptable 75C65M65Y75K.

That GCR in shadows is effectively mandatory has two major consequences.

First, Photoshop's Separation Setup allows us to specify a maximum ink density, forcing GCR in dark areas without necessarily affecting the rest of the picture. Second, to differentiate this species of GCR from the picture-wide varieties, there is another term for it: UCR, for undercolor removal.

You should be aware before going further that the above definitions of these terms are generally but not universally accepted. Some people use UCR and GCR to mean the same thing, or reverse their meaning. In Europe, another term, *achromatic reproduction*, is used to signify the use of heavy GCR.

Figure 8.3 *How heavy a black plate gets generated is governed by Photoshop's GCR function. Clockwise from right, the blacks generated by Maximum, Heavy, Medium, and Light GCR settings.*

We are now ready to discuss values for a typical conversion to CMYK. The total ink limit will depend on the intended use of the separation. For publication or other web work 280 is standard; for sheetfed printing 320 is acceptable. Should you be using very high-quality paper, or printing on a waterless press, an even higher limit may be attainable.

For black generation, if there is nothing to indicate otherwise, use Light. At this setting, regardless of whether we check GCR or UCR, the film will resemble the kinds of separations that printers have the most experience with, and which most people would describe as *no, minimum,* or *skeleton* GCR. This type of black plate is mandatory for many of the curve-based corrections described in Chapters 4 and 5. There, several examples required us to increase black values throughout the image. With a skeleton black, these increases added depth to the picture. Had the black gotten into other colors, increasing it would have made the image muddy.

The None setting for black generation has no practical value and the Maximum setting is dangerous, because any neutral color will appear grainier than the rest of the picture, owing to total absence of three of the four inks.

The Medium and Heavy settings, though, are perfectly workable. It therefore behooves us to inquire whether there may not be certain cases where they would be preferable.

When More Black Is Better

Black is by far the most powerful ink, and once on press, the presence of additional black has several pluses and several minuses. If the pluses seem to match what

we want to accomplish with our picture it will pay to use GCR.

The most obvious way GCR can help is as a defensive measure against some of the problems caused by an ink running too heavy or light on press.

The nice thing about black is that it is perfectly neutral. The more black contained in any color, the less possibility that overinking of C, M, or Y will affect the basic hue. The bad thing is that if black itself is overinked, it is much more noticeable than any of the other three.

The nightscape of Figure 8.4 would consequently be a very bad picture for GCR. The visual strength of this image depends on retaining detail in the three-quartertone area: the dark sky and buildings. If we engineer a lot of black into these areas and the pressman overinks, the detail will close up and image quality will go down the sewer.

You may say, suppose we don't use much black, wouldn't it be just as likely that the cyan or some other color would print too heavily, achieving the same muddy mess? Yes, surely there could be too much cyan, but it would not be nearly as bad. Each process ink only darkens about a third as much as the equivalent amount of black. And as for a cyan cast, in areas this dark our eyes are not particularly sensitive to colors. We would perceive added darkness, nothing more.

From which, we can derive:

• **Rule One**: When the most important part of the image is relatively dark, stay away from GCR.

The image of coins in Figure 8.4 presents the classic neutrality problem. Metallic colors are notoriously difficult to reproduce and silver is the worst of all, because any tendency away from pure gray will be immediately and embarrassingly apparent.

Regardless of how careful we are, there is always the possibility that for any of a number of reasons an ink may run too heavily on press and we will wind up with silver coins that are pink or green.

We cannot stop a determined pressman from doing this to our job. We can, however, make it a lot harder for him by using as much GCR as possible. Nobody can make black ink print any color other than gray. The more black in the silver coins, the less prone they are to take on an offensive off-color.

A less well-known extension of this rule involves items containing a grain, such as the image that is the background of Figure 8.1, or many types of wood. The grain of reddish or brownish wood can become blue rather easily. To prevent this, use higher GCR. Distinguish these cases, though, from the one shown at the start of the next chapter in Figure 9.1. In that image, if the grain takes on the hue of the contaminating color, it is not such a bad thing aesthetically.

• **Rule Two**: When the most important part of the image is a neutral color and it is lighter than the equivalent of 50 percent black, guard against disaster with GCR.

As will be pointed out in Chapter 13, GCR is also useful when producing a duotone effect with process inks. If we are trying to get the look of a green duotone, we will actually use three inks: C, Y, and K. No matter how good our separation is, if yellow or cyan is overinked, some of our image may not have the uniform green tint we want. But the more black we use, the less pronounced the effect will be.

Figure 8.4 *The decision of how much GCR to use strongly depends upon the character of the image. At top, the nightscape is a poor candidate, since even a slight black overinking will ruin the image. Bottom, though, extra black ink generated by GCR will help neutralize the silver coins and prevent them from acquiring an undesirable cast.*

- **Rule Three**: when creating a process tritone or quadtone, use heavy GCR.

Allowing Flexibility on Press

Sometimes color fidelity is so critical that we resort to all kinds of horsing around on press. The best-known examples are mail-order clothing catalogs. If a shirt prints in slightly the wrong shade, tens of thousands of dollars worth of merchandise will be returned by angry customers who believed the book.

In such stressful cases, pressmen and art directors do not rely on contract proofs, but on a real shirt that they hold in their hands as they try all kinds of inking shenanigans to match it.

This is not the time to use GCR, because black neutralizes everything. The more black ink, the less leeway there will be to make an artistic change on press.

- **Rule Four**: When you are expecting careful help for a critical color match during the pressrun, GCR is a hindrance.

These rules can conflict. I once had to work on a clothing catalog where the designer decided that each item should be lit in such a way that a shadow was thrown onto a light background.

As recommended above, the separations were done with minimal GCR, but the shadows handcuffed the press operators. Any effort to color-correct the clothing caused the shadows to take on an offensive cast.

Careful technique by the artists preparing the catalog could have minimized the problem. After arranging for the liquidation of the designer, they should have created two sets of separations, one with light GCR and one with heavy. Then, they should have created composite images, using light GCR for the clothing and heavy for the shadow. The point being, of course, that if the shadow is predominantly black ink it does not matter what gyrations may be occurring in the C, M, and Y.

Project design can also affect GCR desirability if there are areas near the image that require heavy coverage. Ink gets hard to control when a lot of it hits the paper at once. So, if our image is going to be placed on a solid black background, bet on the black coming down too heavily in the picture itself. Naturally, if one is fortunate enough to know about this before converting to CMYK, one uses Light GCR.

Other hints that the black may be hard to handle are large areas of dark gray or black anywhere near the image, very bold headline type, or text type that contains fine lines, Bauer Bodoni being the most glaring example. Any of these factors may motivate the press operator to hike the flow of black ink.

- **Rule Five**: If there is reason to fear heavy black inking on press, avoid GCR.

Repeatability with GCR

Since black ink minimizes hue variation, if the same image appears more than once, there is a good case for using GCR.

This principle seems so obvious that we may forget 95 percent of the things it applies to. An image doesn't have to be a photograph. A flat color will behave the same way. And many designs call for repetitions of the same color, usually a pastel, in large background areas.

Light colors scarcely seem like the place one would want to introduce black. But if we are trying to insure fidelity from one page to the next—as, for example, in a company logo—it can be an excellent idea. This book employs repeating tint elements: the drop caps at the start of each chapter, the pink backgrounds for the sidebar boxes, and the Quick & Dirty section at the end of each chapter. If the mix can be made to contain black ink, there will be less variation each time the element appears.

• **Rule Six**: When repeatability from page to page is an issue, don't forget GCR principles, even when specifying colors in linework and flat tints.

Many people wonder why we use K to stand for black. Mainly, it's to avoid confusion: in the pressroom, cyan is customarily referred to as *blue*, so B is ambiguous. But K is more elegant, anyway. It stands for *key*, and indeed it is the key to the final major uses of GCR.

Black is the key for registration, meaning that the other three colors are supposed to be adjusted to agree with it and not vice versa. When a job is printed out of register, then, the culprit is almost invariably one of the other colors.

This suggests an application for GCR in the growing volume of color work we do for lower print-quality applications, especially newspapers. Because of the speed of newspaper presses, misregistration is very common. A beefy black will minimize it. Warning: before trying this, make sure you understand newspaper dot gain—it is far greater than in other forms of printing, and if the black is too heavy the outcome will not be pleasant.

• **Rule Seven**: Where misregistration is likely, use a heavier black to control it.

The K is the key, not just in registration but in color correction generally. As the most powerful ink, it can add detail and contrast, muddy or clean up colors, and

bulk up shadows in ways that three-letter colorspaces can only envy. So,

• **Rule Eight**: Before making the conversion to CMYK, ask yourself: do I want to correct this image, and can the black plate be of use?

That is a rather deep rule.

The Planned GCR Correction

There are several easy and efficient correction methods that can use GCR as an accomplice. The first is for images that need focusing or definition.

Kodak CD images are the best example. As will be pointed out at considerable length in Chapter 10, they are almost invariably too soft. This dictates more use of Photoshop's unsharp masking filter than one would like. But since these are LAB images, we can specify whatever GCR setting we like on the way to CMYK. If we choose Light black generation, we will get a black that includes only transition areas and anything darker (see Figure 8.3). We can now exaggerate the black plate with curves. This adds snap to the picture in a less obtrusive way than oversharpening. And we could not have done it with any other GCR setting: had we used Medium or higher, there would have been black in the lighter colors, and they would have dirtied up when we applied the curve.

This boosting of black, at least through the quartertones, is so common a remedy for listless images that it, if there were nothing more, would justify using Light GCR as our standard method of converting into CMYK. If the images are produced on a drum scanner that is going to give good contrast and sharpness all the time, there is a better case for using more, but that is not really a Photoshop issue.

Figure 8.5 When looking for crisper, brighter colors, Heavy GCR followed by an overall removal of black may do the trick. The bottom corrected version is more vivid than the original, top.

Figure 8.5 is an extension of the same principle. It comes from a vendor who supplies images in CMYK, but I find that it is too dark overall, and that it has a blue cast. I also object to the color of both the trees and the water as being too dark.

In other words, I want not just a lighter picture but a *cleaner* one. It needs more life, but regrettably, Photoshop's suite of commands does not include *Cleanse.* We can, however, create such a command with the aid of GCR.

I took the unusual step of converting this CMYK image into LAB just so that I could convert it back to CMYK. Before doing this, I set Separation Preferences to Maximum GCR, with a maximum black value of 80 percent. Thus, the new CMYK file had a much heavier black and was much lighter in the other three plates.

The Cleanse command now is nothing more than a curve that jettisons all black 10 percent and less. Remember, GCR works on each color by replacing nearly equal amounts of C, M, and Y with black. If the extra black goes away it will have a disproportionate effect on whatever plate was weakest in the first place, namely, the muddying unwanted color. One could call this GCO—gray component obliteration!

In this image there was an even better option, and I used it to create the bottom of Figure 8.5. Just blasting away the bottom of the black would lose some wanted detail in the water. The better way is to steal the *original* black plate and substitute it for the one generated by Maximum GCR. While I was at it, I also attacked the blue cast, by blending 50 percent of the original yellow plate into the new one. The old yellow was heavier for the same reason that the old black was lighter.

This kind of process can also work in reverse, to give depth to an image that is too brilliant. Figure 8.6 has accurate enough bright colors, but everything is so vivid that it is visually distracting. We need to do something to set them off. Here, the bump we give to the black does not enhance sharpness, as it would if the GCR were Light. Instead, with Heavy GCR, we add weight everywhere except for the brightest areas. This accentuates them and gives a more realistic feel.

The White of Marble

To see more of the impact of black correction, we will now take a world tour. Our first stop is the Acropolis, where we will visit and attempt to repair the ravages of old age—some 2000 years—on the ladies of the Erechtheion.

Marble statuary is appallingly difficult to reproduce. When seen in life, we perceive great depth and detail in comparatively small variations in darkness. The pure white of the marble, which cannot be duplicated on the printed page, and the three-dimensionality of the statues as opposed to the one dimension that we have available, conspire in favor of the sort of flaccid reproduction shown in Figure 8.7.

Figure 8.6 *Here, in the converse of Figure 8.5, GCR is used to dirty up tones for more contrast. The bottom image seems livelier because a heavy black was generated and then exaggerated, giving the brightest areas of the image more apparent sparkle.*

Figure 8.7 *Marble statuary, because of subtle differentiations between neutral colors, is a difficult subject to reproduce.*

We clearly have to emphasize whatever contrast can be found in the marble. Since the lightest areas are already about as light as they can get, meaning they are close to the minimum highlight value of 5C2M2Y, we are going to have to deepen the darker areas of the statues.

This situation is ideal for a black correction. If we just make the black heavier overall, it will not affect the highlight areas, because they don't have any black. It will, however, darken and thus add snap to the other parts of the statue, which contain between 20 and 40 percent black.

The way to improve this picture, then, is to apply a curve to the black plate that will boost these values. The exact method depends on what we want to accomplish. There are at least three possible options.

The straightforward approach is to strengthen detail everywhere, including the wall behind the statues. If we generally increase black, this will occur, and we may not like it.

Since the background wall has more black to start with than the statues, it should be possible, as a second option, to

write a curve that emphasizes one but not the other.

Third, and most time-consuming, we could select the statues only and work on them in isolation. We could then apply a drastic contrast-enhancing curve, and also invert our selection, reducing the clarity of the background by various moves in the black.

Applying a curve to the black is easier than to the other three colors, for two reasons. First, the minimum acceptable value for black is zero, whereas for the other colors, with rare exceptions, zero is a no-no. Since none of the above four curves have any impact on an area that is already zero (in fact, some of them create more zero than there was), they can be used on black, but if they were to be used on cyan, magenta, or yellow, the delicate highlight balance might be upset.

Second, black ink cannot add a color cast. A smooth curve shaped like Curve A in Figure 8.8 is a standard way to correct for a deficiency in any ink, but the other three curves have palpable bumps. Applying such a curve to cyan, magenta, or yellow can lead to unpleasant changes in neutral colors. That can't happen if the curve affects black only.

In fact, because the statue is so full of grays, manipulating the black is just about the only way to correct it. Fiddling with the other three is likely to cause strange-looking local casts.

As always, before writing a curve, we need to measure the existing values that we want to modify. In the darker areas of the statue, the CMY values vary considerably, but the black ranges between 20 and 40 percent. Since we would like to have these areas darker, we drop in a point that changes 30 percent to 40 percent. All nearby values will automatically increase as well, but the further away from 30 percent, the less the increase will be.

This is because the curve contains two other points that we sometimes take for granted. Namely, the endpoints of the curve: 0 changes to 0, and 100 to 100. Unless, of course, we enter our own new endpoints, as in Curve A.

To reiterate the lessons of Chapter 5: The most important concept in curvewriting is that it is a horsetrading operation.

The default curve is a straight line, running at a 45-degree angle from 0 to 100. When we add points, the shape of the curve will change. Some parts will become steeper than 45 degrees. In these areas, there will be more contrast than was originally in the image.

The problem is, if we make one part of the curve steeper other parts have to be made flatter, and in those areas we will have less contrast than we began with.

In other words, our task is to trade contrast in areas we are not interested in for areas that we are.

Consider Curve A. It contains three points: 3 percent becomes 0, 37 becomes 45, and 100 becomes 90. The overall impact is to add black to all areas that previously had between about 8 and 80 percent black. We can see this graphically in that those areas of the new curve are higher than the original 45-degree line.

In addition to the beefier black generally, we will gain contrast everywhere between 3 and 37 percent. After 37 the angle stays at around 45 degrees, until roughly 70 percent, and there it flattens precipitously.

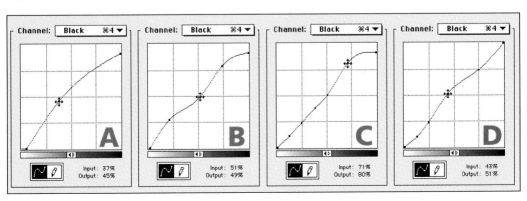

Figure 8.8 *In a typical image, applying Curve A will add both detail and weight. Curve B is designed strictly for contrast, while C aims to correct pictures whose dark areas lack depth. Curve D is a common way to add apparent weight to an image without necessarily sharpening it.*

Figure 8.9 *The original statue image, top left, and three black correction techniques. Clockwise from top right, an overall boost in black; an S-shaped curve intended to emphasize the statue but not the background; and a local correction in which the statue was actually selected.*

This curve suits present purposes well. We have achieved the greater contrast in the statues by exaggerating the black component. The tradeoffs are that we have lost contrast in the darkest areas of the background, and have sacrificed all black of value 3 percent or less, in the interest of a steeper curve. These compromises are a very reasonable price to pay for the improvement we expect.

In deciding where to give up contrast, shadows are the first place to look, as the eye is not terribly sensitive to dark colors. There may, however, be good arguments for taking the hit somewhere else.

You may approve of the results of applying Curve A to the Erechtheion image (Figure 8.9, top right), but you may agree with me that it gives too much detail to the background wall. Curve B is a sensible response to this criticism. By the addition of two points, we make the flat part of the curve fall between 40 and 50 percent, rather than in the shadows. Since that happens to be the value range for much of the wall, the wall will lose contrast, and although it will be somewhat heavier than in the original, it won't be as lovely.

This exemplifies an *S-shaped* curve. Such curves are very powerful, particularly in the black, because the impact is to increase contrast in the lighter areas of the picture while simultaneously boosting the depth of the shadows.

The third variant of the image involved local rather than global correction. The statue was isolated and a curve applied, and the background hit with a different curve. I also took advantage of the selection to sharpen it while blurring the background. Again, these changes were to the

Figure 8.10 *At top, the original suffers from extremely poor shadow density. The corrected image uses a false reseparation to generate a stronger black plate.*

black plate only. Sharpening or blurring the black can cover up a multitude of sins. Because black is what gives definition to the image, sharpening it is highly effective, yet not as harsh and unrealistic as sharpening all four plates.

If We Shadows Have Offended

The majority of pictures, like the one we just worked on, have a lot going on in the black at levels below 40 percent, so variants of Curves A and B should be part of our standard repertoire. But there are plenty of cases where the problem is not insufficient contrast so much as an overall lack of weight. In such a case Curve D or something similar is appropriate.

Figure 8.11 *This street scene is colorful enough, but we do not get much of a sense of how violent the rain is.*

In the Chinese tapestry image of Figure 8.10, the fly in the ointment is the shadow area, which is not even close to being dark enough. Normally, this would call for us to trot out Curve C, which accentuates the heaviest blacks.

To use curves, however, we need a base image that is at least somewhere close to what we are trying to achieve, not on some other continent.

This is a most unsatisfactory image. Lighting conditions were not right when the photograph was taken. As a result, instead of the shiny black background that usually characterizes these wall hangings, we get a translucent and flimsy-looking silk fabric, the shadow of a shadow, if you will.

Too heavy a shadow here might destroy the texture of the fabric. Nor do we want to equalize the depth of the black everywhere, since there is clearly light coming in from the left side of the image. The maximum shadow that I think this book can hold with detail is around 80C70M70Y70K. If we use those values in the darkest region (the upper right) and deduct 10 to 15 points from each color in the lighter parts of the background, we should be in business.

Unfortunately, as matters stand, the black is around 30 points too light everywhere, although the other colors are within reason.

Considering that the black contains a lot of the detail in the fabric, there is no way to alter Curve C or D to accomplish this drastic a move without destroying the image. It may seem like we are left with alternatives involving tedious local selection, or making mathematical blends of the cyan plate, which has a decent shadow, with the black. That strategy would risk contaminating the lighter areas of the picture with black, and those areas, at the moment, are pretty good.

Now that we are GCR experts, a more creative and effective option involves a false reseparation. Using **Image: Duplicate**, make a copy of the image, and convert it to LAB. Change **Preferences: Separation Setup** to UCR, a maximum black of 85 percent, and the ludicrously low maximum ink density of 215. Now bring the copy back to CMYK.

The black of this monstrosity will have heavier shadows, because whenever the sum of the CMY values would otherwise reach 180 or so — which happens throughout the black parts of the silk — extra black will have to be generated instead, to stay within the absurd total density of 215. At the same time, the lighter areas of the black plate will be unaffected, since we specified UCR rather than GCR. This limits the damage to areas that exceed the total density we specified in Separation Setup; the bright colors in the fabric won't change.

The CMY plates of this new separation are of course quite worthless and should be given the burial they deserve. But when we replace the black plate in the original with the black in the second separation, surprise, we suddenly have a decent piece of art.

So Fair and Foul a Day

When a picture is out of focus, as in the rainy street scene of Figure 8.11, sharpening can be counterproductive. Yet the very violence of the cloudburst provides a tantalizing target for the artist. In the original image, we see wetness, but we hardly sense sheets of rain hitting the pavement.

This sort of image is a setup for black manipulation. Obviously, we want to

Figure 8.12 *A black correction emphasizes the cloudburst by increasing contrast in the foreground street.*

increase contrast as much as possible in the street. In the original, the black values in the street range from zero in some of the puddles to 45 near where the two men are standing. While we are at it, we could certainly use more depth in the men's hair, in the man's black shorts, and in the dark areas of the poster behind them. All of these areas currently have about 60 percent black.

Examination of the existing black plate shows very little detail in the men. Therefore, we should be able to sharpen to our hearts' content without creating an overly harsh image. The only area that could cause a problem is the blue shuttering at top center. So we will use that area as a guide, continuing to sharpen the black until we begin to make it too jagged.

The contrast issue can also be treated subjectively. We want to create a curve that is absolutely as steep as possible between the original values of zero and 60 percent. It is nice that we have already decided to increase the 60 to some larger value: that will make the curve steeper by itself. The questions are, how large can we make the 60, and should the endpoints of the curve be anything other than zero and 100?

Theoretically we can increase the 60 by 20 points or so and still hold detail. But what of areas that are already darker than 60? If we let 60 become 80, these will get even darker, and will close up.

Although these points exist in the image, my examination does not suggest that any of them are crucial, so we can let them go higher than normal. On general principles they should probably not go higher than 90, so we will have one endpoint of the curve change 100 to 90.

That endpoint controls black values that we have already decided are useless, but the other endpoint will have considerable impact on the picture. We could leave it at 0=0, but this misses an opportunity. If we move the endpoint to the right—if we let 2, 4, or 10 percent become zero—our overall curve will become steeper, which is just what we want.

The more this endpoint moves to the right, the more the picture will brighten. It will be as if a fog is lifting, when black vanishes totally from areas where there is already hardly any. If we go too far, the picture will become unrealistically bright and cheery. It is purely a judgment call. I chose 5=0. Do you agree with the result?

This clarifying effect of removing black in the highlight area is not critical in Figure 8.12, but, to my sense of aesthetics, it is mildly helpful. When converting the original RGB file into CMYK, I therefore specified Medium GCR, anticipating the benefit of later removing some of the black I was generating.

Methinks I Scent the Morning Air

When brightening the image is of paramount importance, heavier GCR, followed by elimination of light values of black, is the way to go.

Figure 8.14, taken from Victoria Peak in Hong Kong, represents a whole category of images. The problem is that outdoor photo shoots are scheduled well in advance, and sometimes they go ahead even when the weather does not cooperate. I will go further: certain photographers are permanently accompanied, like Joe Btfsplk, by their own personal rain clouds, this for the express purpose of torturing electronic retouchers.

Figure 8.13 *When one of the color plates is as flat as this, watch out. This is the original magenta from Figure 8.14. Can you even tell the subject matter of the image from this?*

You perhaps are thinking that the misty Hong Kong image is romantic as it is, and should not be corrected. If so, forget it. If that cloud over Kowloon were fog, we'd see fog in the foreground, too. That is air pollution, and, unless we are preparing this art for an environmental publication, we are sure to be asked to minimize it.

Duck soup, a major culinary attraction in Hong Kong, is what our color correction ought to be. We treat it exactly the same as the last image, except 1) since we want to cleanse the picture as much as possible, we use Heavy GCR so as to have more black to remove; 2) for the same reason, we move the start of the curve even further to the right, say to 8=0; 3) because this image does not have the other one's problem of lack of shadow depth, we do not make the curve as high. Making 40=50 will emphasize the shape of the buildings, and we can let the rest of the curve go out to 100=100.

One delicacy to add to the menu of black effects is suggested by the magenta plate shown in Figure 8.13. The overall picture will surely get better if we can add definition to this miserable pile of mud. Creating a new magenta that is a blend of the existing magenta and black plates will do this. Experimentation is needed to see how much contrast can be added without a major color change, but 25 percent black, 75 percent magenta is what I used.

Referring all the way back to Figure 3.11, we observe that the sauce of oversharpening the black, though usually a good way to add piquancy, could have caused digestive upset in this picture. The windows in the foreground buildings form a pattern that may cause a moiré. Excessive manipulation of the black will certainly add to the risk.

Attempting professional-level color correction without understanding the uses of black is like trying to cook Chinese food without knowing how to use garlic, ginger, or soy. In both of these fields, an accomplished chef creates dishes that are forever fresh, deliciously different, and consistently colorful.

This concludes our world travels, but not our exploitation of the awesome power of black ink as an enhancement

Quick & Dirty
THE POWER OF BLACK

✓ Although black has no color of its own, it is the most powerful of the four process inks. Generally, adding black has as much impact as adding all three of the other colors simultaneously.

✓ At a minimum, there needs to be enough black to give depth to shadow areas. That is the traditional method of making a color separation. There are, however, instances where more black is desirable.

✓ CMYK is unique in that most colors can be expressed as more than one combination of inks, depending upon how much black is being used. This is the principle behind gray component replacement.

✓ Any time an image goes from another colorspace into CMYK, we have to make a GCR decision. Unless there is a reason to do otherwise, use Light GCR, which will yield a minimum, or skeleton, black.

✓ SWOP standards dictate that the sum of all four ink values should never exceed 300, but most publications request a 280 maximum. This effectively requires greater use of GCR in shadow areas. This species of GCR has its own name, undercolor removal, or UCR.

✓ When the most important part of an image is neutral, using heavier GCR can avoid problems on press.

✓ Overall muddying or cleansing of the brighter colors of an image is possible by first using heavy GCR, then beefing up or eliminating the lighter areas of the black plate.

✓ Contrast-enhancing curves in a skeleton black plate are an excellent way of adding focus to an image. The most common adjustments are an overall increase, or an S-shaped curve that emphasizes both quarter- and three-quartertone values.

✓ Applying unsharp masking to the black plate only is often very effective in creating better definition, without some of the drawbacks of using it on all four plates.

✓ Because the black plate generally has better shape than the other three, poorly detailed C, M, or Y plates can be helped by blending in some black.

tool. Once you master it, you will feel as much pity as I do for the scientists who, with no personal experience in color correction, preach that one should only manipulate images in a three-variable colorspace, and that GCR decisions should be made on the fly by the output device.

If ever you are forced to work under such straitened systemic circumstances, you will be able to produce pretty good color if you have become proficient at writing curves.

But if pretty good is not quite good enough for you, accept that your perpetual punishment for acceding to a three-variable colorspace will be color that can only be pretty good, forever. Through eternity, a voice in your mind, whispering ever so softly, will torment you by repeating the biggest secret in professional color reproduction. As you wail and gnash your teeth over your lack of a good image backbone, over your inability to hold neutral colors, over the missing definition, the highlights that cannot be highlighted, the voice will continue to haunt you; and whatever your color correction talents, however close you get to the sacred territory that is better than pretty good, you

Figure 8.14 Air pollution over Hong Kong in the top image gets an environmentally-friendly color correction at bottom. The technique was to generate a heavy black plate and then to delete the lighter parts of it.

will continue to hear it. And you will know and understand, even without the voice, that if you wish to unlock the cell of your pretty good prison, that if you wish to be set free into a better-looking world, the lifeless, gray door *can* be opened—and the key is the K.

Figure 9.1 *What is the predominant color of this image? What is the most important color in this image? Note: these two questions are not identical.*

CHAPTER 9

The Unwanted Color and Why We Want It

In faces, the most important color is not the magenta and yellow that dominate, but the cyan that gives texture. Yellow governs the sky, and magenta commands greenery. As unlikely as it sounds, the best corrections involve not the obvious inks, but the weakest one.

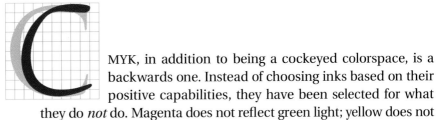 MYK, in addition to being a cockeyed colorspace, is a backwards one. Instead of choosing inks based on their positive capabilities, they have been selected for what they do *not* do. Magenta does not reflect green light; yellow does not reflect blue; cyan does not reflect red.

From this, it is not too much of a stretch to realize that much of the color correction we do is topsy-turvy: that to be effective, we have to think in color terms that are the opposite of what one might expect. When we deal with reds, we should be thinking cyan; when doing greens, magenta; and when portraying blues, yellow.

This is the religion of the *unwanted color*—the color that is the odd man out.

Because the unwanted color is so proficient at poisoning what would otherwise be a bright, clean look, it has a special importance in making an image seem lifelike. The unwanted color, even in slight quantities, is what gives an image depth.

The most obvious example of the importance of the unwanted color is in fleshtones. Caucasian flesh is basically red. That is to say, it is a combination of magenta and yellow. There is far less cyan. Cyan is, therefore, the unwanted color.

And the Last Shall Be First

It would be a tremendous leap of faith for you to accept that cyan may be the most important color in governing a person's face. So, without further theoretical ado, we will go straight to an example.

In Chapter 4, we color-corrected a studio photo of a model's face. The quality is good now, but we would like to find out what part of it is due to the unwanted color. So, leaving the magenta, yellow, and black plates alone, I have applied a curve that drastically flattens the cyan. The average cyan content of the face remains the same; there is simply less detail now.

Figure 9.2 will perplex the infidel. The new cyan plate is flatter, to be sure, but the original cyan was no prize itself in terms of sharpness. Yet, when the two cyans are plugged into the same picture (Figure 9.3) the differences are greatly magnified.

Note that there is technically nothing wrong with the new image. The fleshtone remains within proper parameters. But the picture has gone dead. The original seems to leap into three dimensions by comparison.

Here is another way of looking at this startling phenomenon. The biggest advantage of CMYK in color correction, as we just learned, is the black. There is, however, an interesting corollary.

Cyan, magenta, and yellow, when compared to red, green, and blue, are lighter

Figure 9.2 *The cyan plate of Figure 4.4, left. Right, after application of a curve designed to suppress detail.*

and less assertive colors, subtle rather than straightforward. Their addition to other color combinations can be handled with a little more finesse.

When there are clearly two colors dominating, the unwanted color is so potent in neutralizing them that adding it is almost like adding black. The unwanted color, however, is not quite such a blunt instrument. Also, a much bigger range, and thus a better shape, can be engineered into the unwanted color than into either the two dominants or the black. That is just a matter of numbers: in the original, the cyan ranges from around 5 to 20 percent. There is thus four times as much cyan in the darkest area as in the lightest. Try getting *that* with either one of the dominants.

Best of all, the unwanted color is easy to

adjust, or, occasionally, to create. The two dominant inks must be kept carefully balanced, otherwise areas of the face will start to get too yellow or too magenta. But it will take an enormous move in the cyan before the overall color of the woman goes to something other than a shade of red. Much can be hidden in the unwanted color, and part of the normal technique of working with faces should be calling up the cyan and seeing what improvements can be made. Here, for example, the original cyan seems soft. The picture as a whole cannot be sharpened, in my opinion, but sharpening the cyan only is possible, and that will make a small but significant improvement.

To sum up, when trying to improve sky, the professional thinks of yellow first. To

Figure 9.3 *Changing the cyan plate to the flat version shown in Figure 9.2 has an unexpectedly great impact on the overall image, making it seem two-dimensional.*

correct faces, we concentrate on cyan, and for plants and other greenery we focus on magenta.

This concept is so totally foreign to most people, so much the opposite of what one would expect, that I will retrieve another previously used image to show the principle in action one more time.

Where Is the Impact?

In Figure 9.4 we resurrect a color-correction problem from Chapter 5. The image is almost totally green, meaning that yellow and cyan dominate and that magenta is the unwanted color.

Like any other image, if we want to make it more lifelike, we find the important color ranges and accentuate them. In this case, the important parts have 60 percent and up yellow, 55 percent and up cyan, and 30 percent and less magenta. The correction method is easy. We apply curves that drop the midtone value for cyan and yellow. This will steepen, and thus give more contrast to, the darker cyans and yellows of the image, exactly where we want it. Similarly, we increase the midtone value for magenta, steepening it in its lighter areas.

This is absolutely still the correct way to approach this image. Just because we are unwanted-color worshippers does not mean we shouldn't take easy improvements in the domi-

Figure 9.4 *The original, top, is improved by curves that increase contrast and detail in all green areas of the image.*

nants when they are available. But it might be useful to examine just how much of the improvement results from each method.

Figure 9.5 answers this question. The top image uses the corrected magenta, but the original cyan and yellow. At bottom, the corrected cyan and yellow with the original magenta. Which do you think is more effective?

Obviously, each one achieves its improvement in different areas, and equally obviously, they reinforce one another. In the top image we get more contrast, but the insect is still green. At the bottom, the bug is browner, but detailing is not as good. That is one of the many purposes for which one wants an unwanted color.

If asked to rate one of these hybrid versions against the other, I'd have to call it a draw. Do you agree? If so, consider the meaning. Correcting the unwanted color, the one that most people pay no attention to, had an impact equal to correcting *both* of the colors that appear to be dominating the image.

Creating the Contaminant

One of the great advantages of working with the unwanted color is that, when necessary, we can make one appear out of thin air. That is what we will do with the next two images, in different ways. Figure 9.6 represents a whole class of images that are simply too brilliant to print well.

Figure 9.5 *At top, the image with improvement in the magenta only. At bottom, with improvement in the cyan and yellow only.*

Figure 9.6 *Sometimes an object is so brilliant that it loses all detail. In this situation, more aggressive use of the unwanted color will improve the image.*

The dancer's costume looks fine in person, fine in the photograph, fine on the monitor, and lousy on the printed page. Process inks are not good at reproducing vivid colors like this red. When we bring this image into CMYK, what we get is a kind of red blob lacking most detail, since every part of the costume will be close to the limit of the press's color gamut.

This red is made up of maximum magenta plus pretty large quantities of yellow. (If the two were equal, we would have a costume the color of a fire engine.) What it will not have is very much cyan or black, because these are red-killing colors.

If we take the approach advocated in Chapter 5, the way to create more contrast in the reds should seem as risk-free as it is obvious. After all, there is nothing in the background to be harmed. There are no neutral colors, no highlights to unbalance.

Therefore, we should steepen the magenta and yellow by dropping whatever minimum values of them we find in the costume by 15 points or so. Magenta is probably maxed out already, but we can increase the maximum yellow. As for the cyan and the black, we will steepen their curves by finding the maximum values within the costume and increasing them, presuming that the minimum is near zero and cannot go lower.

The problem is that when the overall effect is so brilliant, the maximum cyan and black are likely to be near zero as well. So, the impact of our correction will not be as much as could be hoped for. In fact, the poor contrast throughout is

Figure 9.7 *When an image with a strongly dominant color improves, frequently it is the doing of the unwanted color. Here, the two cyan plates that produced the images of Figure 9.6.*

because only one of the four plates—the yellow—has any kind of detailing in it. The magenta is essentially a solid color throughout the costume and the black and cyan are basically zeroed out. In other words, three-quarters of our colorspace is not being used at all.

First, then, we should apply curves to maximize whatever small contrast we can find, and along the way, make the flesh-tones more realistic. As for the costume, the way out of this mess is not to be so shockingly red throughout. Whatever the brightest part is, we should keep at the most saturated values possible, (i.e., no cyan or black at all) but we should subdue the rest. For that, we want the unwanted color, and as there is none to speak of at present, one will have to be manufactured.

In practice, we explore the image and find the brightest area. Having discovered this, we proceed to create the unwanted color. Since yellow is the only plate with detail, we use **Image: Calculations>Blend** to create a new cyan plate that is a mathematical blend of 70 percent of the old cyan and 30 percent of the yellow.

This finagling will create a problem. There will now be a certain amount of contaminating colors everywhere in the red. The area that I have identified as lightest will have 8 percent cyan. All other areas will have more.

This conflicts with our previous goal of having the brightest area be absolutely as intense as possible, meaning no cyan or black at all. To restore these regions to

Figure 9.8 *This image has a yellow cast, as measured in the geyser, which should be white. Unfortunately, there is more yellow in the water than in the sky behind it, so if yellow goes out, the sky will become too vivid.*

brilliant red, the correction curve must move 8 percent cyan to zero. That is desirable anyway, since it steepens the cyan curve. Of course, we will steepen it further by increasing the maximum value within the red areas by 10 or 15 points.

In keeping with the theme of this chapter, this was an unwanted-color move only. The only change in the image is shown in Figure 9.7. There was no detail in the magenta to exaggerate, and the yellow

seemed reasonable already. Cyan only is responsible for the substitution of something that looks like an ornate costume for a vague impression of something bright red.

For Intensity, Think Murkiness

One of the reasons that unwanted colors feel unwanted is that they move us away from what are considered to be happy colors. If we are doing real estate advertising we like to have blue skies and green lawns. The unwanted color is our enemy, since it moves us toward gray. We should not get rid of it entirely, of course, but it should be held to the minimum we can get away with, usually 2 percent in the lightest area unless there is a really weird situation like the red costume.

Naturally, on some occasions we actually want to have gloomier colors, as in the opening scene of a murder mystery movie, but human nature being what it is, moves toward the happy side and away from the unwanted color are about a hundred times as common.

There is, nevertheless, an important artistic impetus toward more use of unwanted colors. Just as we open up contrast in the parts of the image that are most important to us, we can downplay areas that compete with them.

A numerical analysis of the picture of Old Faithful in Figure 9.8 yields the following information. The highlight, in the middle of the geyser, is 4C1M22Y. This yellow cast continues throughout. Shadow value, measured in several of the foreground individuals, is 75C55M70Y45K. At the relatively darker top of the sky, it is 85C45M18Y. At the bottom, it is 65C20M12Y.

Although these initial readings are not wonderful, they no longer scare us, for we have written curves to correct worse.

There is just one catch. Exterminating the yellow cast in the geyser presents no difficulty, but if we do it, we will deprive the sky of the unwanted color. Yellow is lighter everyplace in the sky than it is anywhere in the spray. So, if we bring yellow down to 2 percent in the highlight, we either blow the entire yellow in the sky away, or, if we set an endpoint at 0=2, substitute a flat tint of 2 percent, eliminating any contrast.

You can do that if you like, but in addition to a very flat-looking sky you will get one that fights with Old Faithful for attention. While we don't want to make an overcast day out of it, the less vivid the blue of the sky, the more the geyser will stand out.

If the objective is to get more yellow into the sky, curves cannot help us. Photoshop does let us get at this without a difficult direct selection of the sky, however, with **Image: Adjust>Selective Colors**. This is the method of choice in dealing with this image, but it is available in Photoshop 3 only. To cater to users of earlier versions, and also to introduce the HSB colorspace, we will do this correction by means of a command that, although it still exists, is now virtually obsolete: **Image: Adjust> Hue/Saturation**.

Back to Three Letters

These two commands have the ability to act on parts of the image that are of a certain color or colors, without affecting anything else. The spectrum is divided into six pieces for this purpose, RMBCGY.

There are two problems with this. The

Figure 9.9 *Manipulating the unwanted color makes the color of the sky less of a competitor to Old Faithful.*

first is that there is often no neat line between what color is what. In this image Photoshop considers that the top of the sky is blue but that the bottom is cyan. Also, to avoid ridiculous-looking transitions, each color is defined as containing a hint of its immediate neighbors. That is, since we are going to be fooling with blue, there will be a slight effect also on magenta and cyan; and our moves in cyan will also affect green and blue.

The second problem is that we have to use another unfamiliar colorspace to

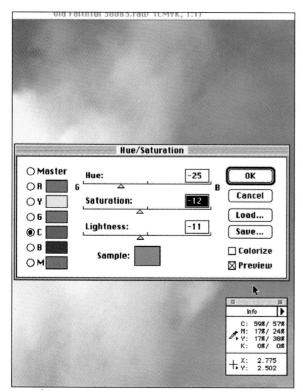

Figure 9.10 *Photoshop's Hue/Saturation adjustment menu lets us change the sky in the Old Faithful image without a local selection.*

make the corrections. This one, HSB, is more complicated than RGB, but you ain't seen nothin' yet, since in the next chapter we will make the acquaintance of LAB, which is roughly to HSB as James Joyce is to John Grisham.

In HSB, each color is defined in terms of its hue, saturation, and brightness components, rather than by any combination of colors. *Hue* refers to the dominant color, which can be confusing. The hue of the model's face in Figure 9.3 happens to be the same hue as a fire engine. It differs in brightness, since the fire engine is darker, but especially it differs in saturation, which can be roughly defined as the presence of the unwanted color. The less satu-

rated a color is, the more it tends toward grayness. A fire engine is completely saturated, which we would translate to mean that we would try not to have any more cyan in it than we could help.

Figure 9.10 shows how I used this option in dealing with the Old Faithful image. Remember, the objective is to get more yellow into the sky, so that we will still have some once we eliminate the cast from the entire image. It also would be nice if the sky got a little darker so that the geyser would be more apparent against it. This is accomplished under Brightness. Yellow is added under Hue, because this option allows us to move a color in the direction of either of its two nearest neighbors. In the case of cyan, the neighbors are green and blue, and obviously going in the direction of green will add yellow to the image.

The most significant move, however, is in Saturation. Any move toward grayness will, by definition, add the unwanted color. In the case of blue, reducing saturation pours yellow into the color. In the case of cyan, magenta comes in as well.

After making the adjustments to the cyan, I turned my attention to blue, and entered values of −18 Hue, −21 Saturation, and −12 Brightness. The Saturation and Brightness moves were for the same purposes as in the cyan. The Hue move was toward blue's nearest neighbor, cyan, and did not add any yellow to the sky. I thought it was a good idea anyway, since the cyan was already moving toward green. Without shifting the blue as well, there would have been more color variation between the top and the bottom of the sky. I decided that I did not want that to happen, though you may disagree.

The result of the Hue/Saturation moves is seen in Figure 9.11. A first impression would be that it made the picture worse than the original, but this is a timorous view. It is true that the sky has turned green in places and that the whole effect is muddier, but color casts no longer terrorize us. For present purposes, the Hue/Saturation move worked if it created more of a differentiation between sky and geyser.

All that remained was to impose curves to correct ranges. Adjusting the brightest area of the geyser to 5C2M2Y called for a drastic drop in yellow, of course. For the reasons stated in Chapter 5, I also steepened all curves between highlight and quartertone. This emphasized whatever contrast could be found in the geyser, at the expense of the remainder of the image. An upward adjustment of all three-quartertone areas, especially magenta, to compensate for the poor shadow, completed the curves and thus the correction. The final result is in Figure 9.9.

This chapter's circle is now complete, since we have made unwanted-color corrections once with magenta, once with cyan, and once with yellow. We'll close with an image that has *two* unwanted colors, but first, a more abstract image may help crystallize thoughts about the contrarian school of color correction.

Going Against the Grain

The interesting marbled-paper image of Figure 9.1 symbolizes a species particularly suited to unwanted-color moves. If an object has a pronounced grain, as this paper does, the unwanted color governs its intensity. When we want to make the grain more or less prominent, the unwanted color is the principal tool.

Figure 9.11 *After the Hue/Saturation move but before elimination of the yellow cast, the image is much muddier, but the geyser is already starting to pull away from the sky.*

Although wood might be a more typical example of where we might want to control grain, the paper image has more possibilities. Images like these are highly suitable for backgrounds, but frequently we will want to make some custom variation of them. Here are a few examples, using a small piece of the overall original.

Curve-based contrast variation in the unwanted color is the best way to affect the grain. In Figure 9.12, compare the

Figure 9.12 *Left, the original. Center, removing all cyan sharply reduces grain. Right, increasing contrast in the cyan makes all patterns more pronounced.*

original to a version with no cyan at all, and one with a steep contrast curve that increases cyan quartertones without adding cyan where there was none.

Unwanted colors do their work best against purer incarnations of red, green, and blue. The overall feeling of this art is less red than magenta, although the yellow plate is much heavier than the cyan. In Figure 9.13 we make the image pure red by duplicating the magenta plate into the yellow channel. Under these circum-

stances, the impact of moves in the cyan is intensified. Note that one effect has gone away: a danger in working with grains is that the grain may take on the look and feel of the unwanted color. This is what is happening in the right third of Figure 9.12. Where the cyan is heavy, the pattern is becoming distinctly blue. That is not necessarily a problem with this art. If we were working on a reddish wood, however, a bluish grain would be just as easily achievable, but far less desirable.

Figure 9.13 *When the image is shifted from magenta-red to pure red, the unwanted color becomes even more prominent. Center and right, adjustments in the cyan drastically change the strength of the grain.*

Figure 9.14 *Neutralization techniques. Left, a single overall reduction in saturation. Right, curves that aim for more neutral colors. Center, swapping the cyan and black plates gives less color variation.*

The center image of Figure 9.14 suggests a way of avoiding this. Earlier, I asserted that adding the unwanted color is roughly as powerful as adding black. To test this proposition, in the center image, I actually transposed the black and cyan plates. If we would like a strong grain, but don't want any of it to have a blue tinge, this is the way to go.

This version is flanked by the right and the wrong way to get a less pink, more neutral effect. On the left, suppose that,

motivated by our success with the Old Faithful image, we open up Hue/Saturation and reduce saturation throughout the image. This floods everything with unwanted colors, and although it does make the image more neutral, it also neutralizes a lot of its appeal.

The blunt instrument of Hue/Saturation adjustment should only be used for its ability to isolate a certain color. When acting on the image as a whole, curves will always be more effective, as in the version at

Figure 9.15 *Special effects. Left, increasing cyan sharply overall by blending 50 percent of magenta into it. Center, an inversion curve on the cyan. Right, using the entire available colorspace through drastic curves.*

the right of Figure 9.14. This was treated just as we would any other image with a cast. I found areas that I wanted to neutralize and forced a gray in them. This retained plenty of interesting color variation throughout the image, since places with relatively heavy magenta, yellow, or cyan continued to display it. The only issue was where to set the highlight and shadow. This is one of the rare images that, in the interest of softness, should probably not make use of all available color space. So, I set my highlight at 10C10M8Y, intentionally retaining a slight magenta cast, and the shadow at about 50 percent in all colors.

Figure 9.15 shows three fanciful variants. At left, a new cyan plate that is a 50–50 split with magenta makes for a lavender image with a much less pronounced grain. Quick! How would we add more grain?

Yes, of course, this change has given us a different unwanted color. The way to add detailing would be to alter the yellow.

The center version has a flipped cyan. That is, the start of the curve is higher than the end, meaning that places that were relatively heavy in cyan are now relatively light. This is not a straight negative version of the cyan, which would overwhelm the image, but a softer variation on the negative theme.

Finally, the right-hand version is a reminder of just how much vitality we can add to any image through curves. I simply set the lightest area of each color to zero and the heaviest to around 90 percent.

This series of maneuvers illustrates some of the potential offered by manipulating abstract patterns. They have interest just by themselves, but they are particularly useful as backgrounds, especially if they are not too assertive. Using such images in this way is itself an extension of the unwanted color principle. If one were to surround the ocean images of Figure 9.16 with a half-inch thick border of pure magenta, that would be artistic suicide. The bright magenta would overwhelm the more subtle colors of the image.

In a way, though, surrounding the image with white (which, in effect, is what the design of the book does) is nearly the same thing. The white clouds of the image suffer in comparison to the whiteness of the blank paper next to it. If, instead, the background page were a much softer and lighter version of the right image of Figure 9.14, full of light grays and unwanted colors, the clouds would appear much whiter, although their color had not in fact changed.

Sky of Blue, Sea of Green

After all this discussion, when you see a picture that is so predominantly blue as Figure 9.16, you should instinctively be thinking in terms of yellow.

Actually, this time we need to pay attention to *two* unwanted colors. The sky and the water are both blue, which means that yellow is the target of close scrutiny. But in the green areas of the pictures, yellow is heavy and the unwanted color is magenta.

This situation is complicated by another yellow cast, as seen by measuring the clouds, which ought to be white, but are instead on the order of 5C0M22Y. This is like what happened in the Old Faithful image (yes, they both came off a Kodak Photo CD, which, as we will see in the next chapter, is prone to yellow casts). In that picture, though, there was less yellow in the sky than in the foreground object. Here, there is more.

In the Old Faithful shot, we intentionally muddied the sky, to draw more attention to the geyser in the foreground. This time, we presumably want a clear blue sky.

The yellow curve will wind up having a zigzag shape, as shown in Figure 9.17. It starts off as a straight horizontal line. Everything between 0 and 22 percent yellow goes to 2 percent. Not dropping it to 0 is simply a safety precaution. There is no specular highlight in this photo, so there is no excuse for the yellow to be missing altogether. I think that I found the minimum highlight, but why take a chance?

In the important areas of this image, yellow is either light (the water and the sky) or heavy (the trees). There is nothing to speak of in between. Accordingly, we can compress the middle of the curve drastically, allowing much steeper curves in the sections we want. The corrected yellow plate, Figure 9.17, shows a much more pronounced cloud pattern. Also, note that rays of sunshine are beginning to appear on the water. They were missing from the original yellow.

Figure 9.16 *Success in correcting the original, above, depends on two unwanted colors: the yellow in the sky and water, and the magenta in the greenery.*

Quick & Dirty

MANIPULATING THE UNWANTED COLOR

✓Areas that are predominantly red, green, or blue are peculiarly susceptible to moves involving the opponent process plate, otherwise known, somewhat inaccurately, as the *unwanted color.* In red areas, including flesh-tones, the unwanted color is cyan; in greens, the unwanted color is magenta; and in blues, it is yellow.

✓Focus-enhancing moves in the unwanted color are very powerful, roughly as effective as moving both dominant inks at once. In adding detail, the unwanted color is the most significant of the three. Steepening its contrast curve will yield dramatic results.

✓Many bright areas appear too flat because they lack an unwanted color altogether. In such cases, one should be generated artificially. This can be done either by blending a small amount of a dominant plate, or by use of Photoshop's Adjust Hue/Saturation commands.

✓When trying to use bright, happy colors, consider reductions in the unwanted color rather than trying to beef up the dominants.

✓In objects with a pronounced grain, such as woods, steepening the unwanted color will greatly intensify the graininess, but at the risk of creating an unwelcome hue. In such cases, consider means of transferring some of the role of the unwanted color into the black plate. Normally this is done by blending some of the unwanted color into the black.

✓Zeroing out the unwanted color in the absolutely brightest area is a good way to add even more contrast to a primary color, even though letting one of the CMY colors drop to zero is normally considered unacceptable.

✓Our perception of colors is influenced by the colors that we see near them. To emphasize a bright color even more, increase the unwanted color in nearby areas.

✓Be alive to the possibility that an image may offer more than one opportunity for an unwanted-color maneuver. If an ink is unwanted in one area of the image and dominant elsewhere, generally it will pay to steepen the curve in the unwanted area even if it penalizes the dominant range.

Having added contrast to the first unwanted color, all we need to do with the second, magenta, is steepen the range that covers the green trees.

The overall shadow in this image was pretty good, but I added more black to the quarter-tone anyway, to try to get more variation between light and dark in the water.

Although standard practice would call for dropping the cyan midtone so as to get a little more range in the important areas of the image, I spitefully left the cyan alone. This was for I-told-you-so reasons. Uninformed Photoshop practitioners look at an image like this and aim the brunt of their assault at the cyan that seems so overwhelming. And yet this highly effective correction completely ignored cyan.

The professional retoucher thinks in reverse. When we see a color that dominates the image, we should not be dazzled and fooled into believing that that is the one we must attack. Instead, we should be more subtle, devoting our energies to courting the color that is prominent by its absence—unwanted, perhaps, but not unnecessary, not unloved.

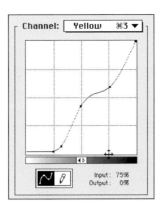

Figure 9.17 *The key to handling the island image is the yellow plate (original below). The drastic curve at left starts out low, to eliminate the yellow cast, then steepens dramatically in areas where yellow is the unwanted color, flattens in areas of little interest, and gets steeper again to emphasize detail in the trees. The resulting yellow plate (bottom) shows far more contrast.*

Figure 10.1
The days when an image like this could come only from a hundred-thousand dollar drum scanner are history. This uncorrected photo never went to film at all: it is a digital capture, direct from camera to computer.

CHAPTER 10

Kodak CDs, Digital Cameras: Is the Future Already Here?

Faster and cheaper than traditional methods, two new technologies take aim at the serious color market. Their images still need some special handling, because certain quality issues are not resolved—yet.

I f you are in the buggy whip business, and somebody has just invented the automobile, what do you do? If you make the world's best slide rule, and somebody has just invented the electronic calculator, where do you go?

These are the kinds of questions facing the professional color industry today.

Photoshop 2.0, which was the first version that really supported working in CMYK, appeared in 1991. Before then, a few hardy souls attempted to do high-level color work on Macintoshes, but they were fighting long odds. Even in 1991, desktop computers and peripherals powerful enough to handle color manipulation were priced out of the reach of most nonprofessionals.

That has all changed in a big hurry. Nowadays even many casual users own computers that outperform in every way the systems that color houses paid millions of dollars for less than five years ago. As of this writing, the biggest advantages that professional color shops have are experience and expertise, not equipment. With a powerful enough computer behind it, Photoshop easily matches the best professional retouching and correction systems.

Another advantage the big color shops currently have is in scanning. As noted at some length in Chapter 3, high-end drum scanners have not yet been dethroned. They have become somewhat cheaper, and continue to clobber all competition, in quality if not in price.

In spite of the great improvement in mass-market desktop scanners, the real threat to the current champions comes from two new digital-capture technologies. Dealing with their great potential and undoubted problems will be the focus of this chapter.

The End for Film?

The two technologies, Kodak Photo CD and digital cameras, are entirely different, but they have two important areas in common. First, they do certain things much faster, cheaper, and occasionally better than traditional methods.

Of more direct impact to us, they require much more of the Photoshop operator. In principle, if we get an image from a top-flight scanner with a top-flight operator, we should not need to correct it at all. All of the curves we have discussed so far can be duplicated and even improved on such a scanner. Sharpening is done automatically and focus is seldom a problem. Yes, frequently such scans have to be corrected just the same. The images coming from the newer technologies, however, *always* need correction.

The correction, though, is sometimes much less than you would be led to believe. Figure 10.1 is the kind of thing that makes scanner operators lose confidence. It is an excellent food shot, about as

perfect a rendition of a slice of pizza as one could ask for. I would not want to make any correction. Yet it is not a conventional photograph at all. It was taken with a digital camera, a device that captures data directly to a computer, rather than film. Photoshop reads the resulting image directly. There is no waiting for film to be developed, no scanning. Finished images can be reviewed immediately and the bad ones discarded. This is a considerable improvement over conventional photography, where we have to develop full rolls of film even if only two or three exposures are any good.

Although the technology is still in its infancy, already the results rival, and in some cases, like Figure 10.1, surpass the quality of conventional photography plus scanning. For the studio photographer it also completely eliminates the practice of taking Polaroids during a shoot prior to wheeling out the big camera. In the digital age, if the preliminary shots unexpectedly turn out to be perfect, we keep them, and if not, we throw them out.

When distributing the same image to more than one party, the digital route is much better than making additional transparencies. There is no deterioration of the image, no problem of physical differences between different versions, no possibility of two scanner operators coming up with drastically different versions of the same cut.

For these persuasive reasons, many observers believe that digital cameras will rapidly take over and that, at least in the professional color world, film will be nearly extinct by the turn of the century.

Before discussing why other knowledgeable people are persuaded that no

Figure 10.2 *At a small fraction of the cost of conventional scanning, a hundred high resolution digital images will fit on Kodak's golden venture into prepress. Each disk customarily comes with an index sheet of thumbnails. As appropriate for this chapter, the image was photographed with a digital camera.*

such thing is about to happen, let's let the other principal actor in this chapter's show strut its stuff.

Kodak's Initial Marketing Mistake

The Kodak Photo CD has emerged from the ashes of a flamed-out initial marketing plan to become a considerable force in professional graphic arts. It is a cheap, convenient, and reasonably high-quality alternative for both reproduction and archiving of images.

Kodak's original idea was that this would be a consumer product, one that would simultaneously protect Kodak's film sales and place the company in the vanguard of the digital revolution.

The plan was that virtually every film processing shop would also become capable of placing images on a CD-ROM. Consumers would take the disk home and insert it into a player hooked up to a normal television set. The pictures could then be displayed on the TV, one after another, for the edification of neighbors, grandparents, etc.

In order to get the pictures on disk, the original film had to be developed and printed as usual. Although Kodak tried hard to keep the price under a dollar per disk image, this was still more than the cost of additional prints. Also, the images displayed on television were of indifferent quality. Standard audio CD players would not recognize the Kodak disks, either.

In short, Kodak believed that people

would be willing to pay several hundred dollars for a new CD player in order to be able to pay more and get less for their images than before, except that they would still have to pay for conventional film processing as well.

This marketing concept did not work.

The idea of converting film into data at a dollar a pop, however, found immediate favor in the prepress industry, since the going price for large-format scans was around a hundred times that. Most serious users were getting CD drives for their computers anyway, so cost of equipment was not an issue. Although the Kodak scans were in a proprietary format, Photoshop quickly developed the capability of reading it. The Kodak format became an industry standard for handling images.

The appeal of this process today is still its efficiency. Starting with positive or negative film (prints and other reflective art are not acceptable, at this writing), the automated Kodak system can process around a hundred scans an hour. We can retrieve the scan in any one of five different resolutions, the highest of which is sufficient for printing at sizes slightly larger than one of the pages of this book. This makes the method ideal for projects where images need to appear both in print and in video or for other purposes that do not require such high resolutions.

Such productivity contrasts favorably to that of high-end scanners. There, if we are producing scans this large, we will be lucky to finish five an hour, although smaller sizes go quicker. There is still a quality difference, but at a twentieth or a fiftieth of the price we will be forgiving. It makes sense in some deadline-pressure cases to scan a huge number of pictures to CD, postponing a decision on which one(s) to use until the last minute.

This format is an extremely reliable and inexpensive way to store images for a long time. A hundred images fit on a single disk. As you can detect in Figure 10.2, the disk itself is treated with a gold alloy that Kodak thinks will help it last longer than an audio CD, a hundred years, perhaps. If you have a large library of images to archive, CD is today's method of choice.

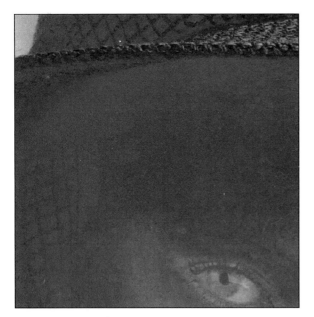

Figure 10.3 *Kodak CD images are compressed, and when restored to their highest resolution, there is some loss of quality. The relics of the chrominance-based compression are commonly found in the yellow plate. In this piece of image, note the squarish areas of no detail in the woman's hairline. This skulduggery is nevertheless difficult to detect—see if you can find it in Figure 10.26.*

The Problem in Shadow Areas

The advantages of these new technologies are huge. Perfection, however, has not yet been achieved. Improvement over the next few years is certain, but for now, at least, certain precautions are necessary.

Both technologies capture their images with CCD arrays, for a start. For mathematical reasons that are difficult to overcome, CCD devices tend to have trouble with dark shades. Sometimes we can correct this deficiency in Photoshop and sometimes not.

Neither one uses any type of unsharp masking, leaving this tiresome chore to us. Kodak CD scans tend to have an exceptionally soft appearance and are often helped by large doses of additional black, as well as heavy sharpening. The scans are also prone to wildly excessive color casts, intensified by the product's choice of colorspace.

PCD images can be opened directly by Photoshop, although different versions do it in different ways. There is also a separate acquire module available from Kodak. In each case, we get to specify which of the five resolutions shown in Figure 10.4 will be used for the Photoshop document, and whether it will be opened as an RGB or as an LAB file.

For choice of resolution, you can follow the rule stated in Chapter 3 calling for 1.5 to 2 times resolution times magnification, but when in doubt, go for the lower resolution. The Kodak images tend to be soft, so lessening resolution can actually help. Plus, as Figure 10.3 demonstrates, there is a certain quality loss at higher resolutions anyway, because of the compression scheme that is used to fit so many images on one disk.

The default PCD resolution is 72, far too low for our purposes. Our first step upon opening, therefore, should be to go to **Image: Image Size**, and with the Constrain Image Size option checked so that resampling does not take place, change

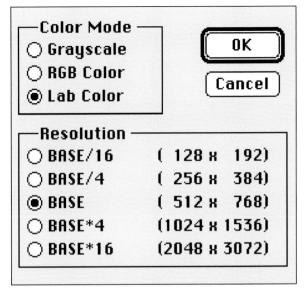

Figure 10.4 *The five resolutions for opening a Photo CD file. When converted to 225 dpi, the sizes of the ensuing files are a) a postage stamp; b) 1.1 × 1.7 inches; c) 2.3 × 3.4; d) 4.5 × 6.8; and e) 9.1 × 13.6.*

the resolution to 225, unless we think we know what we are doing and have decided on something different.

Everyone seems to have a favorite method of opening Photo CD originals, and to feel that all others are inferior. I have tried opening them in every known way, and personally, I can find little meaningful difference, except that there seems to be marginal improvement if the image is opened in LAB rather than RGB.

Perhaps LAB works best because it is a relative of Kodak's proprietary YCC colorspace, the native language on these disks, or perhaps because LAB is Photoshop's own internal choice for color definition. It certainly is not because LAB is the colorspace that any rational retoucher would think of using.

The LAB model (written, by true believers, as L*a*b* and pronounced Ell-star-eh-star-bee-star) is the current favorite in

Figure 10.5 Difficult images, like this cloud-covered Puerto Rico scene, can cause breakdowns in calibrationist systems such as Photo CD. Below, selective color correction on a high-end scanner cuts through the haze so effectively that it is hard to believe the two versions come from the same original.

calibrationist circles, and Kodak's view of color reproduction is as purely calibrationist as can possibly be. The inner workings of LAB are known only to a few disciples, although I will attempt to enlighten you momentarily. First, though, to understand the uses of the Kodak product, we have to return for a moment to the debate that was introduced in the very first chapter. Should we be attempting to match the photograph, or what the photograph means?

The Views of Kodak Management

There is a lot to be said for an orderly and predictable scanning process, particularly if you start with the assumption that the original photograph is always perfect. If you are unwilling to make this assumption the case for calibration becomes much tougher to make.

Arguing in favor of the use of Photo CD images by magazines, the head of Kodak's team that developed the product was quoted as saying, "With the exception of some publications, I don't think it pays for most customers to do their own scanning—because they don't do enough of it. Making sure the color is right and the system is in calibration are also serious issues involved in scanning, and it's a really *boring* kind of operation with no effect on the creative process."

Those who find scanning boring fully deserve to be saddled with the type of reproduction shown in the top half of Figure 10.5. This difficult image comes from a transparency shot by a professional photographer. Even so, under these adverse lighting conditions the chrome came out flat, so the PCD version did too.

You may find it hard to believe that the lower image comes from the same original photograph. I scanned this one myself on a drum scanner. Rather than yawning and rubbing my eyes at the thought of having to engage in such a boring operation, when I scanned I treated it exactly as if it were a Photoshop color correction. That is, I spent a few minutes analyzing the picture, tried to imagine how a human would have perceived this scene, and changed the color values as necessary. I found the lightest value in the clouds and set it to 5C2M2Y, darkened the shadow, increased magenta at all points 15 percent and over, and, with almost all of the image being light, drastically darkened quartertones in all four colors. Moves this big are not possible in Photoshop. If we try, the picture will begin to lose continuity. There will be abrupt jumps in colors and a generally ragged look. If the curves are imposed at the time of scanning, these problems don't exist, because there is far more color information to play with. Photoshop is at present limited to 256 levels per channel, or 8 bits. Digital drum scanners tend to be 12 bits per channel, 4096 levels. All this extra data gets thrown away before Photoshop gets into the act, but it can be used for correction during the scan.

So much for "boring," for "no effect on the creative process." Time for another thought from Kodak management.

The head of Kodak's color characterization team advocates use of PCD in conjunction with a rather expensive Kodak calibration package for Macintosh, which includes a circuit board controlling monitor response and an extensive array of calibration curves. This package, he has been quoted as saying, "provides accurate color measurement of device response, creation of correction tables, and the combination of correction tables in sequence for Adobe Photoshop. This approach challenges and often surpasses the color quality achieved by expert drum scanner operators who calibrate their scanners in CMYK for one specific proofing system."

Those prepress professionals who react to this statement by rolling on the floor, helplessly convulsed with mirth that anyone might think that PCD images could compete in such lofty company, would do well to read it more carefully. There is a lot of truth to it, and a lot to think about.

The Same Results Every Time?

Kodak's commitment to repeatability and predictability over the entire production process is impressive. The company does not manufacture a press, but it is a major supplier of printing plates, in addition to a contract proofing system, imagesetting and other graphic arts film and paper and a complete array of supporting chemicals. It also markets a sophisticated color correction system based on heavy-duty workstations. Although Photo CD is a relatively new product, Kodak was already in the scanner room, and not merely because so many professional photographers use Kodak film.

Figure 10.6 *Most pictures have at least some points of reference where we know or can guess at what the colors should be. This one is an exception. There is a moon, so it is night, but we don't know how dark the scene is supposed to be. Since it is a PCD image based on an amateur photograph, there is no guarantee that the current colors are even remotely accurate. What moves, if any, would you make? To see the different thinking of two Photoshop professionals and a scanner operator, turn the page.*

Figure 10.7 *Possibly the most reproduced image in the world, the famous Kodak shot of three musicians stands as a challenge to every scanner operator.*

Most professional scanner operators use an excellent package of test images known collectively as the Q–60 set. Kodak makes it, and it consists of photographs on different types of film and paper. The idea is to find and maintain good default settings for the scanner. It makes sense to be able to say that we can make the musicians image of Figure 10.7 look the same whether it is supplied on Kodachrome, Ektachrome, Fuji film, or, for that matter, as a paper print. Different scanner settings will have to be found for each kind of original, because each has its own quirks.

Accurate reproduction of the color grid of Figure 10.8 is an important test of scanning settings. The color perception of a good scanner can be changed. If we conclude that the greens of the target image are too vivid, we can change defaults so that next time we will get more cyan, less yellow, more magenta, or some combination. This change would not affect any

color but green. Now, if we were scanning an original with weak greens, we would change this setting, but we need to know what numbers to go back to afterward.

Leaving scanning for a moment, if we have gotten a musicians image that we like into our computer and our job is now to get film and a contract proof, we want great precision from the whole process. If we run the same job tomorrow, next week, or next year, we would like to get a proof that looks exactly the same as today's. We therefore require stringent quality control and repeatability from Kodak graphic arts products and those of its competitors.

No sane individual would possibly argue this point. If we have corrected the image in Photoshop, we have to be able to get identical reproduction of it every time. But should this be taken further? If we scan the original photograph of the musicians once today and once next week, do we want the two scans to be identical?

The Kodak people have gone to great lengths to try to make it so. To start the discussion of whether they are right, have a look at Figure 10.6. How should it be corrected, if at all?

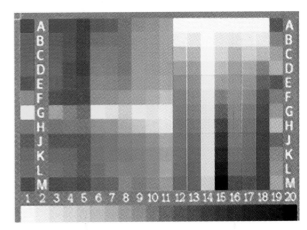

Figure 10.8 *The Kodak Q–60 targets.*

Figure 10.9 *Without known colors or an original photograph to adhere to, two professionals came up with these radically different color-corrected versions of the original Photo CD image of Figure 10.6.*

In trying to improve the color correction skills of the people who work for me, I frequently pass out digital images to several people, and have them each, independently, correct them if they see fit. Only global corrections are allowed. Then, they get together, examine each other's efforts, and draw conclusions about what the best technique was. Naturally, I do the color corrections also.

By mistake, Figure 10.6 was put into a group of these images. This picture is unlike any other in the book in that there is no way to figure out what any of the colors should actually look like. There is a moon, so it must be after sunset. Who knows how dark it is? Clouds are usually white, but maybe they *should* be as red as they are. Trees are usually green, but maybe in this setting they should be black. Furthermore, this is a PCD image, and as such it may have a heavy cast and bear little relation to the actual photograph.

Without anything to go by, when my turn came to correct the image, I decided to concentrate on the rock formation. Since it is primarily magenta and yellow, I steepened the curves in those two plates in their upper ranges. Although I believed that the clouds should have a magenta cast, reducing it somewhat would help me make a steeper magenta curve, so I did it. Cyan being the unwanted color in the rocks, I increased it slightly for all values under 50 percent, accepting a quality loss in the foreground tree. The black I moved only as necessary to get a proper shadow value. My final version is the top half of Figure 10.9.

The bottom half is the entry of a second contestant, Crawford Hart, who took a significantly different view. He felt that the

Figure 10.10
A high-quality professional scan of the same image, where the scanner operator had an original photograph to refer to. This, therefore, is accurate color—but is it better color?

photograph was taken in the early evening but that the reproduction was generally too light. He disagreed with my opinion that the clouds should be somewhat red, thinking that this effect was caused by an overall magenta cast in the PCD file. He therefore neutralized the clouds completely, although the general shapes of his cyan, magenta, and yellow curves were similar to mine. In keeping with his interpretation that the image was too light, he boosted quartertones in all colors and gave an especially violent boost to black so as to get a much darker foreground.

Which of us do you think was right?

As I said, this picture got into our correction exercises by mistake. I was not aware that it was one of my own PCD images, or that a high-end scan was available for comparison. In preparing files for this book I found an original color print of the photograph, and I realized that I had a professional scan lurking in my computer.

That scan, Figure 10.10, is accurate for color. It closely matches the original photograph. With my memory appropriately jogged, I can now tell you that this picture was taken in Capitol Reef National Park at about half an hour before sunset. Although the moon was out the sun was still shining.

If you are a calibrationist, that clinches it for you. Both correction efforts are total failures. The high-end scan is the image you want.

Me, I am not so sure. The viewer of the printed piece won't have the original photo to look at. The original is history. It has no further meaning for us. The only issue now is which of the three digital versions appeals the most. To my way of thinking the "correct" scan of Figure 10.10

is the worst of the bunch by a wide margin. The other two are very different interpretations but they both work. Reasonable people would probably split their vote on which one was better.

This is a strange result. The PCD scan appears to have captured more detail than the supposedly superior drum scanner. On the other hand, for a calibrationist system, PCD missed badly on color, putting in a heavy magenta cast that did not exist in the original.

Everyone has slightly different preferences in color. There is no reason at all to think that your taste would or should be the same as either mine or Crawford's. As long as the scan has captured all necessary detail all three of us can correct it in our own way. If we each then think we have the best version, *vive la différence.*

Therefore, whether scanning settings are precisely the same from day to day is of little relevance. As long as the result is somewhere in the ballpark, we will be able to live with it. If you try to color-correct a certain image today, and then, without referring back to what you did, try your hand at the same image next month, do you suppose there is the slightest chance that your two versions will be identical?

Let us go back to the start of this discussion: the Kodak spokesman's assertion that PCD scans, in conjunction with other products, are at least as predictable as those made by experts. I think he is basically right. The Kodak approach rigorously measures and attempts to correct for all variables in the process. If Ektachrome tends to have a bluer look than other films, fine, we make a special curve, developed by painstaking measurements, that automatically applies to Ektachrome images. Gray balance is ruthlessly enforced by other curves, based on analysis of the scans of gray scales that are known to be dead neutral.

Few professional scanner operators if any are this conscientious. They may take densitometer readings of the Q–60 targets of Figure 10.8 and make relatively gross adjustments. They may, as a matter of course, scan certain films with different default settings. And some try to guarantee gray balance by placing a known gray target strip (supplied by Kodak, of course) alongside the original art and making sure that whatever adjustments are made do not turn the gray target some other color.

Personally, I endorse the first technique, but not the other two. The use of a gray scale as a crutch I find particularly repellent. If my assignment were to reproduce the Kodak gray scale, I could and would make sure it stayed neutral. If I were scanning something else, my settings could turn the Kodak gray scale flaming crimson, for all I would care, so long as the real image had the right balance.

In sum, the statement that Kodak's technique "challenges and often surpasses the color quality achieved by expert drum scanner operators who calibrate their scanners in CMYK…" is correct in a manner of speaking. Its underlying assumption is the problem, for expert scanner operators *don't calibrate*. Except, of course, to the only thing that is important—the individual image.

The Common Corrections

You might not guess it from looking at the artwork in this chapter, but the images from either a Photo CD or a digital camera are treated similarly in color correction.

It is certainly true that the original digital camera images shown here are vastly superior to the original PCD ones, but a leisurely look at Figure 10.11 might suggest a reason. Examine the second hand of the watch. Digital cameras tend to be rather slow in doing their exposures. And there are other significant drawbacks as well. They need a power supply, unlike conventional cameras. Their images can be quite large (the ones used here were originally more than 12 megabytes apiece), and popping in a new gigabyte hard drive is not exactly as simple as loading a new roll of film. Also, they work much better if they are physically hooked up to a computer where the work can be previewed.

Good digital cameras, though the price is coming down, are still priced in five-figure territory.

While all these problems are being addressed, for the moment digital cameras are too cumbersome to use outdoors, too slow for shots involving live action, too dependent upon a computer to be portable, and too expensive for casual users. Effectively, then, the current major use for them is by professional photographers for product shots and other still-life images, normally under carefully controlled studio conditions.

If all Photo CD images were made this way, they'd be pretty good too.

Neither digital cameras nor PCD scans apply any unsharp masking. It is almost unheard of, therefore, for us not to want to add some ourselves. The fundamentals of doing this were covered in Chapter 7. There is no easy rule for how much to use on one of these images. Unsharp masking of a large image takes time, so it isn't practical to just guess at the value needed and take the risk of having to redo it several times. Instead, using the marquee tool, select a small portion of the image in an area that interests you. Then apply **Filter: Sharpen>Unsharp Masking** at 75 percent amount, 1.0 pixel radius, 3 threshold, which are reasonable minimums.

Assuming that the selected area now looks better than it did before, cancel the sharpening with a Command–Z, and reapply it at a stronger setting. And so forth, until the picture seems to be getting too grainy or you see other signs that your moves are becoming counterproductive. When you think you've found the right value, cancel your selection and apply USM to the entire image.

If you are working with a PCD image, in all probability you will have to reinforce the sharpening by also boosting the quartertone and midtone values in black, once you have converted to CMYK. Such a move adds detailing and focus, and PCD images generally are too soft.

As both of these technologies use CCDs to capture data, one expects to see some quality deterioration in dark areas, and certain countermeasures may be needed. The weakness in shadow areas is not limited to dark browns and blacks, but can happen where colors are bright. In Figure 10.12, the problem is occurring in a brilliant red. When the scan has lost this much information, recovering it is difficult, but we do have some resources that will be discussed momentarily.

Figure 10.11 *Hidden in this picture is a reason that digital cameras are primarily used indoors and almost always to photograph still-lifes.*

Living with L*a*b*

Editors are trained to sniff out the phrase *exponential increase* and to mercilessly delete it (oops, mercilessly to delete it) each time a writer is so unimaginative as to use this tired cliché.

I bring this point up to alert my editor to the following sentence.

When we open a Kodak Photo CD image for the first time, the odds of a serious color cast increase exponentially.

The majority of PCD images are reasonably in balance, but scattered throughout this book are examples of some real whoppers. We just saw, in Figure

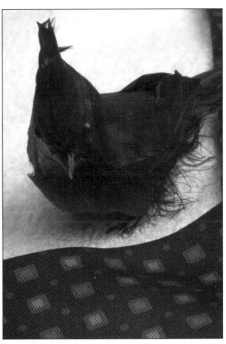

Figure 10.12 *CCD devices have difficulty with shadows, and not necessarily black ones. Here, the bird is so saturated in red that the digital camera starts to lose detail. Compare the quality of the bird to that of the tie. At right, the blue plate of this originally RGB image (in RGB, darker areas print as white) shows the magnitude of the quality loss.*

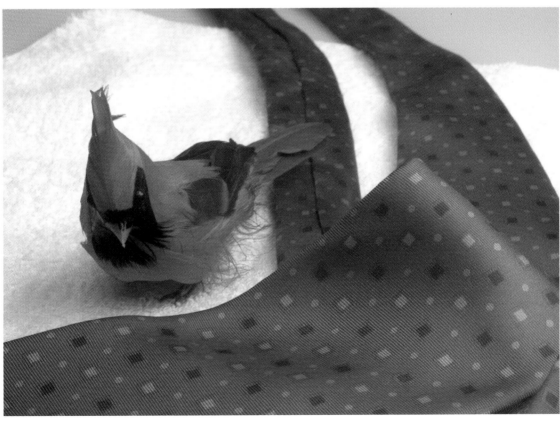

10.6, the mother of all magenta casts, and later, in Figure 10.19, there will be a cyan cast that is just as bad. Excruciatingly heavy yellows are on display in the PCD images of Figures 4.1, 9.9, and 9.16, and there is a gruesome green in Figure 14.4.

As we enter yet another colorspace, it is sobering to learn that these problems are to some extent created and tolerated in the name of calibrationism.

This is not to suggest that we should not attempt to exploit the advantages of LAB, as we would any other potential weapon in the war against poor color. This particular firearm, however, is one of those with the tendency to blow up in the user's face.

L*a*b* Made Easy: The CIE Equations

$$L^* = 116 \sqrt[3]{\frac{Y}{Y_n}} - 16$$

$$a^* = 500 \left[\sqrt[3]{\frac{X}{X_n}} - \sqrt[3]{\frac{Y}{Y_n}} \right]$$

$$b^* = 500 \left[\sqrt[3]{\frac{Y}{Y_n}} - \sqrt[3]{\frac{Z}{Z_n}} \right]$$

where X, Y, and Z, the so-called *tristimulus values,* are the theoretical reflectance readings of the object in question under three different varieties of light. The three different lights are imaginary, not existing in nature, although they correspond very roughly to red, green and blue. The Y source, for example, contains all colors, but with a green emphasis. X_n, Y_n, and Z_n add a further imaginary factor: they represent the theoretical reflectance of a perfectly white object.

The above equations are valid unless X/X_n, Y/Y_n, or Z/Z_n ≤0.008856. In that case, for each X/X_n, Y/Y_n, or Z/Z_n so affected, the cube root expression is eliminated in favor of the one below, (using L* and Y/Y_n as an example)

$$L^* = 116 \left[7.787 \left(\frac{Y}{Y_n} \right) + .138 \right] - 16$$

Figure 10.13 CMYK and RGB are highly intuitive colorspaces. Changes in the values of their components are easily understood. LAB is not quite as simple to comprehend.

And, (to irritate the editor with a further hackneyed phrase) in LAB, a miss is as good as a mile.

In Figure 10.14, we see how minuscule changes in LAB values can annihilate the whole structure of an image. The two variants at top and bottom are caused by a single mild bump in the curve of one channel only. We have applied curves several times as violent to our CMYK images without doing apparent damage. What is going on here?

In CMYK, changes are straightforward. If you apply a curve to a color that changes 50 percent to 60 percent, well, those parts of the image will become 20 percent (10 percentage points, that is) darker than they were. It works the same way in RGB, and for that matter, in HSB. To get mathematical, these are *linear* colorspaces.

Even if you do not fully comprehend the equations of Figure 10.13, you probably grasp that LAB is a different animal altogether, and one that should be approached with great caution.

Even at its most basic level, LAB is difficult to fathom. Of the three spaces we have worked with so far, it most closely resembles HSB, because the L channel in LAB is essentially the same as the B channel in HSB. They both govern luminosity, or brightness. They are somewhat akin to the K channel in CMYK, but more powerful.

In HSB, one of the two remaining channels governs hue. It can specify red, blue, orange, or anything else. The other, the saturation channel, controls how clean or dirty the dominating hue is.

In LAB, A and B are *both* hue channels.

Figure 10.14 *LAB may be mathematically precise, but it is not very forgiving. A slight maladjustment can result in a huge color cast. The original image is at center. Note the extraordinarily large effect of modest moves in a single channel, the A.*

What we call saturation is determined by a very complex interplay of the two. They are sometimes termed *opponent-color* channels, because A goes from red to green, whereas B goes from blue to yellow. Colors in the middle of each channel are more or less neutral.

This would be hard enough to handle if the curves behaved in normal linear fashion, but they don't. Instead, they rely heavily on the cube roots of certain fractions. If you have not taken arithmetic recently, you may not be aware that the cube root of a number smaller than one can be many times larger than the original number. The cube root of .001, for example, is .1, which is a hundred times as large.

That is, quite literally and quite technically, an exponential kind of increase, and it ruins any hope of manipulating the A and B channels, at least, through curves.

By now you may be on the verge of concluding that LAB is an invention of the forces of darkness, specifically for the purpose of tormenting true believers in color fidelity. This is not so. It has many valuable attributes (of which ease in color correction is clearly not one) and some perspective on it is in order.

Forgetting the graphic arts for a moment, the use of color in industry is so pervasive and so critical to success that a clearcut method of identifying small variations is essential. If the paint on a car is just slightly the wrong color, if a detergent package has an offensive hue, consumers won't buy it. Considering that we all see color differently, an objectively perfect color identification scheme is nearly impossible.

Although the inner workings of the human visual system are still poorly understood, color science is blessed with highly accurate spectrophotometers and other such measuring instruments. The question has been how to use them.

A system is needed that will respond to very small changes in color, that will be independent of the color judgment of individuals, that will cope with colors that are unknown at present, and that can handle the phenomenon of *metamerism*. That is an optical peculiarity whereby two objects can appear to be the same color under one type of lighting conditions, yet different in another.

Color-defining systems used to be based on HSB principles, but since the time of the second world war the models favored by color scientists have been opponent-color variants of LAB. To avoid metameric difficulties, these

Figure 10.15 *The image of chocolates in Figure 3.4 had poor detail in the darkest pieces, at extreme left and right. Looking at the blue channel of the original RGB file coming off the digital camera, it is easy to see why.*

colorspaces have all defined individual colors not just under standard lighting conditions, but as mathematical combinations of their values under three different light sources. Frequently (but no longer) these three sources were red, green and blue.

The leading worldwide authority, the CIE (Commission International de l'Eclairage, or International Commission on Lighting) recommended use of LAB in 1960, but issued a revised mathematical model of the colorspace, involving cube roots and three imaginary reference colors, in 1978. Because there have been so many LAB variants over the years, this one should properly be called either CIELAB or L*a*b*, but in the interest of typographic sanity, I have been and will be referring to this model, shown in mathematical form in Figure 10.13, as LAB. This is Photoshop's native colorspace. It is related to Kodak's YCC, which is also an opponent-color model, but uses considerably different mathematics.

Which Plate Has the Contrast?

Practical uses for the A and B channels of LAB in color correction are limited because the resulting changes are too violent. The L channel is a much more likely candidate. There are many times when (thinking in CMYK for a moment) we would like to add black to punch up contrast, but are unable to write a drastic enough curve without ruining the

image. The L channel is more powerful than black, since the A and B, unlike C, M, and Y, carry no darkness information. Moreover, because of the exponential nature of the colorspace, a slight change in the L curve will have spectacular results. An example of this can be found all the way back in Figure 4.7.

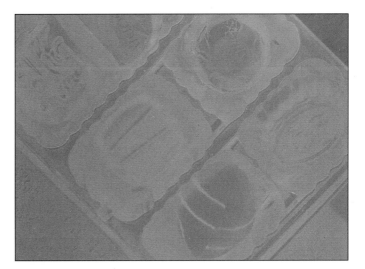

Figure 10.16 *The advantage of switching colorspaces: when one channel (the A of LAB, above top) is hopeless, the contrast must be hiding out in one or more of the other channels. Above bottom, the L channel carries good contrast in the darker chocolates.*

LAB can be used more subtly to solve another problem shown earlier, in Figure 3.4. There, although the general quality of the digital-camera image of a box of chocolates was exceptional, the typical CCD problem of poor shadow contrast crashed the party. The molded patterns on the two darkest pieces of chocolate were scarcely visible.

To see why this was, have a look at Figure 10.15, the blue channel of the original RGB image. Note what a contrast catastrophe the extreme right and left pieces of chocolate have become. Although, once we convert to CMYK, none of the plates will be quite this horrible, they will be bad enough, especially the cyan.

Supposing that our assignment is to do whatever we can to increase detail in these two pieces of chocolate, even if there is a slight color shift because of it.

We have seen several times that a sensible way to create contrast where there

Figure 10.17 *After selecting the two contrast-deficient chocolates and blending 65 percent of the L channel into each of the three RGB channels, the detailing begins to be pronounced, although blue chocolates are not exactly what we had in mind.*

isn't any is to use **Image: Calculations>Blend** to average some of the strengths of a high-contrast plate into a poor one. In the CMYK version of the chocolates photo, the best plate to attack our problem with is the black, but even that is not too hot. This varies from previous experience. In most images, there is at least one channel with excellent contrast, as where a person's face is weak in cyan, and we blend some of the magenta into the bad plate.

Just because we have examined each of our four channels and found nothing to our liking does not mean we should stop the search. There are six more channels to look at. If we make two new copies of the CMYK image, and convert one each to LAB and RGB, maybe we will find a channel somewhere that is better than the current black. Can you guess where?

You can look at all 10 channels if you want, but if you think about it, you will realize that the winner has to be the L of LAB. In all of these colorspaces, there is a certain amount of contrast that has to be distributed. The blue channel of Figure 10.15 and the cyan channel (if we convert to CMYK), do not get very much, but whatever they do get is subtracted from the other, stronger channels.

If you had not seen the gray blur that is the top half of Figure 10.16, you could still figure out that that is what the A must look like. The A is an opponent-color channel. The lights represent red and the darks are green. There happens to be nothing in this image that can remotely be considered red, nothing that is green.

When contrast was being distributed, the A channel had stepped out for a beer. The A is so flat that, if you did not know it was a picture of a box of chocolates, you would be unlikely to figure it out.

The B channel, blue vs. yellow, is a little better (the golden wrappers are heavily yellow) but not much.

Accordingly, with two flat channels, all of the contrast winds up in the third. That makes the L channel not just the best one in LAB, but of all the thirteen channels. The pattern embossed into the dark chocolates is clearly visible.

We have not yet converted the original RGB digital camera image into CMYK, so we have the opportunity to do a little blending first. The L doesn't have much in common with any of the RGB channels, so we are forced to select, and feather, the two problem pieces of chocolate.

With the chocolates selected in the L channel, we copy into memory with a Command–C. Then, we pass the selection path into the RGB file, using **Image: Calculations>Copy**. Opening one of the three RGB channels after another, we now paste in the chocolates from the L channel. Since we have arranged for the chocolates to be selected in the target image, the pasted chocolates will land in exactly the right place.

The only question is how forcefully we will make this blend take place. The L chocolates are so much lighter than those in any of the RGB channels that it is

unthinkable to make an outright substitution. This means we have to establish a layer and change the opacity of the pasted object to something other than 100 percent. There is no need to use the same value in each channel, but I did anyhow, putting in 65 percent in all three.

This finagling accounts for the blue chocolates of Figure 10.17. Silly as it looks now, it is a lot easier to correct than the

Figure 10.18 *Before and after correction.*

feeble detailing of the top of Figure 10.18. With both images side by side on the monitor, we can write curves to alter the blue chocolates (remember, we can affect them alone; we never deselected them) until they assume more or less the values of the originals.

No question, the final version in the bottom of Figure 10.18 shows the detail we were looking for, but I am a little ambivalent about the result. Neither you nor I know whether we would accept this image as real if we could magically develop

Figure 10.19 *Despite the blue cast, this is a very respectable photograph, and Kodak uses it on a promotional disk that advertises the high quality of PCD images.*

amnesia and forget that we know what was done. My feeling is that the two chocolates we worked on were convincing, but the giveaway is the middle chocolate, the one that we first said had enough contrast, but now is being overshadowed by the other two.

When we were doing this correction, did you say to yourself, let's save the selection paths for the chocolates, just in case we need them again? Did you make a mental note that 65 was the blend percentage? Did you remember to save the CMYK curves we used to make the blue chocolates brown? If you did, redoing this job to include the third piece in the blending will be quick and easy. If not, take advantage of the digital camera's quick turnaround. Reshoot the job, but before doing so, eat the middle chocolate and leave the space empty. That's what I would do, anyway.

Makeover, Digital Style

Occasionally having to play Photoshop tricks to get decent shadow contrast is a small price to pay for the convenience and high quality offered by a first-rate digital camera. For all the advantages that Kodak CD offers, we sometimes find ourselves in even more untenable positions.

A lot of quality problems get hidden when an image is not very large. Properly handled, professional results can be dredged out of most PCD images at sizes up to, say, six square inches. When they get much larger the weaknesses of the scan get harder to hide.

Since the final example of the chapter also will be the last standard color correction in this book, we may as well make it a tough one. Large portraits of faces are notoriously the most difficult subjects in professional work. The face shown in Figure 10.19 is impressive enough that Kodak decided to include it on a promotional CD, one that was distributed to professional users as an advertisement for the quality of the process.

This image has a blue cast of mammoth proportions. It could be that this is the inevitable result of automated scanning using a fractious and unpredictable colorspace. It is also entirely possible that the bluish effect is deliberate. As it stands, the picture has certain artistic merit. The composition is good, and if the color is unnatural, it creates an interesting soft effect. It reduces contrast in the face, smoothing it out.

For present purposes, however, please assume that it is a mistake. Our assignment is to create a more lifelike version, one good enough to print on a full page. Standard PCD images have enough data for this. It is reasonable to use them at up to 8½×11, if resolution is going to be the only criterion. Color quality is, alas, another story.

Space limitations dictate that the preliminary files used for illustration of this correction be smaller than a full page. Those shown here were resampled down in Photoshop to a reasonable resolution for the smaller sizes.

Figure 10.20, you will agree, is a big step in the right direction. This

difficult correction used a combination of techniques that are by now familiar. The investigation began with the Info palette telling me exactly what my eyes did, that a blue cast permeates everything. The proof of this is easy. There are no less than four areas of known color in this image. Three of them—the necklace, the whites of the eyes, and the teeth—are plainly supposed to be close to neutral. Instead, they are buried under six times as much cyan and magenta as yellow. The fourth area, the skin itself, ought to have at least as much

Figure 10.20 *Standard correction curves make an enormous difference in bringing this image to life, but there is a long way to go yet if it is to appear at the size of a full page.*

Figure 10.21 The striking improvement shown in Figure 10.20 is almost entirely due to changes in the cyan plate. Above left, the cyan of Figure 10.19; below left, the totally transformed version of Figure 10.20.

yellow as magenta, and maybe a quarter as much cyan as magenta. Instead, a typical value is 40C50M40Y10K.

All this adds up to the weird cyan plate shown at the top of Figure 10.21. The idea of my correction was to transform this disgrace into the usable plate at the bottom of the figure.

About the only hopeful sign here was that we had an excellent black plate to work with. And no wonder! The original face was so gray that large amounts of black were generated when the image went to CMYK. So, the black was crisp throughout.

I therefore made a new cyan consisting of 40 percent of the black and 60 percent of the old cyan. Then, I applied curves to maximize contrast in all colors. With the new cyan rapidly taking shape, I blended in 15 percent of magenta, and then 10 percent more black.

The yellow plate, while not as dreadful as the cyan, was also very flat, so I blended in black there as well. The final step was to impose a new set of curves that placed a 5C2M2Y value in the lightest part of the white necklace and an 80C70M70Y70K in the black parts.

Although this surgery may be considered a qualified success, one cannot expect the patient to jump out of the hospital bed and run a marathon. That is exactly what we would be doing if we suggested that this image was now ready for a full page. There are still the following glaring deficiencies:

• The skin is still too cyan, too neutral. I take this woman to be fairly light-skinned, given her hair and eye color. This argues for pinker flesh than for most people. Despite our best efforts we have bronzed her more than is believable.

• In a similar vein, one expects that a person of this general coloring will have blue eyes, but all of my plate blending has turned them into a mousy color.

• The curves I used could not correct every instance of a cast. For example, I was able to get the half of the necklace that is to our right to be more or less white, but the left half is heavily magenta.

• The basic contrast problem with the image is that three important elements, the face, the hair, and the fabric background, are close to being the same color. To get more differentiation, it looks like we will have to select each of these sections individually. The background is taking on a pink appearance that I find objectionable, and the hair is appearing to blend into the forehead.

• The question of focus lacks a satisfactory answer at this point. Because PCD scans do not have any kind of unsharp masking applied, we almost invariably have to do it ourselves in Photoshop. This image may be the exception. Many areas could use better focus, but the skin itself is a poor candidate.

As usual, we will be adding contrast to the face. That will, unfortunately, accentuate any irregularities. Sharpening will make them worse still. This model has a good complexion but she is a human being, after all, not an alabaster statue. Like any other human, she has scars, pimples, birthmarks, and blackheads. These may not be noticeable in Figure

10.20 but at full page size, they will be.

Makeup should be unobtrusive, but at full size it becomes very obvious. Under the woman's right eye, for example, the makeup artist missed with the eye pencil and a dark line appears. Worse yet, the model is wearing a heavy layer of foundation that is not quite her natural skin tone. The last thing we need is to advertise that by doing anything that would exaggerate the powder.

For all these reasons, the outlook for further improvement is one of gloom and tedium. Yes, the picture can be made substantially better, with a large investment of time. No, I would rather not be the one to have to do it.

Instead, I would like to suggest a different option. Not that it will make things easy, of course; what we are trying to do is just too extreme. Starting out with the CMYK file of Figure 10.20 has proven too difficult. At this point we will, therefore, despite the considerable improvements that were made, abandon that approach and start from scratch.

Organizing Before the Conversion

We begin from the beginning, by opening the PCD file at 16x base size, the highest resolution on a standard Photo CD. As always, we choose LAB as our colorspace, and per Kodak's documentation for this image, we use Ektamatic defaults.

The first order of business is to verify that even so large a file will have enough resolution to produce the size printed image we want. The pages of this book are 9.25 inches tall, and the image is set up to *bleed,* meaning that it will print to the very edge of the top and bottom. The printer will require about an eighth of an inch more image at the top and the bottom, to be sure that when the pages are trimmed after printing, an inaccurate cut cannot result in white space on the page. Therefore, the total image will have to be almost 10 inches tall.

Image: Image Size reveals that the image is currently more than 40 inches tall, but that is because PCD images are set to a default resolution of 72 pixels per inch. With the Constrain File Size option checked, we reduce the height down to the 10 inches that we want, and the resolution automatically adjusts to 270.

This book prints with a 150-line screen, and the rules explained in Chapter 3 call for a picture to have a resolution between 1.5 and 2 times the screen value. That means between 225 and 300, so we are in fine shape, though this is the sort of image where a higher resolution would be agreeable, since that would soften the skin.

This image occupies around 14 megabytes. On a file of this size, certain Photoshop transactions take a long time to execute. Even with the most powerful computers now available, some of the things we would like to do will not exactly go like a bolt of lightning.

As a practical matter, therefore, we would like to do as much as possible of the preliminary work *before* converting to CMYK. This is because LAB has only three channels to CMYK's four. In CMYK, the file size will be almost 20 megabytes.

To reduce system overhead even more, we will start by cropping the image as much as possible, discarding unnecessary data. Next step will be a thorough examination of the image for gross defects. This tiresome procedure is always necessary in images this large, because no matter how

stringent the quality control, small problems get in, and at the size we plan to print, they will be visible. I found four such areas. In the woman's right cheek, there was the water stain previously shown in Figure 7.5. High up on her neck on the left of the picture was a series of white scratches almost a quarter of an inch long. In the extreme upper right of the background there was a large white gouge in the pink fabric. These three problems were all corrected in the same way: by selecting an adjacent piece of image, feathering it heavily, copying it to memory, and dropping it on top of the defect. The fourth problem, a tiny hole in the fourth white link of the necklace at left of the picture, was fixed by airbrushing.

While doing these things, it of course makes sense to also fix up any other undesirable details. So, the moles on the model's left shoulder and the left side of her face were taken out as well, along with various small facial blemishes. Normally this kind of work would be done in CMYK, but there is no technical advantage in doing so, and in a picture this large, we get faster performance in LAB.

Thinking along the same lines, I also drew and saved four simple paths: for the whites of the eyes, the irises of the eyes, the teeth, and the lips. Having worked on many portraits of female models, I was very sure that these would be useful later.

No great accuracy was necessary in those four paths, but two others required more effort. I felt that success depended on having more differentiation between the colors of the skin, the hair, and the background. As they were all almost the same color to begin with, it was impossible to write a curve in any colorspace that would affect one but not the other two. There was therefore no alternative to manually selecting the areas and changing them individually.

Selecting the background can be done either with the lasso or the pen tool, but there is a tricky part. Parts of the background show through the mesh of the hat. I doubted that it would be noticeable if they were a slightly different color from the rest of the background, but was not willing to risk it. So these elements had to get into the selection. The obvious method was to use **Select: Similar** to rope them in. This tactic may also succeed in rounding up part of the face, but that can be easily deleted from the overall selection by means of the Command–lasso.

Complex as that selection is, it can still be saved through the Paths palette. The hair, however, cannot. There are too many individual strands falling over the forehead. In some areas the strands are less than a pixel wide, so even if we tried to take the time to se-

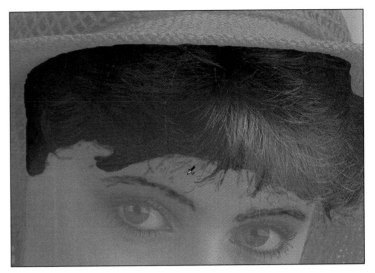

Figure 10.22 *Above, using the airbrush tool at 50 percent intensity to add suggestions of strands of hair into the final mask (below). Photoshop's masking tools, which allow use of airbrushing and other softening techniques, let one cater to amorphous areas like the eyebrows.*

lect every one, we would pick up skin as well, which we don't want. Furthermore, if we are to change the hair color we certainly want to change the eyebrows at the same time, and they can't be selected easily either.

The only workable approach is to create a mask, because masks can have areas

of partial intensity. We can use these to offer the suggestion of a color change in the problem areas, without swinging a sledgehammer at the underlying skin.

To make the mask shown in Figure 10.22, I started by lassoing the part that was exclusively hair, and feathering two pixels. This selection did not include any

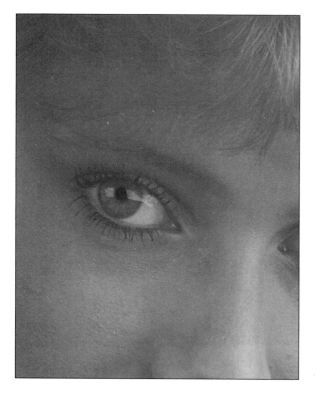

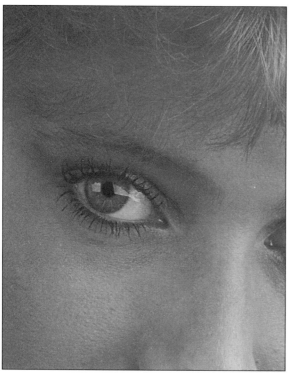

Figure 10.23 *Because it has no hue component, the L channel of LAB is a convenient place to use unsharp masking: no disagreeable color shifts will take place. Above left, the original L channel. Below left, after USM and a contrast-enhancing curve.*

individual hairs or the eyebrows. However, changing into Quick Mask mode lets us edit the selection using any tool we like. I mostly did the work with the airbrush at 50 percent strength, but the paintbrush tool would have done just as well. Photoshop allows working on the mask while the image is visible (Figure 10.22), so it is easy to trace. To do this, open the Channels palette and turn off the ability to write to the CMYK channels, while leaving them visible.

When the mask is completed, it makes sense to save it as a separate grayscale Photoshop 3 document, rather than as an additional channel, if for no other reason than that this file is so large already. **Image: Calculations>Composite** allows the use of any channel in any open file as a mask, so having a separate mask file like this is no problem, and it will be easier to edit should we discover problems later.

This concludes the preliminary work, so it would be appropriate to hit the save key now, but let's not convert to CMYK just yet. The very explosiveness of LAB will be used to blow some blue away.

The B Channel Beats the Blues

Before charging into the B channel, consider the advantages of the L in solving our focusing problem. As we know, in CMYK it frequently pays to sharpen the black only. The same arguments apply to the L, maybe more so because the L is a heavier channel. Sharpening the L rather than the entire file avoids the problem of accentuating color breaks in the face, since the L affects lightness and darkness only, not color. Coupled with a very, very mild S-shaped curve to add contrast, sharpening made the difference between the top and bottom halves of Figure 10.23.

To avoid having to wait forever, I first tested my sharpening and curves on a small section of the document. When I thought I had good values, I applied them to the entire channel.

Manipulating the A and B should be rare, because they are so counterintuitive and so volatile, but here the blue cast is pervasive enough that a B alteration may be our best option.

In writing a curve to alter the B, lighter values move the image closer to yellow and darker ones toward its opponent color, blue. Even the smallest moves will have a drastic impact, not only because of the exponential nature of the colorspace, but because so few of the available colors have any relevance to printing. Given how bad cyan inks are, most of the blues that the B channel can define, though they may be useful in other contexts, cannot be printed with process inks. This is yet another argument for doing color correction in CMYK, all of whose colors are useful ones.

But CMYK has no method to transform blue into yellow. So, with great trepidation, we embark on the adventure of curving the B.

As one might expect, the B is almost entirely gray. This is because, as the image stands, practically

everything is a standoff between blue and yellow. The fleshtones certainly *ought* to be more yellow than blue, but they aren't. About the only objects with a pronounced difference from the average are the eyes, which are clearly more blue than yellow. However, we would not mind if they got bluer still. This is good news, because it will allow a steeper curve. We will be able to reduce the B where it is currently

Figure 10.24 *After the moves of Figure 10.23, the application of the inset curve to the B channel, and a slight adjustment to the hair color, this image is far from perfect, but it is a much better starting point than Figure 10.20 was.*

lightest and increase it where it is darkest. This will translate into greater contrast between yellows and blues everywhere, just what we want. Also, once we find our values, we will push the entire curve to the right, eliminating blue and favoring yellow throughout the image. To get a start on the curve, the eyedropper option in the curves dialog box is a big help. Without it, it is hard to know exactly where the B values we want to affect are located on the curve. When we click on that eyedropper and then place our cursor anywhere in the image, Photoshop will show us where it is on the curve.

After applying this mild curve to the B, it was time to try to put more impact in the hair. I thought that the hair should be more yellow and less of a neutral color, so it was back to the B. I duplicated it into a new document, and applied the smallest possible shift toward yellow to it. Then, I composited it back into the existing file, using the mask for the hair shown in Figure 10.22. This made the hair yellower without doing anything to the rest of the image.

At this point, I converted to CMYK. The result is Figure 10.24. The blue cast is roughly cut in half. We still have a ways to go, but we are much better off with this as our starting point than with Figure 10.20.

Back in the CMYK Saddle

Now that we are back on our home turf, corrections will seem much more manageable. Many of the problems noted in Figure 10.20 are still present, but they are less severe. The cyan plate, for example, is poor, but it is not the hideous abomination of Figure 10.21. As before, mixing in some of the black plate data will help, but

I chose only a 35 percent blend this time. There was no need to blend anything into the yellow.

One application of curves now sufficed to get acceptable color. As before, I set the highlight in the right side of the necklace and the shadow in the dark parts of it. As cyan was still too heavy in the fleshtone, my curve, shown in Figure 10.25, brought down the quartertone values without doing anything to the heavier cyans in areas like the eyes.

The image was now all right for color, except that the overall reduction in cyan had damaged the background to the point that it had become a timid pink. I had anticipated this, so I opened the Paths palette and loaded the path that isolates the background. I made this area the current selection, feathering it one pixel, and then opened the original, uncorrected version of Figure 10.19, blue cast and all. Using **Image: Calculations>Copy**, I passed the selection from the new file to the raw one. Then, clicking into the raw file, I copied the selected background into memory. I now closed the raw file to return to the new one, whose background was still selected. A Command–V placed the background from the raw image into the good one. Feeling that this background was now too purple, I saved the floating suggestion as a layer, opened Layer Options, and adjusted the opacity settings until I was satisfied with the change in the color. I settled for 60 percent of the old background and 40 percent of the new.

That finished the hard part. There was now no further serious defect in the image. Correction had ended. Enhancement was about to begin.

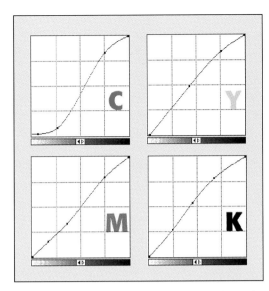

Figure 10.25 *The correction curves that brought Figure 10.24 into striking range of the final version shown in Figure 10.26.*

Local Touchup Where It Counts

When an image is printing this large, techniques that would not be noticeable at smaller sizes are no longer a waste of time. Here is a summary of the things I did to try to get more out of this image than merely acceptable color. If you compare the full page raw and corrected images of Figure 10.26, I think you will see the difference these local corrections make.

• Activating the magic wand, I clicked into the lightest area of the hair. This generated an irregularly shaped selection covering about half a square inch. I feathered this by 6 pixels and applied a curve that reduced all colors by about 10 percent. Thus, a soft and attractive highlight was added to the hair just above the model's left eye.

• Loading and feathering the path that isolated the irises of the eyes, I applied a curve that increased cyan and decreased yellow, making the eyes bluer. Also, the curve increased black values in shadow areas only, making the pupils more pronounced.

• While there, I deselected the iris path and loaded the one for the whites of the eyes. One cannot go too far with lightening these (or they would compete with the whiteness of the necklace), but the whites of the eyes started out rather gray and bloodshot, so a mild lightening curve helped.

• On to the teeth. Same idea, same curve, same lightening.

• And the lips. Loading and feathering the path that isolated them, I applied unsharp masking to get them in better focus. Then, I added further contrast by steepening the curves of the dominant colors, magenta and yellow, in the shadows, and of the unwanted color, cyan, in the highlights. This helped compensate for what I thought was too heavy an application of lipstick.

• Back to the eyes. The eyelids are one of the most important features in facial work, regardless of the sex of the model. There is a tendency for them to appear soft, because eyelashes are so delicate that they often lose definition in printing. Therefore, in most cases one should do what I did here, namely, activate the sharpen half of the blur/sharpen tool, set intensity to around 30 percent, choose a wide feathered brush, and sweep over lashes, brows, and the eyelids. To add further depth still, I also went to the airbrush tool, chose black as the foreground color,

Figure 10.26 (overleaf) *Full-page renditions of the original, uncorrected PCD file, and a version manipulated as described in the text. Are Photo CD originals, however much corrected, suitable for professional purposes at this size? You be the judge.*

Quick & Dirty

KODAK CDs AND DIGITAL CAMERAS

✓Rapid, high-resolution image capture, without conventional scanning, is the big growth area in professional imaging.

✓Digital cameras, which evaluate live art with a CCD array similar to that found in many scanners, dump their data directly into a computer: no film is ever used. Unsatisfactory exposures are merely discarded, so there is no need for preliminary shots with an instant camera before a shoot begins. Although there is some loss in shadow detail, on the whole quality may exceed that of conventional film plus graphic arts scanning.

✓Kodak's Photo CD approach lets us give original positive or negative film (prints not acceptable) to our local supplier, who scans it on Kodak equipment and writes it to a compact disk that should last a lifetime. The cost is a small fraction that of conventional scanning, the files can be read directly by Photoshop, each image contains enough resolution to print a full magazine page, and 100 pictures will fit on a single CD.

✓For technical reasons, high-resolution digital cameras are not yet very portable or very fast. Their big advantage is in studio conditions, photographing objects that do not move.

✓PCD images always require some correction in Photoshop. They are generally soft and need sharpening and boosts in local contrast. Most images have proper color balance but the process is capable of incorporating color casts of epochal proportions. As the aim of the process is faithful reproduction of whatever is on the film, unsatisfactory originals will remain unsatisfactory and defects may even be magnified.

✓The LAB colorspace into which we open PCD images uses a non-linear, opponent-color model to define its channels. Though scientifically sound, it is counterintuitive and difficult to use. The L is a lightness channel, the A slides between red and green, and the B between yellow and blue.

✓Careful and conservative moves within LAB occasionally accomplish things that would be more difficult in CMYK. Sharpening or adding contrast to the L channel is the most common example. However, images with severe color casts can sometimes be corrected most efficiently by manipulating the A and/or the B. These channels are both highly volatile and definitely not recommended for most jobs.

30 percent intensity, narrow feathered brush, and traced the outline of the lower eyelids, darkening them.

• The human eye (ours, that is, not hers) is much less sensitive to reflected harsh light than the camera is. Accordingly, where the camera is picking up catchlights, realism suggests they should be minimized, though not eliminated. In this image there are such catchlights in the irises of the model's eyes, on the bridge of her nose and on the tip of her chin. There is also such an area on her left shoulder, but leaving it alone is probably correct, since we don't want anything to compete with the face.

The best way to fix these catchlights is to use the burn third of the dodge/burn/sponge tool, setting it to Highlights, about 30 percent intensity, wide feathered brush. However, before using it one must click open the Channels palette. As the burn tool affects all four colors equally, using it unmodified will darken the catchlights, but will do it with gray, not with whatever the dominant color is. The solution to this is to disable black and the unwanted color before proceeding. That way, only magenta and yellow will be built up when the brush is dragged through the catchlight area. Similarly, when fixing the irises, turn off yellow and black, making the correction in cyan and magenta only.

• With the catchlights now taken safely out of range, there was nothing of importance left in the image where either magenta or yellow was between 10 and 20 percent. Unwilling to waste this opportunity, I wrote a global curve flattening this area and giving the extra contrast to the face.

• Finally, I wanted to darken the hints of shadow in the face. This is along the same lines as lightening the highlight in the hair. I was trying to hoodwink the viewer into perceiving more range between light and dark areas in the face. When successful, this technique makes the image look more three-dimensional. To accomplish it, I set the burn tool to midtones, 30 percent intensity, wide feathered brush. Then I ran it over the dark areas beneath the left eye, on the sides of the nose, and the dimples.

This complicated illustration of how an inferior original can be brought up to professional standards is a fitting end both to this survey of new technologies and to our discussion of color correction generally. The two topics really go hand in hand. Digital cameras and Photo CDs are not going to go away. They have too many advantages in cost, speed, and flexibility. To the extent that they (for the moment) do not meet the quality standards one would hope for, well, there are ways of compensating, as the last two examples have shown. We may not particularly like the extra work, but it is worth it. This is where professional imaging is now headed, although how fast it is headed there is not clear. There is no reining it in. The fates of the crafters of buggy whips and the manufacturers of slide rules stand ready to remind us of the perils of failing to adjust.

Figure 11.1 *One of the most commonly requested Photoshop maneuvers is to move a person out of one picture and into another. It seems simple: we merely silhouette and feather as described in Chapter 6, select and copy the person into memory, and drop her into a new layer the revised picture. Unfortunately, it is usually just as simple for a discerning viewer to recognize the new image as a composite. What do you think of the example above? The background is Rocky Mountain National Park in Colorado. Was the woman in the foreground really there, or is it a Photoshop trick?*

CHAPTER 11

On the Marriage of Images

Photoshop makes it easy to pick up a piece of one picture and paste it into another. Making the union believable, though, is another story. Here, we'll discuss the four common mistakes that give away an image as a composite, the least-common-denominator approach that lets us avoid them, creating seamless merges with masks, and why divorce is so much less painful than marriage (at least in imaging).

 ll the moves we have made so far have been designed to enhance the overall appearance of a picture. We have improved upon the photographer's work in many ways, but we have not actually falsified the picture by adding something that is not really there, or cutting out details that are.

There is nothing inherently evil about doing so. We may need to add a person or a package to a preexisting layout, enhance an image by incorporating a detail that is more attractive than those currently in the picture, clone objects, or replace items that are so poor we have no hope of resurrecting them.

The straightforward way to merge is by selecting the new object from the source picture, copying it to memory, and then pasting it into the target picture. Upon doing this, the moved object "floats" on a layer above the image. We can move it around, resize it, rotate it, alter its perspective, etc., without worrying about what is happening beneath it, and we can retain the layer for later alterations. It is only when we are done fooling around and merge the new layer into the background that it permanently replaces the area beneath it.

Figure 11.2 *The sign in right foreground, nominally prohibiting the use of computers in Zion National Park, is a late addition to this image. You probably figured that out yourself. The question is, how did you tell?*

The first example of the power of this technique will involve another imaginary picture. Consider an image of a plate of spaghetti with tomato sauce, for use in food advertising. On top of the sauce are two or three green flecks of oregano. The advertiser is likely to think that this small amount of spice looks chintzy, and ask us to add half a dozen more flecks.

We therefore, using the lasso tool, select the best-looking existing piece of oregano, copy it to the clipboard, and paste it in six different strategic locations on the sauce. Of course, that is not *all* we do, because nobody would be fooled by six pieces of oregano that were so identical that they might have come from a cookie cutter. No, we have to introduce some randomness, so each time we paste a new piece in, we go to **Image: Effects** and make a few changes. We rotate each piece to a different angle, resize each one to be larger or smaller than the original, skew a few of them to get shape variations, and probably apply a modest curve to each one so that none will be exactly the same color.

Because oregano flakes are so small that one does not perceive much detail in them, we rate to get away with this simple deception. But marrying two or more images undetectably, creating a new reality, is not always this easy. Indeed, it is one of the most difficult techniques in all of the graphic arts. Some composites simply cannot be created to an acceptable quality level. Each combination of pictures presents a new challenge. We can, however, generalize about what we should consider before embarking on the arduous task of trying to trick the viewer.

It is a snap in theory to make a composite image, so success is not so much a matter of doing things right, as of avoiding doing them wrong. In Figure 11.2, I have supplied a merged image where almost everything that could be bad, is.

As you will no doubt have gathered, I am an aficionado of our western National Parks. Zion, in Utah, is an idyllic environment, conducive to leaving the troubles of the office behind. So I thought that perhaps the scenery would be enhanced by a sign prohibiting the use of computers.

To understand why so many "undetectable" composites look almost as amateurish as my example, specifics are needed. Mine is a bad merge, no doubt about it, but you can't avoid my mistakes until you figure out what they are.

The Four Deadly Sins

The problem with the face of the sign, strangely enough, is not that it is so bad, but that it is so good. It looks cartoonish because it is grossly out of character with the rest of the image, not because of any defect. Nowhere else in the image are there whites nearly as white, blacks as black, or any color remotely rivaling the red in its intensity. The images on the sign are crisp and sharp—as perfect as the resolution will allow. If anyone is going to believe that this sign is for real, we will have to make it considerably rattier, in addition to toning down the colors and reducing the ranges from highlight to shadow.

The opposite problem plagues the sign's post. There, image quality is just terrible, wholly inappropriate to the rest of the picture. There is no way to fix this. This should have scotched the whole concept before I began.

Next on the list of grievances is the lack of attention paid to the lighting issue. This is a very common problem with pictures taken outdoors.

In this picture we seem to have intense sunlight coming from high and to the left. We surmise this from the shadows of the trees, which are strong, but very small. The rock formations likewise are casting small, crisp shadows. Therefore, if our sign were real, it would have to be lighter on the side that is to our left, to simulate the impact of the sun that we know is hitting it. This is where to use the dodge/burn/sponge tool, which makes this sort of smooth lightening or darkening of random areas of images much easier than before. Since the sign is a neutral white, the dodge or burn tool would not pick up and exaggerate a color cast.

Next giveaway: the sign is preposterously outsized. To believe in this sign one would have to imagine it as tall as the trees in the background. The face of the sign is also too large relative to the post.

This is a problem in image merging only when there are items that are of a size the viewer knows or can guess. We know how big signs usually are; the same goes for trees. In cases like this, we have to take special care to bring the sign in at a reasonable size.

If the trees were missing and the background nothing more than a rock formation, it would be extremely hard for the viewer to get a sense of scale. We therefore would have much more leeway in sizing our sign.

Last, and most difficult, when we bring a new element into an existing picture, we are altering reality. In planning the alteration, we must also imagine the ways in which it logically would have to change the rest of the picture.

That's a mouthful, because the effect of a new object can be very subtle. Here, however, it happens to be straightforward. If there were really a sign there it would have to cast a shadow. In the hypothetical example, we reasoned similarly: if there *were* six extra flakes of oregano, they would *not* be all of the same size, color, and angle on the plate.

To summarize, I should never have attempted this composite in the first place. That aside, the image is a disaster for the following reasons:

•   **Quality Variation**. The general photographic quality of the pasted-in object does not match that of the background picture.

•   **Lighting Discrepancy**. The background indicates that light is coming from a certain direction, but there is no hint of this in the foreign object.

•   **Faulty Scale**. The new object is out of proportion, given the known size of objects in the background.

•   **Reality Check**. The artist failed to grasp certain logical consequences of the addition—consequences that the viewer expects, even if unconsciously, to see.

One or more of these four shortcomings is almost always the reason that a composite image fails.

The Sky Is What Limits

Now let's move on to an example that embodies one of the most common real-world reasons for our wanting to marry images. Take a look at Figure 11.3, and suppose that we are involved in travel advertising and would like to use that picture to promote the dramatic beauty of Bryce Canyon National Park. One thing we might find objectionable is the color of the sky—very dull and overcast. Another problem could be that we want to suggest the grandeur of the image by having a *lot* of sky over the arch, and, as can be ascertained from the image's failure to reach its top border, there is not much at present.

The only way to correct these things is to find a suitable sky from some other picture and drop it into this one. So, let's go back to the Figure 11.2, the Zion picture, and make up for what we did to it there by borrowing its beautiful sky for our present purposes.

From the silhouetting point of view, this is not much of a challenge. Where the mountains in the background will meet the new sky, the Bryce image is very soft. We won't have to worry, therefore, about any obvious seam showing, provided we feather adequately before we merge.

Before investing any time in merging pictures, the artist should always spend a few minutes thinking over what the problems are likely to be. If you have not done this very much in the past, check your plan against the four sins named on the preceding page before commencing.

So, let's examine this merger proposal, starting with comparing the photographic quality of the two images.

The Zion picture seems to me to be the better focused of the two, but this would only matter if we were bringing in some of the rock formation, which has more detail than the sky.

The Bryce picture is a little grainy. It's hard to get rid of that, so we should try to imitate the effect in the Zion sky. Since the predominant colors in any sky are cyan and magenta, we can add a small amount of noise to these plates (but not to the unwanted color, yellow, or to black, which would be very obvious) to get the grainier feeling that we want.

Color balance and range appear to match in both pictures, so we can now say that quality overall is suitable for a merge.

We also have to consider the lighting of the new sky. That's easy, too: skies can never have a lighting problem, since they, in effect, carry their own light source.

Next on the list is scale. Since there is no object in the new sky that the viewer can assign a size to, there is no reason to worry. We can use whatever piece of the Zion sky we like at any convenient size.

The final test is the reality check. We must ask ourselves, if the new piece were really there, would any part of it, by logical extension, change any elements of the existing picture? One of the reasons this is a very deep question is that we have to consider not only what is actually in the new picture, but also things *we cannot see but must be there anyway.*

The Zion sky is a deep and iridescent azure. There is not a cloud to be found. The hue is pure and not tending toward grayness at all. These facts tell us exactly what the rest of the Zion picture does, namely, that the sun is shining brightly.

When we import this sky into the Bryce picture, we create the irrefutable inference that there is brilliant sunshine. The rest of the image does not support this. Compare the intensity of the light hitting the rocks, and the shadows that are cast, in the two base pictures.

Bringing the Zion sky into the Bryce picture cannot be made to work. The two pieces are logically inconsistent with one another and cannot be reconciled without an entirely unreasonable amount of effort. (If you have never tried to pick up clouds from one sky and drop them into another, don't suggest that as an option.)

Figure 11.3 *This photo's sky is dull and overcast, and, furthermore, there isn't enough of it. The top of the image does not fill the desired space.*

No, what we need is a blue sky that contains a few clouds. I happen to have one available, in a picture from Arches National Park. Unfortunately, the sun was not behind one of the clouds when the shot was taken. I know this for the same reasons I knew it in the Zion picture. The sky is a dark blue, suggesting that the harsh lighting caused the photographer to underexpose the film in the interest of capturing all detail. The blueness of the sky is not contaminated to any extent by yellow and/or black.

These things, however, can be fixed. After correcting for graininess as discussed previously, I made the sky a little grayer by introducing the unwanted color, yellow. Since there was almost no yellow in the sky to begin with, applying a curve to it would not have been effective. I therefore, using **Image: Calculations>Blend**, created a new yellow plate that was a combination of 90 percent of the existing yellow plus 10 percent of the existing cyan. This added about six percentage points to the yellow dot in the sky. Normally, this would risk a color change elsewhere, but since I intended to discard the rest of this image, I did not particularly care. Then, by a curve, I also reduced the overall amount of magenta and cyan in the sky. These moves subdued the sunlight.

Using Masks to Merge

Finally, the merge. Although this could be done using the same cut-and-paste technique described earlier, for more complex merges it is better to use a mask— a Quick Mask in this case. The reason is not so much quality as it is ease of correction. If we merge and are slightly dissatisfied with the result, we retain all the partial elements that made up the merge and can edit them quickly and recomposite. If we instead try cut-and-paste and it fails, we tend to have to start again from scratch.

To create this merge using masks, the size and resolution of both images have to be the same. Neither one is correct at the moment. We need additional space at the top of the Bryce image to accommodate

the additional sky we are intending to generate.

We therefore add an additional inch to the top of the Bryce picture by choosing **Image: Canvas Size** and increasing the height by one inch, specifying that the current image is to be centered at the bottom of the new canvas. Thus, the new blank area will be at top.

Now, we do a quick Command–A, Command–C, Command–N. This is shorthand for select the entire image, including white space; copy it to the clipboard; open a new, blank image.

By Photoshop default, the new image will be the same size and resolution as whatever is in memory. By dropping the new sky into the blank file first, we avoid the tiresome procedure of equalizing the resolutions of the two originals.

We therefore open the Arches sky file, select whatever part of it we need for the merge, and copy it into the top of the new, blank image. It does not matter whether the bottom of the blank image stays blank, since it will not be used in the merge. Using **Image: Effects>Scale,** we resize and/or reposition the new sky so that it completely fills the desired width.

So that we will have a way to get back to it later if we want to make a correction, we save the sky image, leaving it open on the screen. Now, returning to the Bryce Canyon picture, we use the lasso tool to select the entire overcast sky, including the white space above it, and we apply a feather of 2 pixels. For safety's sake, we also save the selection path so that it can be edited if we are not satisfied with our first effort.

By clicking on the Quick Mask icon in the toolbox, we create a temporary channel through which the new image will show when the two pictures are merged. The actual marriage takes place through **Image: Calculations>Composite**, which creates Figure 11.4.

The beauty of doing it this way is that we can inspect the new image carefully, and if there are any areas where the merge is not smooth, or if we want to have the sky come in at a different size or angle, we can redo it easily by modifying our base files. In particular, the mask can be edited, just as if it were an image itself, using the standard airbrush, eraser, smudge, and pencil tools, not to mention curves. The new sky will come in at full strength in those areas of the mask that are solid black. In places, such as the feathered edge, where the mask is a shade of gray, the merged image will have some characteristics of each of the parent pictures.

Before leaving the masking function, a major use in color correction of absurdly bad images should be pointed out.

A common problem in dealing with skintones is that, due to a poor photograph or a poor scan, the skin is excessively pink. In Chapter 9, we learned to correct this deficiency by accentuating the unwanted color, cyan. This is impossible, however, if the original is so bad that there is no cyan at all in the skin.

Since flesh should have about a quarter as much cyan as magenta or yellow, the way to fix this is to create a 25 percent mask for the flesh, being careful not to include eyes, teeth, etc. Now, **Image: Calculations>Composite**, using the cyan plate as target image, checking the invert option in the mask and the magenta (or yellow) plate as Source 1.

Figure 11.4 *A more appealing version of Figure 11.3.*

The Least Common Denominator

In Figure 11.4, we purposely degraded one part of an image so as to let it merge more naturally into another. We muted the tonality of the sky and deliberately made it grainier.

This theme recurs almost every time two elements are merged, and sometimes the sabotage we inflict is quite severe. The two images must match in quality if we expect the viewer to believe they are part of the same scene. It is much harder to make a bad image better than a good image worse. The problem is magnified when we are supposed to perceive that one is well in front of the other.

Before seeing what this means in a typical setting, note that some of the silhouetting problems and techniques discussed in Chapter 6 come into play here. The owl photo (Figure 11.5) is more troublesome to isolate from its background than the skies we have been considering so far.

When the background is white, about all that is needed for a good silhouette is a grasp of the **Select: Feather** function. Even though one might argue that this image is, ahem, a pre-feathered one.

Feathering tries to make a believable transition by averaging some of the pixel values where the foreground object hits the white background. Trial and error can be the best approach to learning this tool. If the transition is too harsh and the foreground appears jagged, there is not enough feathering; if there seems to be a halo around the object, there is too much.

When the background color contrasts sharply with the foreground object, things get tougher. This is because of the appearance of a transition color. If the background is white, a transition color that is halfway between white and the brown of the owl's feathers will be unobtrusive.

Using exactly the same amount of feathering will not work, however, if the background is brick red, as in the right half of Figure 11.5. A transition color that is halfway between brick red and brown will not have much in common with either the owl or the background. Accordingly, that color will be visible as an annoying halo

around the owl. Photoshop provides a quick fix for this in the **Select: Defringe** command, which looks for such halos and eliminates them by forcing more of the interior color outward. In my experience, this method does not always work well. One really has to examine every area where the images adjoin, and retouch out the most obvious transitions.

At least, though, the backgrounds we have worked with so far have obviously been artificial. The viewer, understanding this, will cut us a little slack. Nobody would suggest, for example, that we should manufacture a shadow of the owl on the red background.

Now, let's go for the hard stuff: not just brick red, but real bricks.

A Believable Background

Brick walls are much more cooperative than wildlife about being photographed. It is therefore no surprise to learn that the photograph of the brick wall is sharper, crisper, cleaner, better detailed, and in every other respect superior to that of the bird. That will not do. If the owl is going to be in the foreground, it must be not just of equal quality, but substantially better than the background wall.

If there is doubt as to whether there is a quality difference, a good way of checking is to blow the two up on the monitor, which will emphasize it if it is there. Here, the harshness of the detail in the brick should convince us that the bird is the softer of the two images.

In Figure 11.6, the image on the left shows what happens if we blithely ignore this disparity and marry the images in the prevailing slapdash fashion. Maybe the colors are nice and bright, maybe it's an

Figure 11.5 *When the background is pure white (left) silhouetting is relatively easy. But when there's a contrasting color in the background (right) the merge becomes much tougher.*

interesting artistic effect, but it won't convince anyone of anything—except that it's possible to cut an owl out of one picture and paste it into another.

There is also an issue of scale. We all know how big bricks are. I am not certain of how big the owl really is, but I *am* sure that if he is seven bricks tall, I do not care to meet him.

Finally, if you look back to the first time we encountered this particular owl (Figure 11.5), you will notice how out of focus the background grass seems. This is more or less the effect we will have to achieve with the brick wall.

When our eyes focus on a close object, all aspects of the background suffer, not just sharpness. As we concentrate on the browns and yellows of the feathers, we desensitize our eyes to the reds in the distance. The *range* of colors in the background does not seem as great.

In other words, just unsharpening the bricks will not be enough. We also have to reduce both the contrast and the intensity

of the redness of the bricks. There are many ways to do these things. Here is the method I used.

I first isolated the black plate and hit it with **Filter: Blur>Blur More.** As the red gets toned down, there will be relatively more black in the bricks. And because black is the most powerful ink and the black plate is mostly for added depth and sharpness, any time we emphasize black we are likely to add detail. Adding detail is the last thing we want to do here. Thus the blur, which counters the black plate's strength.

Next, I made the image flatter. On the magenta and yellow plates, I applied a curve 0=5, 100=80. This darkened the highlight, but more importantly, it reduced the amount of color in the bricks. Both the magenta and yellow values had been around 60 percent before the move. They came down to the 40–45 percent range. Cyan I curved 0=5, 100=90, not needing the additional reduction in the heavier areas. The black plate remained unchanged.

Figure 11.6 *The least-common-denominator principle in action: on the left, the composite image is unconvincing because the brick wall is in sharper focus than the owl, which makes no visual sense.*

Now that color balance was more reasonable, I used Blur More twice on the entire picture. Further blurring would have been inadvisable because then the bricks would have become too smooth. To preserve some roughness, I went into the magenta plate only and added noise, ran unsharp masking, and then ran blur more. I applied this three-step process two more times on the magenta, twice on the yellow, and once on the cyan. This type of horsing around is less noticeable in the colors that dominate the picture.

With the background image now as out of focus as I cared to get, all that remained was to consider the lighting. In the owl picture, there is a light shadow on the left leg. This suggests a mild light source coming in from the left. Therefore, using the dodge tool, midtones option, large feathered brush, I slightly lightened the left side of the wall. Also, after the merge I added a hint of a shadow (by selecting a heavily feathered area, choosing 70C70M70Y100K as the background color, and using **Edit: Fill** with 25 percent opacity) on the wall to the right of the bird. The result is Figure 11.6.

It is no accident that we have been dealing with nonhuman objects so far. Adding a person is much tougher than an owl or a sky. Artists can run into figurative brick walls more daunting than the literal one we just reworked.

Please go back to the opening of this chapter and examine Figure 11.1. By now, you should be able to ascertain whether the picture is real or a merged image. The woman is my sister-in-law, Joanne. Do you think the general quality of her image matches that of the background? Is there a discrepancy in lighting? Is she weirdly out of scale with the background? Is there anything in the background that must logically be happening, but isn't?

Of course, it *is* a composite, but anyone who doesn't think that the quality of Joanne's image matches the background has some explaining to do. They match perfectly. They ought to. They are both from the same original.

The shrewd observer, however, will wonder how sunlight can be hitting the background from the right and Joanne's face from the left and will correctly deduce that I took the image of Joanne out of the picture, flopped it, and put it back in. The position of her jacket pocket, which normally is on the left side, should also be a giveaway.

Pre-Merge Retouching

Most of us are acutely sensitive to variations in the reproduction of skin tones and are therefore unwilling to accept composites that involve people. There are just too many problems: if we can match the skin tone and texture, we cannot match focus, or the overall feeling of depth.

Before we discuss these people problems, let us dispense with one item that terrorizes beginning artists: What do you do with someone like Joanne, who has a shag haircut? The shape of her hair appears to be too complicated to isolate.

With big hair the rage today, this situation comes up a lot. Any attempt to silhouette by conventional methods will likely fail. Even if all the complexities of

the hair are captured in some revoltingly deep selection path, the feathering and merging process will destroy the texture. And, if the silhouette is to be employed as a clipping path for use in another application, that many points in the path could very well mean that the job won't print (at least, not in the PostScript world).

We'll deal with the hair issue in Figure 11.7, where Joanne has moved from Rocky Mountain National Park into Zion. The background is stolen from Figure 11.2. Naturally, it had to be deintensified for this merge, as in the owl-and-bricks composite. Otherwise, we would have had a background that was sharper than the person in the foreground.

That is the same general concept as in the owl-and-brick-wall marriage we previously worked on. The complication here is the hair. It is moving from a light, neutral background in Rocky Mountain to a bright blue one in Zion. If we proceed to silhouette and merge in the usual fashion, we will get a transition-color halo, and it will be worst around her hair (although the jacket, which moves from a dark to a light background, will have it too).

The best way to prevent this is to correct the background before the merge takes place. In other words, we should go into the *original* picture and paint in some background blue in the places her hair is straggly. This may seem annoying, but it is a good deal preferable to having to go in and retouch the hair in an image like the one shown to the right of Figure 11.7. It is also marginally easier than creating a special mask and then modifying its edges to accommodate various strands of hair, as was shown in Figure 10.22. There, we had no choice but to use masking, as the area around the hair was too sharply focused for us to get away with adding any false colors. Here, it's a very soft blue sky, and nobody will ever suspect that we cheated on the silhouette.

Adding by Subtracting

Unlike real life, in digital imagery divorces are usually easier to obtain than marriages. When removing details, we can ignore some problems that might afflict an image merge.

For example, in Figure 11.7, there is a large tree sticking into the sky on the right side of the picture. Suppose we decide we don't want it.

We can take care of that in short order by replacing the tree with cloned areas of the sky. We are fortunate that the sky has almost no detail, so it won't be obvious that we have duplicated parts of it. If the tree were hiding some of the rock formation it would be somewhat tougher.

Compare this exercise to *adding* a hypothetical tree from a different picture, and you will see why it is usually easier to delete. If we are adding a tree, we have to check that it more or less matches the background. We may be forced to color-correct or otherwise mess with it first, to satisfy the least-common-denominator approach. If we are subtracting the tree, we don't have to do any of these things.

And a tree that we are adding must not be the size of a giant redwood. It cannot show up with light shining on one side when the rest of the picture indicates that the light comes from the other. But if we are subtracting the tree, we need not worry about either factor.

Whether adding or deleting, however, we have to ask, what if? In this picture the ramifications of removing the tree are so obvious that we hardly notice we thought about it at all; but the fact is that we did, and we concluded that if the tree were

Figure 11.7 *Here, a complex subject, Joanne's hair, gets dropped onto a background much darker than the original. In these cases, we should retouch the image to add the new background color, before we merge. The alternative is a difficult correction (below).*

truly not there, *we would see the sky*, not blank space, another tree, Joanne's ears, or any other such irrelevant item.

Nor should we confine our thinking to what is behind the object we are deleting. Just as when we add an object, there may be a logical impact on some other part of the picture, some other area may need to change as well when we subtract. Removing this tree will not have any such effect, but what if the picture showed a lightning bolt hitting the tree we were about to delete? The more complex the deletion, the more likely it is that there will be one of these inferential problems, and some of them are exquisitely easy to overlook.

For example, suppose we are asked to remove Joanne's glasses. This is deceptively difficult.

Before undertaking any deletion involving skin tones, look it over carefully for hidden traps. Some of them have been given numbers in Figure 11.8.

Area 4 is easy. There, the frames of the glasses can be taken out in no time flat by cloning some of the adjoining light skin. The rest of the frames can be removed in much the same manner, except for area 5, where the glasses are covering up so much of her face that certain gyrations will be necessary to restore it.

There is no obvious glare or distortion from the glass inside the frames, so if we successfully get rid of the frames, we are done, right?

Wrong.

Even though we can't see the actual glass in the original, logic tells us that it must have an impact. It's hard to believe that area 3, for instance, would be as dark

Figure 11.8 *Before undertaking a complicated revision like removing a person's glasses, it pays to identify the problem areas and have a plan for each (right). The case of the missing eyebrows necessitated a quick trip to the spare images folder. Even though this person's hair, skin tone, and gender don't match Joanne's, any port will do in a storm.*

as it is, were the glasses not blocking some of the sunlight.

Moreover, a person wearing glasses will be more sensitive to sunlight. If she were not wearing glasses, Joanne would not be squinting. In area 1, we would have to open her eyes wider.

But the biggest challenge of all is in area 2. The problem is, most human beings have eyebrows. Where are they?

That is a most disagreeable complication. Drawing in eyebrows ourselves is likely to make Joanne look like Groucho Marx, and there is nothing in the rest of the picture that we can pick up and clone. There is no choice: we need eyebrows from somewhere else. So, the job that we thought was simply subtraction actually involves some tricky addition as well.

This is a good argument for careful consideration before saying you can alter reality in a given image. You may not be so lucky as to have a set of spare eyebrows of approximately the right resolution available. I happened to have a pair, but

Quick & Dirty

MERGING IMAGES AND ELIMINATING DETAILS

✓ Before wasting any time on complicated work, careful planning is needed. Many planned image merges are technically impossible. Also, decide on a general approach. Should layers be saved? Will masks be necessary?

✓ Once two suitable candidates for merge are identified, they must be made to match size and resolution. Usually, this is done by reducing the resolution of the larger image, when the two do not match.

✓ Examine the two images closely at high magnification to be sure that they roughly match in terms of color balance and range, grain, and sharpness. If the two do not match, it may be necessary to sabotage the better picture somewhat. This is called the least-common-denominator approach.

✓ Check the lighting of both images. Does the light appear to be coming from the same direction? If the intensity of bright areas and shadows differ, use the dodge/burn/sponge tool to correct them.

✓ Are there any objects in each picture that we know or can guess the sizes of? If so, be sure that the two images are scaled correctly. It will not do to have a person who appears to the viewer to be nine feet tall.

✓ Most important, remember that you are creating a new reality. Close your eyes, and try to imagine: if these objects were really in the same image, would there be some *other* effect, like a shadow, that would have to be created? Include in your imagination items that are not in either picture, but must exist by inference.

✓ When the task is to take something out of an image rather than adding to it, most of these problems don't exist. It is usually just a matter of recreating some background, but one must still consider what the impact of the subtraction would be in real life. Frequently enough, the deletion will have impact elsewhere in the image.

✓ Careful preparation and feathering of the image that is to be moved can save difficult correction later. There are several ways to execute the actual merge. Silhouetting, cutting and pasting is one option, but in difficult merges it is usually better to composite the image using a mask, because it is easier to make changes in technique this way, should the first effort not be satisfactory.

they belong to a man — a man whose hair is much darker and whose skin coloring is lighter than Joanne's.

Getting a believable, constant skin tone and texture is a challenge in a picture like this. In area 4, the flesh is almost the same color inside and outside the frames, so direct cloning will work. In virtually all other areas, however, the skin is slightly darker inside the frames than outside. That means extra work, because any sudden transition will be glaringly obvious. Each of the four plates has to be handled individually and delicately. Furthermore, the impact of light coming in from the left must be attended to with the dodge/burn/sponge tool.

The eyebrow merge is another headache. Before doing it, the eyebrows have to be narrowed, as men's eyebrows are normally thicker than women's. The eyebrows must be color-corrected drastically to more or less match Joanne's hair, and the man's skin color and texture has to be altered to match in the same way.

Next, we have to do something about the color of the skin beneath her eyes, which is much too dark. That calls for first a light clone (perhaps at 35 percent opacity), then the dodge tool used on each individual plate.

Finally, we must open her eyes wider. I did this by isolating the lower eyelids, striking the down cursor twice to move them two pixels down in the image, and then building on and adding more snap to the existing eyes to fill the extra space. Even so, in Figure 11.9 it looks like she is

Figure 11.9 *In most cases removing a section of image is easier than adding one, but here the exception is when a difficult background must be created behind the object that was removed.*

suffering from allergies. But the point is, if you had not seen her with glasses, you would not guess the truth.

Let It Be Your Secret

It is perhaps unfair to the reader to discuss this most complex of topics in only one chapter, when an entire book would not suffice to cover every possibility. Nevertheless, the general techniques we have discussed are broadly applicable to most kinds of image marriages.

"That's incredible!" is the sort of compliment we usually like to hear, but in this kind of work, we don't want it. We would much rather imagine some knowledgeable viewer jumping up and shouting, "That's *credible!*"

If you plan and execute marriages carefully, people will not say that your work is incredible unless and until you reveal that the image is actually a composite. But perhaps you would rather keep that a secret.

Figure 12.1 *Using black and white as a foil for color. This cheetah is a majestic beast no matter what the surroundings, but she seems to jump out from the monochrome background.*

Keeping the Color In Black and White

Color images *can* be converted into snappy, effective black and white files. Provided, that is, that we make the necessary corrections in CMYK *before* we hit the convert key.

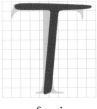

he ease with which we can produce and manipulate color images on the desktop has made some of us view the whole idea of black and white as antique, primitive, foreign, even contemptible.

Though it may be all of these things, we cannot ignore it, because black and white printing is not going away. Adding color printing units to web presses is not a cheap proposition, and we can expect large daily newspapers and many trade magazines to remain monochrome for decades to come.

This unpleasant reality causes us color publishers a considerable technical problem. We frequently have to produce materials that will print in process color in one publication and black and white in another. Often the black and white version is more important than the color one.

As in Figure 12.1, even when color is readily available, there are frequently sensible artistic reasons to use black and white as a foil. There are significant examples of this throughout the history of our culture. While it is incongruous to mention Steven Spielberg in the same sentence with Michelangelo, the greatest masterpiece of each involved the intentional use of monochrome when color was not only readily available but also cheaper.

Good conversion to B/W is also a prerequisite for effective duotones, which are currently very popular and which will receive a full airing in our next chapter.

Digital conversion of color photographs to black and white is a very recent phenomenon and those who have tried it have generally gotten burned. Most trade shops, being experienced at producing murky black and whites out of perfectly fine color, prefer to have the conversion

Figure 12.2 Certain types of contrast convert well to black and white, but other varieties completely dry up.

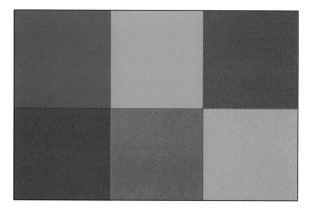

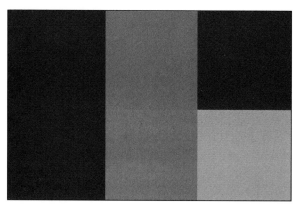

done by photographers. This is a bad attitude. The job is not easy, but if we give the matter proper attention we can do a much better job with desktop technology.

The Fatal Flatness in B/W

Color pictures almost invariably appear flat when they go to B/W. A lot of the contrast we saw in the color original is gone and we can no longer distinguish some of the subtler details. Recognizing this, a photographer making a B/W print from a color negative will almost always use some kind of high-contrast filter. We have some even niftier desktop tools to get rid of the flatness—provided we understand what is causing it.

In discussing these techniques, we will assume a CMYK picture from which we need to generate a B/W version. When we ask Photoshop to make the conversion, it uses a weighted-average method to compute what the new image should look like. In doing this, it refers not to CMYK, but to a hypothetical RGB rendition of the image. Each new B/W pixel, in the Photoshop algorithm, gets 59 percent of the value of the green component of the RGB, 30 percent of the red, and 11 percent of the blue. As usual, there are some calibrationist scientists out there who claim that this magic formula will always give the most "accurate," and hence best, rendition of a quality 4/c photograph.

Figure 12.2 is a little test of this assertion. Let's see what happens when we convert this "picture" to B/W using this infallible formula.

In a proper conversion, the B/W image should be crisp and legible. The viewer should be able to form a mental picture of what the color image must look like. If

Figure 12.3 Conversion problems using Photoshop's defaults exist not just in artificial images like Figure 12.2.

these are our objectives we have obviously failed miserably. What went wrong?

In a B/W world, there is only one kind of contrast, which can be called lightness, luminosity, or dark vs. light. If the original color image has this kind of contrast, we are in good shape. This is what is happening in the right-hand third of our checkerboard. The B/W conversion of this third is entirely reasonable.

When we convert, however, we lose completely two other kinds of contrast. In the left third of our checkerboard there is a huge contrast in colors. In the second third the contrast is there not because of color difference but because of purity difference. We easily distinguish the muddy green at the bottom from the clean one at the top. As color and purity variation are

irrelevant in B/W, however, our attempt to convert these parts of the picture was not exactly crowned with success.

This unsatisfactory effort should convince us of a somewhat subtle point. Even if we can visualize in our mind's eye what the B/W version should look like, we cannot possibly get there by correcting the bottom image. We have to do something, but whatever it is, it has to be done to the color version, before we make the switch to B/W. This is a most important concept. A good 4/c image can produce an unacceptable B/W one. Sometimes it takes an unacceptable 4/c image to produce a good B/W one.

Of course, this artificial "picture" was designed to be atrocious when converted, but such pictures do exist in real life. If

Figure 12.4. *A default conversion of this image to B/W will have difficulty holding contrast in the bear's fur and in the red background.*

you doubt it, have a look at Figure 12.3. There is plenty of snap in the color original, yet the B/W version is garbage from the word go.

Planning the B/W Conversion

Because the samples so far are extreme in the problems they illustrate, they are also extreme in terms of the ease with which one can fix them up. By the end of this chapter, you should know how you would handle them. Let's go on to more interesting work. Our assignment will be to take four color pictures of various subjects, and create the best possible B/W representations of them. Per our normal policy, no selections of local areas are permitted. We will limit ourselves to moves that affect the image as a whole. The general approach will be similar in each case.

The first step is a very obvious one. Unfortunately it is also very hard. We have to visualize what is going to go wrong when our color perception is taken away. It takes a close look at the *color* to realize what we will be missing in the B/W.

We must identify what parts of the picture are likely to convert well, and which not. In Figure 12.4, our first challenge, we will have no problem with the bear's nose standing out from his fur. That is strictly lightness vs. darkness and it will look just fine in B/W.

On the other hand, the bear's coat will suffer for sure. Most of what we take for contrast in the color version is a subtle variation in the red and yellow shading in his fur. Ditto for the background rocks: we see contrast in the purity of the reds there, and a lot of it will vanish in B/W.

Our second step, therefore, will be to formulate some method of exaggerating the contrast in the areas we expect to have trouble with. In effect, we will intentionally louse up our color picture.

Our principal tool will be, as always, curves. There is more flexibility than usual, though, in that we no longer have to worry about keeping grays neutral. When they get to B/W, they *will* be neutral, believe me. Also, we need not be too careful about highlight and shadow values. Once in B/W we will be able to correct these easily with a supplementary curve. We can also make liberal use of plate blending to emphasize certain details, since what happens to the color balance makes no difference. Fixing up this bear will not require any such gyrations.

The third step will be the actual conversion, and any minor tonal range correction that's needed once we are in B/W.

Those of us in need of ego gratification usually add a fourth step, which is to go back to the original, uncorrected color picture, convert it to B/W exactly as is, compare the result with the corrected B/W version we just made, and pat ourselves on the back for the improvement.

Back to the bear.

Fuzzy Wuzzy Needs Some Hair

To add contrast to the bear, we have to steepen the curve that affects his range of colors. We would like to do that even if the image were staying in color, except that we can go much further now. If this were a standard correction, we couldn't do much more. Spots of color are already starting to appear in inappropriate places in the bear's fur, and further contrast will make them worse. If we are intending to go to B/W, however, we care not a fig for this.

The whitest part of the bear is his forehead. The darkest parts of the fur are in the areas where we see traces of red, yellow or blue shading. What we need to do is to increase the difference between the lightest and the darkest, thus providing a bigger range of colors, and hence more detail and contrast.

The bear's forehead is a perfect highlight of 5C2M2Y. That shouldn't go much lighter, so we'll have to make the dark spots darker.

Measuring the red spots above his left rear leg, the yellow spots in his midsection, and the bluish area near his neck, we observe that the predominant color—whether it is magenta, cyan, or yellow—is in the neighborhood of 25 or 30 percent. We need to push those values up.

In this set, the most important curves (Figure 12.6) affect the black and the magenta. Changing the black, the most powerful tool we have in color retouching generally, is even more prominent in B/W conversions. Beefing up the black accentuates detailing, such as the darker areas of the rocky background in this picture. Such a tactic should be semi-automatic when converting from CMYK to B/W. The exact move depends on the image.

Correct handling of the magenta plate is the key to this particular image. I am so anxious to steepen the range that is originally 10 percent to 60 percent, that I am willing to obliterate all magenta less than 5 percent, and have no difference at all between 90 percent and 100 percent. In this way, I have drawn an extremely vertical curve and have gained detail in important areas at the expense of areas I care nothing about.

Figure 12.5 At top, the polar bear image of Figure 12.4 converted directly to black and white using Photoshop defaults. Bottom, when the CMYK image was adjusted first to exaggerate the contrast areas that were going to be hurt in the conversion.

Manipulating the cyan and yellow in the bear picture is largely a reaction to the moves made in the magenta and black. I have, as described previously, intentionally blown out the magenta highlight; there will now be areas that have no magenta at all. That would not be acceptable if the picture were to print in color, but as our goal is B/W, it is irrelevant.

However, we must be sure that we don't allow anything like it to happen in the other colors, or we may find ourselves with areas of the final B/W that have no dot. To guard against this, I add slightly to the highlight values in cyan and yellow.

Much the same thing happens in the background. The moves in magenta and black will increase the contrast, which is what we want, but they will also darken the background overall, which is undesirable. I compensate by reducing yellow and cyan in the heavier ranges.

Both the cyan and yellow curves, then, go like this. Highlights: a little more, to make up for the lack of magenta in these areas. Quartertones: much more, to add contrast to the bear's fur. Everything else: much less, to compensate for all the extra magenta and black going in these areas.

Applying these curves to the color picture creates a horrifying result. The background turns cranberry, and the bear becomes every color of the rainbow, making us wonder whether he is a polar bear or a grizzly who has just trashed a paint store. I won't even show how bad it looks, because what matters is how it looks after we change it to grayscale.

And there, strange to say, it works.

So, compare the two B/W images of Figure 12.5, one converted without correction, one with the curves of Figure 12.6

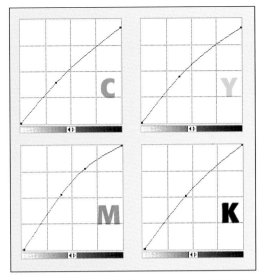

Figure 12.6 *The correction curves applied to the polar bear image prior to converting it to B/W.*

applied to the color first. One is much more alive than the other. Every detail of the picture is snappier. The uncorrected version might strike us at first as a reasonable rendition of the 4/c—but to those who know, it is, er, bearly acceptable.

When "Good Enough" Isn't

Converting the bear picture had a very obvious problem, the bear's fur. We are not always so lucky. To see what happens to a picture that will actually convert well without intervention, we'll have a go at a color image familiar to all professionals. Figure 12.7 is part of Kodak's Q–60 calibration kit for scanner operators. It is full of the light-dark contrast that converts to B/W so nicely. There is no area where contrast apparently depends on purity or on radically different colors of the same lightness.

Consequently, we expect a reasonable B/W if we simply convert it as is. But can we do better?

Offhand, there are only two minor reservations about a straight conversion. First, as usual, tweaking the black will probably help, since it will enhance the details of the building and the foliage. Second, the sky in the 4/c version is a very deep blue, which will clearly turn into a dark gray. Although this is not a contrast issue, we may want to write a curve that reduces 100 percent cyan to 80 percent or so, to create a more believable sky. This, however, will risk flattening the water and the grass.

When we are not sure of how to attack a picture, it pays to get more information before commencing hostilities. The best way to do this is to examine each color plate individually.

As we might expect, each plate shown in Figure 12.8 has different strengths and

Figure 12.7 *This Kodak quality-control image is a good test for color scanning fidelity, but what are the considerations if it needs to go to B/W?*

weaknesses. The cyan has great contrast in most areas but is poor in the building. The yellow has a good building but no sky. The black shows detail, so our initial plan to beef it up will probably work.

The magenta in this picture is a big disappointment. The plate is very flat overall. This is only natural, since all of the colors in this picture have a significant magenta component. We can't make too many changes to it without risking red water and purple sky. But in black and white, we don't care what color the water is. This plate is a tempting target for correction.

Figure 12.8
Checking the individual plates of the color image before conversion to B/W gives us clues. Here, the magenta plate clearly lacks contrast. Also, we can see which has the best building, the best lake, the best sky and so on.

Figure 12.9 *At top, the original converted with default values. Center, a straightforward color correction. Bottom, an alternate correction intended to lighten the sky and emphasize the details of the building.*

Here, then, is my conservative plan for dealing with this conversion.

• I will hit the black plate with exactly the same curve used in the bear example.

• In magenta, I will impose a sharply vertical curve that is really a straight line, setting the zero point at what was originally 10 percent and 100 percent to what was 90 percent.

• Using **Image: Calculations>Blend**, I will create a new cyan plate that consists of 80 percent of the old cyan and 20 percent of the yellow. My purpose is to lighten the sky. The yellow is perfect for this because it has no sky at all and yet is strong in all other details.

The results of these moves are shown in Figure 12.9, below an uncorrected conversion. I show an alternate corrected version for anyone who seriously objects to the sky being darker than the building. This was done by further diluting the cyan plate with more yellow and some black.

Although the uncorrected version must be considered acceptable, either corrected version is significantly better, even at this small size. That is food for thought, because this example is the most unfavorable one I could find for the treatment I am suggesting. When an image has elements in all color ranges, as this Kodak image and the one shown in Figure 10.7 do, it's tough to find areas that we are willing to sacrifice.

To get back to a more drastic improvement at a respectable size, have a look at the colonial tavern in Figure 12.10.

Figure 12.10 *Several juxtapositions of colors in this image will lose contrast when converted to B/W.*

What to Lighten, What to Darken

There is plenty of color in this image, but it is all relatively light, and full of the kind of contrast that is great in 4/c and terrible in B/W. The dark windows will certainly convert well, and the bricks will be moderately successful, though some of the color-related contrast in the bricks will vanish.

In order of importance, the problems:
•   The sign over the door is likely to vanish into the background bricks.
•   In the color image there is great contrast between the light blue shutters, the red bricks, and the white areas at top and bottom of the windows, but this will go away in B/W.
•   Maintaining some semblance of life in the doors.
•   Helping out the bricks.

The shutters vs. bricks problem raises the interesting issue of which should wind up darker. If we want differentiation in B/W, we will have to make a choice.

Inspection of the individual plates (Figure 12.11) can give us the clues we need. The bricks are in all plates, but the sign is heaviest by far in the yellow, and the shutters are concentrated in the cyan.

In image enhancement, there is a time for delicate instruments and a time for sledgehammers and crowbars. This is one of those latter instances.

The fastest way by far to make an object darker is to get some black ink into it. Therefore, my first step was to blend 20 percent of cyan into the black. My second was to blend 20 percent of the yellow into the new black. The black was now much

Figure 12.11. *The four plates of the original image, used to plan the transition to B/W. Here, we should be looking for places to add weight to the sign and to the shutters.*

darker overall, but, more importantly, it had a pronounced sign and blue shutters. To kill the surplus black generally, I wrote a curve that dropped out all of it under 10 percent. But I increased quartertone black drastically, to get even more punch into the sign and shutters.

This left less black than before in the bricks, so to compensate, I increased magenta above midtone, but I killed the magenta highlight, to make the light areas even whiter and thus give more contrast to the bricks.

I left the yellow alone, but in the cyan, I also dropped out the highlight. Although this left a highlight of yellow only, I reasoned that if this was inadequate for the final B/W, it could be fixed easily enough after conversion, by a curve that set the lightest possible black to 2 percent. I also increased the cyan midtone; in the doors, cyan is the unwanted color, so any change in it will have a big impact. I wanted to stress the grain of the wood. This move would not have been possible in 4/c, since the grain would have become green.

Looking at the final results in Figure 12.12, you must certainly agree that there would be no hope of ever correcting the top image to equal the one at the bottom. There is as much quality difference as in some of the head-to-head competitions between desktop and high-end scanners shown in Chapter 3.

Figure 12.12 *Raw, above, and corrected versions.*

If you want your B/Ws to look their best, you therefore, by logic, must also agree that initial corrections must be done in color. Taking it further still, you must also agree that the quality of Photoshop's CMYK-to-grayscale conversion is really a secondary issue.

Recall that all we are doing when we go into grayscale is forcing our image into a smaller colorspace of drastically different shape. It is precisely analogous to an RGB (or LAB) to CMYK conversion, where the data is forced into a colorspace that effectively has no blue.

If you concur that the corrected B/Ws in this chapter are overwhelmingly superior to the default conversions, you have become an anti-calibrationist. Whether you realize it yet or not, you have also rejected the need for great control over the RGB to CMYK conversion.

Balancing the Checks

The final example (Figure 12.13) is a variation on the theme of the artificial checkerboard. In the checkerboard, we saw that dark reds and blues, though drastically different colors, aren't so different when brought into B/W. Here, the checkerboard is the woman's jacket.

It is so glaringly obvious that we will have to compensate for the jacket that we may miss two other areas where contrast will suffer: the woman's hair, which is various shades of yellow now (and the baby's hair too, for that matter); and the flesh-tones seem quite flat, in addition to being too light.

There is also a nasty trick lying in wait for us. The red checks in the jacket appear marginally lighter than the blue ones. So, clearly, we will try to lighten them even

more. If we reduce the magenta overall, however, we will have a woman who looks like a ghost, considering how light her face is already. We need to add red to the face yet remove it from her jacket.

That can easily be done with curves, but there are enough other problems with this photo that it once again pays to examine each plate. This reveals that such contrast as there is in the hair is mostly in the cyan, and that such contrast as there is in the face is mostly in the magenta. Therefore, my strategy will be:

• I will emphasize the hair by blending 20 percent of the cyan into both the black and yellow plates.

Figure 12.13 *The checkerboard pattern in the woman's jacket is a warning flag that a direct conversion to B/W may not work well.*

Quick & Dirty
KEEPING THE COLOR IN BLACK AND WHITE

✓There are times when we have to use black and white, and times when we want to. B/W can be a very effective foil for other color images. Until recently, it was unheard of to take a digital color image and convert it to monochrome. Now, with most images coming into our computers in color, it is commonplace.

✓Any time an image goes from color to B/W viewers complain that it loses contrast. This is inaccurate. The image loses those types of contrast that are associated with color, but fully retains light/dark distinctions. A color image of a black cat in a blizzard will convert brilliantly to B/W.

✓Conversion candidates should be examined carefully for the kinds of contrast that *don't* convert well. Different colors that are of roughly the same lightness (e.g., the reds and blues in the flags of various nations) will reproduce as nearly the same shade in B/W. Similarly, different saturation values of the same color are readily distinguishable in CMYK, but not B/W.

✓Having identified the areas of a color image that will not convert well to B/W, apply correction curves or other methods that will exaggerate the differences, forcing different colors further apart.

✓Before the conversion, examine each plate of the CMYK image individually. Often one or more plates are very flat. If curves will not suffice to add contrast, think about blending in portions of other plates to add definition. The black plate, in particular, tends to have more shape than the other three and is a good candidate for blends.

✓Photoshop's default conversion to B/W is a mathematical formula. It takes no account of the individuality of the image. If we were not allowed to color-correct before conversion, it would probably be the best formula. As matters stand, however, practically *every* image can be improved by CMYK moves before going to B/W.

✓Do not worry about strict adherence to highlight/shadow settings in making the first correction. These can easily be fixed once we get to B/W, but whatever contrast we lose on the way will be gone forever.

✓RGB images generally should go to CMYK first before conversion to B/W, so as to get the full benefit of a color correction.

- My curves will boost all quartertones. The magenta plate gets a drastic increase in all values through about 30 percent, thus putting oomph in the fleshtones, and then drops off precipitously, deflating the red checks in the jacket. A similar decrease in the cyan shadows is needed; otherwise, the foliage will be too dark (remember, we blended some of the cyan into the black and yellow plates).

As black and white is meant to symbolize the more complex color image, the strange-looking 4/c picture that produced the excellent B/W of the right half of Figure 12.14 symbolizes the difficult art of B/W conversion. At first glance it seems terrible, but that is because we see color where we have to imagine B/W. The effectiveness of the conversion will depend upon the effectiveness of our imagination.

Figure 12.14 *Top right, the correction curves made for a much worse color image, but a much better B/W one (bottom right). At bottom left, a default conversion from the original image shown in Figure 12.13.*

Figure 13.1 Because duotones have been traditionally difficult to construct, some authorities still propose doing them by means of a flat color tint over a black and white picture (below). Above, Photoshop makes it simple to produce a much livelier and more effective tinted image.

Duotones

Printing a monochrome image with more than one kind of ink is a weird hybrid. Some different rules apply but in many ways it is just another curve-based color correction. The results are usually interesting, and often quite attractive.

aking images from color into black and white is like running them through a meat grinder. If there only will be black ink on the printing press, we can make a more tasty hamburger than our competition by using the techniques discussed in the last chapter, but it will be hamburger nonetheless.

In the opposite situation, where we have a black and white image yet are permitted to use color in printing it, well, we can't exactly turn the meat grinder into reverse. But the proficient color chef can serve up some tempting dishes with the ingredients at hand.

The subject of multitones, like many others, can be divided into the aesthetic and the practical. Forget, for the moment, that Photoshop provides an extensive and impressive multitoning routine. Let's get down to practicalities with a hypothetical exercise.

Please imagine, then, that the reason we did all the black and white conversions in the previous chapter was that the pictures have to appear in a brochure that is to be printed in two colors only. The colors will be black plus a purple, similar to the purple of the capital T at the top of this chapter. The reason for this, let's say, is that the company printing the brochure has a logo that is supposed to be purple.

We have recently rampaged through plate blending, cranberry-colored polar bears, and curves that would make honest folk shudder. As color desperados, is it morally consistent for us to scruple at making use of this new resource?

I can tell you what I would do in this situation, assuming that I had never heard of duotones. First, I would inform the printer that whatever was labeled cyan on my film was actually purple. And I would play with my page layout files so that the purple logo would wind up on what is labeled as the cyan plate.

Next, I would open each one of the B/W images that we had painstakingly created, and go through the following process.

I would Command–A, Command–C, Command–N. This is shorthand for **Select: Select All; Edit: Copy; File: New**. The new file, by default, comes up at the same size as whatever has been saved into memory, i.e., at the exact size of the current picture. Grayscale, the same as our picture, is the default, but I would change this to CMYK before clicking OK. I would then use **Image: Calculations>Copy** to place a copy of the existing B/W into the black channel of the new, empty CMYK document and into the cyan channel as well. The magenta and yellow would stay blank.

The black channel I would leave as an exact copy of the original B/W. On the cyan (purple) channel, however, I would impose a staggeringly steep straight-line correction curve. All points that were previously 60 percent or smaller would go to zero. However, the 100 percent endpoint would stay the same. This curve, in other words, would obliterate everything from

midtones down. Darker areas would have enormous contrast, starting from almost no dot but leaving the very darkest areas almost as heavy as they were before the bomb of this curve fell.

Comparing this new purple and black collage to the original B/W, the two are identical up to around 60K. As the image gets darker, however, 65K, for example, will become 65K12P. 70K will become 70K25P. And 90K will become 90K75P.

Do you suppose that anybody will notice that the darker half of the picture has gone purple? Fat chance! When black is that heavy, color perception goes away. What they will think they notice is that I am a B/W wizard. And why not? I have just invented a painless way to extend range. My 90K75P shadow is *much* darker than can be gotten with a conventional black and white. That translates to a bigger range, more contrast, more lifelike feeling, and many other good things.

How Strong a Duotone Effect?

The above-described technique is a brutal, barbaric, buccaneering introduction to duotoning. It presupposes that we are trying to hide the fact that a second color is involved. And it ignores some powerful aids that Photoshop can offer. Barbaric or not, it works: see Figure 13.2.

In real life, of course, we do not apologize for or try to hide the use of duotones. In their classic form, we use the second ink not only for a deeper shadow, but for a better highlight as well. Purple is a dark ink, but it is lighter than black. A highlight of 0K2P is better than one of 2K0P. More range equals more contrast.

This method will, unlike my first example, give the image an overall purplish

Figure 13.2 *Even when we have no desire to create a colorized black and white, if a second ink is available on press it can give us better reproduction. At right, the image appears to have more contrast because the shadows have been subtly deepened with a shade of purple.*

cast. We would have a purple picture with black used for depth only, more or less the same way it is in full color, not just a black and white with reinforced shadows. Clearly, one could split the difference between the two extremes in several ways. The decision would depend on how much of a purple feel we wanted.

That purple feel is much prized by designers in the 1990s. Duotones are an important part of many of the best-looking of today's advertising campaigns. Every now and then you find one where the reason

for the duotone was that the original images were black and white—a series of ads based on 1940s movies, for example.

More than likely, though, any images used in a duotone campaign originally were in color, but the agency went to the extra expense and aggravation of converting them into B/W in order to convert them into duotones. Duotones have many artistic purposes, in addition to simply setting a mood. When an image's natural colors are not vivid, or when we fear that they might compete with other graphics that are more important to our design, a duotone is a sensible choice.

Some writers, scientists and other benighted individuals have actually suggested that the way to achieve the purple look is to plaster a flat tint of purple over a B/W picture. That obsolete approach dates from the days when decent duotones were difficult. Adding a tint of a second color gives the image a certain flavor, all right, but in the nostrils of the professional it also gives it a certain smell. Figure 13.1 shows the difference between such an effect and a properly constructed duotone.

The Definition of a Multitone

This chapter concerns itself with all images that are based on a single monochrome channel—an original black and white—but that are printed with more than one ink. Usually, as in the case of Figure 13.2, each plate, although based on the same original image, is produced by the application of a different curve. Since the last chapter produced some pretty fair B/W images, we'll pick them up and use them as examples here.

A *true duotone* consists of two inks only. Although Photoshop permits construction of duotones using any two colors, in prac-

tice one of the colors is almost always black. The other color can be black as well. Black-black duotones, also known as *double-dot printing*, greatly increase the dynamic range and detail in a black and white image. This method is popular in Europe, especially in art books.

In true duotones, the second ink is usually not cyan, magenta, or yellow, but a custom color that is selected especially, or happens to be available on press because of the nature of the job, as in the hypothetical example of the purple logo.

Far more common nowadays, however, is the *process duotone*—the use of CMYK inks to produce the look and feel of a true duotone. All of the examples in this chapter, naturally, are process duotones, since I don't have a fifth ink available. Some purists would say these are technically not duotones, because they wind up using more than two inks. If we are trying to simulate a green duotone, for example, we will create what some would insist on calling a *tritone*, because it will use, at least, cyan, yellow, and black. A sepia, or coffee-colored, look requires a *quadtone*.

Technically incorrect or not, for the sake of sanity I will henceforth refer to as a *duotone* any image that uses multiple inks but has only one dominant hue. As Figure 13.5 suggests, it is entirely possible to create a variable-hue multitone, using curves only. What anybody would want to do this for escapes me, and no further time will be spent exploring its ramifications.

The Four-Color Black and White

Under my expansive definition, an attempt to enlarge the range of a B/W image by printing it in CMYK, rather than in black only, qualifies as a species of

Figure 13.3 *Unexpected color casts ruin duotones. An important way of guarding against surprises on press is to convert to CMYK using Heavy gray component replacement.*

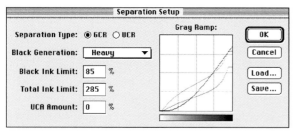

Figure 13.4 *Printing B/W images using all four CMYK inks is the way to go when possible, especially if they appear near full-color images. The CMYK version, top, has more tonal range than the black-only version, because the shadows can be made darker with four inks rather than one. Perhaps more important, the halftone screen pattern is less pronounced when there are four times as many dots.*

duotone. Figure 13.4 shows the extra snap that this technique can add. The top image seemed pretty good in the last chapter when compared to an alternate version that also was black only, but it looks a little anemic now.

Where B/W and 4/c images are in close proximity, there is really no argument for doing things any other way. News-magazines, for example, have to use monochrome historical photographs right next to normal color images. If printed in black ink only, they would look not only

colorless but lifeless. The color images would have richer blacks (since 80C70M70Y80K is far darker than 90K), and the screening pattern in the B/W would be much more noticeable. An un-wary reader might conclude from these factors that the magazine's production staff was incompetent, but a better adjective would be thoughtless.

Creating a four-color B/W image is as easy as changing from **Mode: Grayscale** to **Mode: CMYK**, but there is one small catch. Before doing it, we should go to **Edit: Preferences>Separation Preferences** and change the setting to Heavy GCR, as in Figure 13.3. The reasons for doing so are amplified in Chapter 8. Any time an image is predominantly composed of neutral grays (and this one will be *entirely* so composed) we are in danger of being torpedoed by careless presswork. The more black in our CMYK version, the less likely that an ink imbalance on press will cause a disastrous color cast.

Note the curves appearing at the right

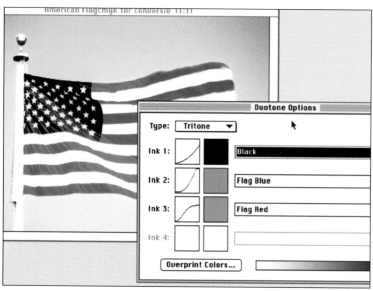

Figure 13.5 It is theoretically possible, if rarely seen in practice, to use multitone curves (bottom left) to so twiddle a monochrome image that it appears to take on more than one color (top left).

of the Preferences dialog box. As with any duotone, we are applying different curves in each channel to the same original monochrome image. As you would expect, the magenta and yellow use the same curve. The cyan curve has to be somewhat higher, since neutral colors require more cyan than magenta and yellow. And the black curve is a law unto itself.

It is also perfectly workable to copy the original black and white into two or more plates of a blank CMYK file and then apply curves in the normal way. This is how I made the crude duotone of Figure 13.2. There exists a commercially available Photoshop duotoning package, complete with an extensive book of samples, that works in this way.

Photoshop's **Mode: Duotone** controls are, however, one of the strongest points of the program, and the remainder of the examples in this chapter will use this method of applying curves.

Curves, Preset and Otherwise

Figure 13.6 shows Photoshop's duotone dialog box, which is accessed by changing

Mode: Grayscale to **Mode: Duotone**. In Photoshop, one cannot convert a CMYK or RGB image directly into duotone; they must go to grayscale first. The basic two colors can be changed freely by clicking on the existing ones. They can be defined either as CMYK percentages or by their Pantone identification number.

Once we click OK, the monitor will show us what looks like a duotone, and one would expect the new Photoshop document to have two channels, just as an RGB file has three channels and a CMYK file four. Frustratingly, it does not, which causes some handling problems. There is no way to display either half of a duotoned image by itself, and duotones cannot be manipulated using the subcommands of **Image: Calculations**.

Certain problems, such as producing a hybrid image duotoned in only a certain area, can only be resolved by converting the duotone file into CMYK. If the duotone will eventually print in CMYK, we should convert the file as well, even though page-layout programs can break a CMYK separation out of a Photoshop duotone file. As

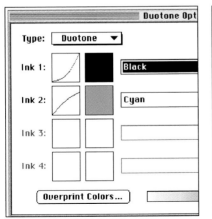
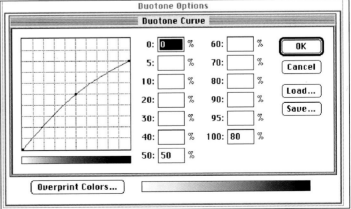

Figure 13.6 The duotone dialog box, left, showing Photoshop's default first curve for a cyan duotone. The curve structure, right, differs from what we are used to, but is easily understandable.

in the four-color black and white of Figure 13.4, process duotones should be separated using Heavy GCR, and it won't happen unless we do it ourselves. If we are printing a true duotone using a fifth color, however, there is normally no choice but to print out of a Photoshop duotone file. Duotones can't be saved as TIFFs, incidentally; one has to use EPS.

Each half of a Photoshop duotone is the original black and white image, modified by a curve. The curve is clearly necessary in at least the black plate, since if a significant amount of a second color were added to an unaltered black, the image would become too dark. If you have become proficient with curves, you will be able to come up with adequate duotone curves but it is not particularly easy. What the second color is makes a big difference, assuming black is the first. It also depends on what kind of look you are trying to achieve with the duotone, for there are many possibilities.

The curve dialog box for duotoning differs from the one we are used to. On the one hand, we can only place points at spots corresponding to original values that are multiples of 10 percent. On the other, we can, if we wish, type our desired values in, which beats the heck out of doing it with the mouse. You should have

Figure 13.7 *As a rule, subdued colors work much better in partnership with black than bright ones do. Brilliant colors like the red at left are ineffective in lighter shades, and in shadow areas, they are overmatched by black.*

Figure 13.8 *Photoshop's preset curves give considerable flexibility as to how much colorization will occur. Clockwise from top left, the four default cyan duotone curves applied to the image of Figure 12.9.*

no difficulty making the adjustment.

Writing the actual curves, however, is another story. Assuming we are doing a duotone with black plus color X, it's a safe bet that we want the highlight to be 2X0K and the shadow to be 90X90K. Thereafter, complications set in. If X is something heavy like a purple or brown, its curve will probably have to dip in the middle. If X is light, like cyan or yellow, the curve may actually have to bulge to make the X plate somewhat heavier than the original B/W was. And if X falls somewhere in between, like red or blue, we may not need a curve at all.

If this sounds troublesome, it is. Adobe

The Perils of the True Duotone

Although Photoshop makes the creation of true duotones far easier than at any time in the past, leaving the comfort of the CMYK womb can still be hazardous. The two biggest problems are predictability and the relationship with the page-output program.

First of all, if you up and decide to produce a duotone using black plus some uncommon PMS ink specification, bear in mind that you may well be the very first person in the history of the graphic arts ever to try it.

If you think that there is a printed sample book somewhere that will give you an idea of what a duotone with that ink looks like, forget it. Also, you can't rely on your screen: Photoshop's monitor settings are based on CMYK equivalents of the Pantone colors. The ink you will use will be custom-mixed and have nothing to do with CMYK, so this display method is inaccurate.

Possibly worst of all, there is no adequate method of predicting press reproduction. The leading brands of contract proof permit mixing toners to emulate a special ink, but these are far from reliable. If close to the proof is good enough, fine, but if you are going to be super-critical, there is no alternative to an expensive press proof before the job is printed.

If you are not dissuaded already, imaging Photoshop duotones, though possible, is fraught with snares for the unwary. Most output programs make the asinine assumption that a fifth color should be output at the black angle. This guarantees a moiré for a duotone user who forgets to correct the angle to either cyan or magenta (*never* yellow).

Also, great care must be taken in the output program to give the fifth color the *exact* same name that it has in Photoshop. An extra space-band, even a letter that is not capitalized, will result in the duotone separating into CMYK rather than printing as a fifth color.

has responded well by packaging many preset curves with Photoshop. If you have installed Photoshop normally they will be located in a subfolder called Duotone Curves and can be loaded directly from the dialog box shown in Figure 13.6. In each of the colors that are included (and there are around 20), there are four variations. The first one is the one that most emphasizes the second color. The fourth is mostly black with the second color added for emphasis only. The other two come down in the middle.

Figure 13.8 shows one image as modified by each of the four preset curves for a black-cyan duotone. Which look is best? It is purely an artistic call. One may be right for a certain project and not for another.

Aesthetically, though, there is no doubt that certain colors work better in duotones than others. Figure 13.7 illustrates this by making duotones out of black plus a brilliant color (PMS 485, which is emulated as 100M91Y) and one subdued color (PMS 478, which is 69C87M100Y.) In each case the image was created with the Photoshop first default curve for the specific color, and at the top of each is a sample of the unmodified second color.

The singular lack of success of the red duotone is a warning against using bright colors instead of earthier shades like brown. 100M91Y is a powerful color, but we never get any of its impact in this image. At values less than 30 percent, it is a sorry-looking pink, and at values greater, it is eviscerated by the presence of black. Overall, there is a red feel, but there is no bright red anywhere, since the heavier the red gets, the more black is added to it.

Those who are successful in designing with duotones almost invariably stick with

Figure 13.9 *Although Photoshop's supplied duotone curves give excellent results (above, the second blue default curve applied to the B/W image of Figure 12.5), writing custom curves can emphasize detailing in critical areas. Below, a rendition seeking more weight in the fur.*

darker, subtler colors in combination with black. Maybe one of the reasons that duotones are so fashionable in 1990s advertising is that there is currently a taste for "earthtones." Dark greens and browns are the in colors in the fashion industry, and there have been several reports that consumers are tending to shy away from bolder colors in all their purchasing.

As you can see, the duotones produced by Adobe's default curves are of quite respectable quality. And there is enough of a selection to let us find a curve for just about any of the infinite number of duotone colors we might be motivated to use. For example, in Figure 13.7 I used PMS 485 as a second color because it happens to be included in the defaults. But the specific colors and curves are easily edited. The default red curve should not be used to define a cyan duotone, but it will work for just about any red. So, if we decide that the existing red is too bright and we want a dirtier-looking second color, we simply open the default duotone curve, click on the color box that specifies PMS 485, and change the value to 20C80M80Y or whatever. Since the alteration takes seconds, we can try one color after another until we get the desired effect.

Excellent as these default curves are, however, they are only defaults. Pictures with special characteristics need special handling. Normal rules of curvewriting have not been repealed just because we have entered a new colorspace.

In Chapter 12, we corrected a B/W image of a polar bear to accentuate whatever contrast we could find in his white fur. If we are now asked to make a duo-tone of this image, building heavier fur is still going to be the objective. While we are at it, it would be nice to get more detail in the background as well. Being so much less familiar to viewers than conventional black and white images, duotones give us room to make moves that might be unacceptable in different settings.

Whether the image is color, grayscale, or multitone, we build contrast in the same way. We find the values in the area we want to accentuate, and then arrange for the curves to be steeper there. In the bear image the fur ranges approximately from 2 to 30 percent. The background is roughly 55 to 90. Photoshop's default curves do not realize that nothing of interest is going on between 30 and 55 percent, and give that range just as much emphasis as the bear and the background.

Remembering always that black will have more of an impact than any other color, even the comparatively dark blue of this image, we find the default curve that gives the closest overall feel to what we want, and start juggling. I elected to keep the lightest part of the bear blue only. I started adding black at levels of 5 percent or more. This enabled a steeper black curve than if I had started at zero. It also causes a sudden jump in the animal's near shoulder when the black ink starts to kick in. It does not have as much emphasis on the individual hairs, but it makes for almost a shadowy look on the bear's side. Perhaps more important, having the quick jump in the face emphasizes the areas that are still white and makes for the meaner-looking beast at the bottom of Figure 13.9.

Figure 13.10 *This image, full of dark, subtle tonal contrasts, is about as tricky a duotone candidate as could be imagined.*

From Start to Finish

This modest change of look brings us to the end of the the discussion of correction that began in Chapter 4. Some of the adjustments shown along the way were dramatic and others subtle, but they all were aimed at the same target: a more lifelike and believable image.

To remind us of how the little techniques add up, let's close out with a start-to-finish exercise, a nasty one at that. Given the original of Figure 13.10 (a bear of a different color, you might say), we are to produce an earth-colored duotone.

Even the most experienced professional would have trouble with this one. Yet though the subject of the photograph is tricky, the quality of the digital image is surely acceptable, much better than the average original seen in this book. Photo-

shop's CMYK-to-grayscale conversion is endorsed even by the most ardent calibrationists, and we have already seen the excellence of its duotone methods.

For these reasons, one should theoretically be able to deal with this picture in the 30 seconds or so it takes to convert to grayscale and apply the standard duotone curve. The results ought to be quite satisfactory. We shall see.

Alternatively, one can take the few extra minutes to evaluate what is really going on in the image and do things in a way that will take advantage of what strengths can be found in it.

The highlight of this image appears to be in the belly of the unfortunate fish, at 3C6M18Y. The shadow is in the animal's rear leg, at 74C75M68Y60K. Yellow sunlight must be affecting the right side of

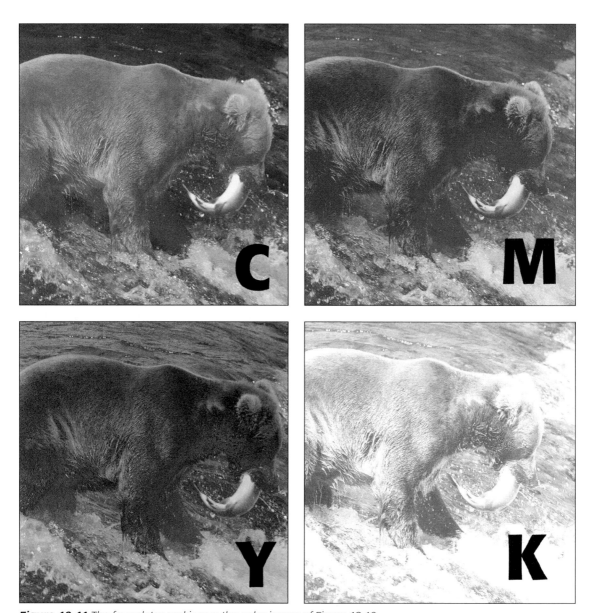

Figure 13.11 *The four plates making up the color image of Figure 13.10.*

the picture, because not only is the fish's belly yellow, the whitewater beneath it is 20C12M25Y, which is green, whereas at the left side of the picture, the whitewater is a more neutral 35C31MC35Y.

The big worry in this conversion is obviously going to be keeping contrast not only in the bear's fur but also in the dark water behind her. It may even be tough to differentiate the animal from the background. If only she were a polar bear, as in the previous example!

Measurements of the fur find values of 58C73M86Y29K, 57C72M85Y24K,

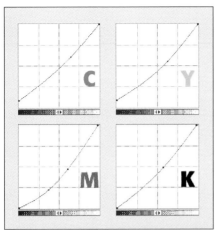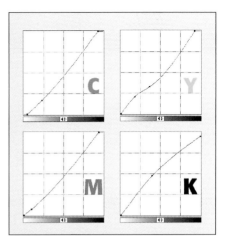

Figure 13.1 After applying the curves at left to the image, the black plate was sharpened. It was then blended into each of the other three plates. This move made the CMY plates lighter and thus weakened the shadow, so a second set of curves (right) was needed to produce the final color image (below).

61C74M83Y30K; and 62C75M84Y32K. That is hardly any variation. The dark water is not a whole lot better, at 76C51M51Y13K, 82C65M65Y29K, and 80C61M52Y19K.

The situation is desperate, for sure, though far from hopeless. A certain amount of extra range can be squeezed from the highlight and shadow, but we will have to scrounge for the contrast we need in the bear and in the water. That calls for an examination of the four plates of Figure 13.11.

As usual, each plate has good and bad features. The best bear, by far, is in the black, but everything else about the black is ill-defined. The cyan has good transition in the light areas of the water but is poor everywhere else. Being the unwanted color, yellow has the best detail in the blue water, but the yellow bear is terrible, probably a relic of JPEG compression. The magenta has average contrast everywhere.

As this is the most difficult conversion to B/W we have yet encountered, it needs the most involved correction. The plan will have to be to blend the black plate into the other three so as to have a more acceptable bear. First, though, all four plates need to have their better areas emphasized. We need not worry so much about their weak points; there is only so much worse we can make them.

The pivotal black plate can be beefed up by the curve shown in Figure 13.12. That is not, however, the only shark in our tank. With the other plates being as soft as they are, we can afford to apply unsharp masking to the black. Even if the result looks too rough by itself, the other plates will cover it up.

Meanwhile, the cyan gets a curve that adds contrast to the whitewater, while the yellow and magenta have their upper ranges stretched to get more detail in the darker water.

Time now for **Image: Calculations>Blend**, for new magenta and yellow plates that are the average of 85 percent of the old plate and 15 percent of the sharpened black. With the cyan plate being so terrible, I used a 75–25 split there.

Since, as always, the black plate was the lightest of the four, all this averaging and blending made the CMY plates lighter. Thus, the shadows that we had gone to such trouble to darken are now once

again too light. So, back to curves to darken them again. Naturally, we will use this occasion to try to engineer yet more contrast into the bear, by making the curves steepest in the ranges of each plate that encompass her.

The resulting color image appears in Figure 13.12. A lot more is going on there than just better highlights and shadows. Although the water is no longer blue, the bear is pulling away from it. We see much more detail in the animal's coat. It seems shinier, because the areas where the sun is reflecting off it have been lightened as they were pushed farther away from the darker fur. Note also how the bear's eye, practically invisible in the original picture, is starting to gain definition.

After converting to **Mode: Grayscale**, where no further correction is necessary, we now switch to **Mode: Duotone** and choose a weapon with which to mount one more assault on the fur.

I selected Photoshop's second mauve duotone curve, and in the interest of enabling a fair comparison of the two pictures of Figure 13.13, left the second color, PMS 4655 (0C24M43Y18K), alone. The actual curves, though (Figure 13.14) did not have enough punch in the critical midtone-to-three-quartertone area.

The Final Curves

Before beginning this series of corrections, I suggested that just converting the original image to B/W and applying the default duotone curve would yield a reasonably good product. Considering the difficult subject, it does.

It would be absurd, however, to pretend that it is in the same league as our corrected version, which was produced

Figure 13.13 *The top image was produced by taking Figure 13.10, converting it directly to grayscale, and applying Photoshop's default second mauve duotone curve. Bottom, a competing version using the techniques discussed in the last few pages.*

Quick & Dirty
DUOTONES

✓ If you have a monochrome image, but the ability to print with more than one color on press, you should be thinking about duotones. Many color images become more useful when made monochrome.

✓ Even if there is only one other color available, and even if you do not want anyone to know you are making a duotone, you can use the second color to deepen shadows undetectably, making for a superior B/W.

✓ True duotones involve the use of only two inks, one of which is almost always black and the other usually a special color. This look can be duplicated, however, by breaking the color components into CMYK and printing it with two or more process inks.

✓ Photoshop duotones can only be generated from a grayscale file. Files in other colorspaces must be converted to grayscale first.

✓ The key to getting a good duotone is a good, high-contrast B/W image. If you are planning to make a *color* picture into a duotone, be sure you grasp the concepts of color-to-B/W conversion explored in Chapter 12.

✓ Photoshop provides an excellent array of editable preset duotone curves. There are four curves for each color, each of which emphasizes black more than the last. The colors can be changed easily, and so can the curves. But the defaults are quite satisfactory for most multitones.

✓ True duotones using a non-process color are easily manufactured in Photoshop, but a lot can go wrong afterwards. There is no good way to proof them, for example. Also, screen angling problems are common.

✓ As a general rule, brilliant colors are not good choices for duotone work. They can never print at their full intensity, since the darker they get, the more black appears. Earthtones and other subdued colors work better.

✓ In Photoshop, a duotone is a single channel, which is not what you would expect. Certain manipulations, such as a retouch of one duotone plate but not the other, can only take place if the duotone is brought into CMYK.

✓ In a process duotone or 4-color B/W image, press problems will be minimized by running a heavier black than normal. Before separating into CMYK, therefore, change Photoshop's Separation Setup to Heavy GCR.

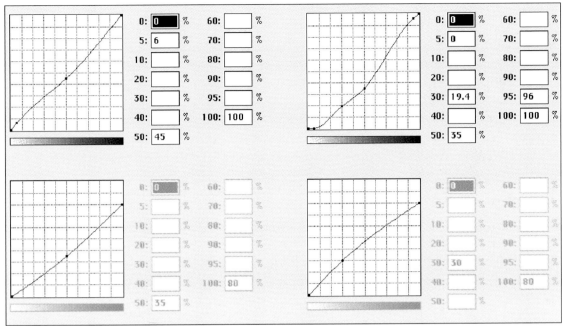

Figure 13.14 *Photoshop's second mauve duotone curves (left) and the customized contrast-emphasizing curves (right) that produced the competing duotones of Figure 13.13.*

without trickery, without local selection, using only curves, blending, and a smidgen of sharpening on a single plate.

The techniques we used are all closely related. Assuming a color original, you cannot produce a decent duotone without knowing how to get the most out of a black and white conversion. You can't do *that* without a good grasp of standard professional color correction. And you can't do professional-level correction without curves, curves, curves.

Plenty of improvements can be expected from Photoshop over the coming years. Version 3 is not the last word.

Without a skilled operator, however, one is hard pressed to see how the Photoshop of the future will be able to improve on today's performance. The original image was fine. The conversion to B/W was theoretically perfect. The default duotone curve cannot be faulted. How can Adobe improve any step of this procedure?

Five years, 10 years from now, the bottom half of the figure will still be laughing at the futility and lack of definition of the top half. If you have mastered color correction and enhancement, perhaps you will manage a wry smile at it yourself, for your skills will still be much in demand.

Figure 14.1 In this image it is very clear who the most important person is, not just because we know he is the President, but because of the way the photograph is set up to focus on him. But what if we need to emphasize not the speaker, but the individuals at the left of the image? Photoshop 3's sponge tool was made for situations like this.

Flexing the Muscles Of Photoshop 3

The big four improvements in the newest Photoshop are selective color correction, layering, lighting control, and a new tool, the sponge. Each allows certain kinds of maneuvers that previously were difficult.

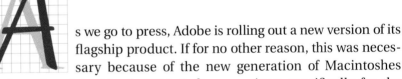

s we go to press, Adobe is rolling out a new version of its flagship product. If for no other reason, this was necessary because of the new generation of Macintoshes introduced in March 1994. Software written specifically for the PowerPC chip on which the new Macs are based runs several times faster than before, and slow performance has plagued Photoshop as well as every other image-processing application.

Because Photoshop 3 requires more RAM than some users have available, it will likely be some time before earlier versions vanish. Those making the upgrade will find the transition a smooth one. Photoshop 2.5 is a highly competent program, fully capable of color work at the highest level. The overwhelming majority of jobs are handled in Photoshop 3 exactly as they have been in the past. The mainstream examples of our first 13 chapters illustrate this. Although there were some cases where version 3 would have been more efficient, every one of the corrections could have been done with version 2.0, let alone 2.5.

In this chapter, we will seek out the areas where Photoshop 3 has expanded our capabilities. The corrections we will discuss here *are* possible with older versions, but they are considerably more difficult.

Four Major Improvements

While there are a number of useful minor additions to the program, such as the ability to shrink or spread paths, more accessible palettes and dialog boxes, and a monochrome noise option, they all pale in comparison to the four biggies I am about to summarize.

• **Selective color correction**. This, standard practice on high-end scanners, is the ability to add or subtract specific inks from every occurrence of a given color, or even of neutral colors. Plus, we can now create automatic, feathered masks that isolate a color, so that we can apply all kinds of curves to it in isolation.

• **Layering**. We can now make multiple, independent layers. Each can be moved about freely, and its attributes changed. Previously, once we pasted a piece of one image into another and deselected it, that was it. Whatever used to be underneath the object was there no longer. Thus, moving the new object was impossible. For simple merges of the type discussed in Chapter 11, this was not such a big deal, but if there were more than two or three merges in the same image the inability to move things became most unwieldy. Images with layers must be saved in Photoshop 3 format; to print them, we have to merge the layers before saving them as TIFFs or EPSs.

• A new tool, the **sponge**, is a third option to the existing dodge/burn. The tool either saturates or desaturates the underlying color, using the usual assortment of feathered, variable-opacity brushes. This lets us enjoy the advantages of the HSB colorspace, such as they are, in CMYK. Because the sponge's main job is to control the unwanted color, it is highly useful, for reasons pointed out in Chapter 9.

• In Photoshop's first foray into the 3-D world, a **Lighting Effects** filter is introduced. This lets us simulate the effect of light hitting objects in an existing image. We have control over the color of the light, what angle it comes in from, the type of reflection that will occur, and how far away the light source theoretically is.

For the remainder of this chapter, we will examine how these four new capabilities let us resolve difficulties that were previously formidable.

Preparing a Layer Options Merge

The image of two tropical birds in Figure 14.2 represents the Kodak CD process at its best. The full range of colors is captured nicely, there is no cast anywhere, and every area of the picture has reasonable color values. It had to be sharpened in Photoshop, of course, but outside of this it must be considered completely acceptable for professional work right off the CD.

Notwithstanding the excellent start, we can do better, as the bottom image indicates. Check the level of detailing in the bright areas of the two birds. The focus is plainly much better in the corrected version. Without Photoshop 3's color selection controls, this improvement would have been very difficult.

Superficially, this image is like others we have seen, notably Figure 9.6, which featured a brilliantly costumed dancer. The basic problem, though, is that too much is going on. To add contrast to the

Figure 14.2 *Although the raw image, top, has excellent color balance and range, improvement can be engineered into the brightest areas of plumage through Photoshop 3's density masking capabilities.*

areas we care about, we have to find tonal regions that are unimportant, and there are very few of those here. Consider the cyan plate, for example. It is a highlight in the yellow chest of the rear bird, a quarter-tone in the red plumage of the forward one, a midtone in the darker areas of both birds, a three-quartertone in the background greens and at the top of the rear parrot's head, and a shadow in the blue areas of both birds. In short, every value is in use. We cannot sacrifice anything.

Accordingly, if we want more detail in the bright plumage, we will have to do some local correction. Unfortunately, there is no easy way to isolate the areas we want to work on.

Therefore, using **Image: Duplicate**, I made three additional copies of the file. I color-corrected each one to emphasize detailing in one of the three plumage colors: the red of the forward bird, the yellow of the rear bird's chest, and the yellowish-cyan feathers of both. In doing so, I completely ignored what was happening to the other parts of the three pictures.

The approach was the same throughout. In each case, I found the typical values for each of the three inks that made up the important color, then wrote curves to steepen them drastically in these areas. Where there was an unwanted color (cyan in the red and the yellow; magenta in the cyan), I allowed it to go to zero in the brightest areas, ignoring the normal minimum dot requirement. Also, I applied unsharp masking to the weaker plates of each color. In the image that was optimized for yellow, I sharpened both cyan and magenta; in the red one, I sharpened both cyan and black, which was creeping into the darker areas of the plumage.

This yields four images: one original, slightly corrected for a deeper shadow; plus three copies, each having either good yellow, good red, or good cyan, with nothing else to recommend any of them. The problem becomes one of bringing the strong areas of each into a single image.

Merging the yellow is the easy part, because the yellow chest is so well differentiated from the surrounding colors. Starting with the revised yellow image, we make a rectangular selection that completely includes the bird's chest, and copy this to memory. With **Image: Calculations> Copy**, we pass the selection area into the original image. That way, when we **Edit: Paste**, the revised version that is now in memory will fit exactly over the same area in the original.

At the moment, this leaves a very obvious demarcation at the edge of the rectangular selection. Since the moves we made in the revised yellow also affected the background, it no longer matches the background of the original image. But this is easily sidestepped. First, we go to the Layers palette and save the floating rectangular selection as a new layer. Then, by bringing up the Layer Options menu (Figure 14.4), we can limit the merge to a certain area, as was done in Figure 7.18. As long as it is possible to define that area in terms of any combination of process colors, we are home free. Here, it will be any area within the rectangle that consists of both a lot of yellow and not much cyan. Since nothing except the chest meets these criteria, the definition will work.

This maneuvering was entirely possible in earlier versions of Photoshop, even though there was no Layers palette. The defunct command **Edit: Composite Controls**

Figure 14.3 *Photoshop 3's Color Ranges command calculates a Quick Mask for whatever color we specify, top. At bottom, the resulting cyan mask is saved as a separate channel.*

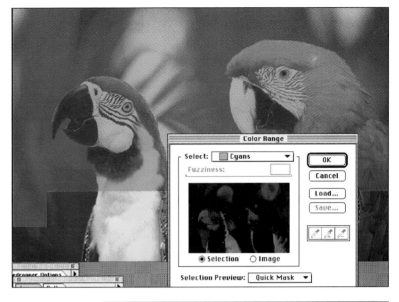

brought up a similar options menu. Once we start to have trouble defining the merge area, though, a different approach is needed, and Photoshop 3 provides it.

Creating a Density Mask

The cyan feathers, unlike the yellow ones, are surrounded by areas of similar color. We will not be able to use the above technique to isolate them. Instead, Photoshop 3 gives us **Select: Color Range**, otherwise known as a density mask.

As with most such menus, we can make any of the six RYGCBM colors a starting point. Choosing cyan causes Photoshop to evaluate the entire image and select those areas that it considers to be that color. This is, importantly, not a complete selection, but one whose intensity depends on exactly *how* cyan Photoshop finds the area to be. Areas that are green or blue will be considered partially cyan, and so will be partially selected. Now, using **Select: Save Selection**, we can automatically create a heavily feathered, variable-

intensity grayscale emulation of the area of the picture that is thought to be cyan. That is just the thing we need to bring in our corrected cyan image.

In the current image, this will be all we need. There will be cases, however, where we need still more control. Using the eyedropper to choose the color of the selection, rather than one of the preset colors, enables use of a "fuzziness" slider. This lets us decide how loosely or rigidly the color will be defined, and consequently how extensive the mask will become.

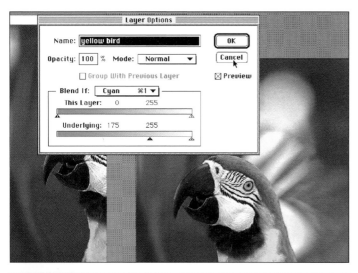

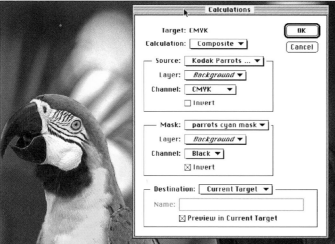

Figure 14.4 The yellow chest of the bird is so well differentiated from the other colors that one can paste a corrected version in directly, top, using layer options. The other colors have to be merged using masks, bottom.

Saving the default red selection as a channel (and it should be as a new document, saved in Photoshop 3 format, which is much more efficient than making a fifth channel in the existing document) yields the grayscale image of Figure 14.3. This will now be used as a mask. The darker the area, the more pronounced the composite will be.

The mask channel can be adjusted or edited just as if it were a photograph. That is what we would like to do here. Since no area of the image was absolutely cyan, no area of the mask will be at absolutely full intensity. The parts we see as being cyan will show up at around 80 percent. The parts we perceive as green or blue will be less than this, but they will be there.

Since we would like our corrected cyan image to replace the cyans of the original image almost completely, we apply a soft curve to darken the already dark areas of the mask. If the parts representing green get lighter, that is a plus, but it will not make a big difference.

We now go back to the original document, but leave both the mask and the version corrected for cyan open on the screen. The original thus becomes the target image when we go to **Image: Calculations>Composite**, so we have to define the corrected cyan version as the source image. The mask, naturally, will be the grayscale document we have created.

If we leave it at that, we will get a final version that changes everywhere *except* in the cyan—exactly the opposite of what we want. The source image replaces the target except where the mask is dark, which happens to be in all the cyan areas. Fortunately, this dialog box has a checkoff option that lets us use an inverted version of the mask, as shown in Figure 14.4.

Applying the red correction is done in much the same way, creating a mask for the red areas and then compositing. In this image, the red is less ubiquitous than the cyan, which shows up in many areas of the plumage. This leads to a slight variation in handling. The only area outside of the red feathers that Photoshop places within the red mask is the yellow chest of the rear bird. Admittedly, there is a very slight orange flavor, which translates to about a 10 percent presence in the red mask. But there is no need for this. Thanks to our previous moves, the yellow is already as good as we can make it. Therefore, it makes sense to delete this area from the mask by drawing a rectangular selection around it and hitting the delete key.

If you are wondering why we used density masks rather than selective color correction in this example, the answer is that selective color correction would have been a good way to add or subtract certain inks from the red, yellow, and cyan areas that interested us. That is not a particularly good way to generate an unwanted color. What is needed is contrast, not quantity. To get detail in the feathers, we don't need a heavier unwanted color, just a better one.

Selective Color to the Rescue

Moving right along from the sublime to the preposterous, Figure 14.5, the worst Photo CD image in this book, demonstrates a more plausible use for selective color correction.

The woman's shirt, plainly supposed to be white, averages 29C16M33Y. The flesh tends to be around 50C50M90Y10K. These lamentable numbers tell us what

our eyes do, that this image has a green cast of epic proportions.

One would hope that it would be possible to discard this abomination and start off with something more suitable. Regrettably, life is not like that sometimes. This cast is bad enough that, as shown in Chapter 10, it is worthwhile to attempt an LAB correction before bringing the image into CMYK.

Moves in LAB are highly volatile, so just bringing the image closer to where we would like it must be termed a success. Here, we have options available in each of the three LAB channels. In the A, which is a red vs. green channel, we clearly want to steer the image away from green and toward red. In the B, a slight move away from yellow and toward blue will help. And the L, which has no hue but is lightness only, could use the application of an S-shaped curve for more contrast, plus some unsharp masking.

The left half of Figure 14.6, the result of these LAB maneuvers, is a distinct improvement, but falls well short of the numerical guidelines we would like to meet. For that, we need the accuracy of CMYK curves.

Following the standard curvewriting rules laid down in Chapter 4, however, serves up the right half of Figure 14.6. With the image starting out so green, there was virtually no contrast in the magenta channel. The magenta in the faces was as heavy as in the shadow area at the top of the lamp. That translates into a face that is grossly too red after application of any curves that would insure a proper shadow.

In earlier versions of Photoshop, we would now confront the disagreeable choice of somehow selecting all the flesh

Figure 14.5 *The startling transformation of the original, left, into something approximating a usable image was assisted by Photoshop 3's selective color correction capability.*

in the image and correcting it locally, or else dealing with the awkward **Image: Adjust>Hue/Saturation**. Now, however, we have the infinitely preferable **Image: Adjust>Selective Colors.**

This command works in the same fashion as the **Select: Color Ranges** that served us well in the last example. Photoshop isolates a certain color and works on it alone. We can specify an increase or reduction in any CMYK plate within the chosen color. The fleshtone in the right half of Figure 14.5 hovers around 8C85M80Y15K.

Ghastly though it is, this color is *red*, not magenta, not yellow, and we can fix it right up with a selective color correction.

Unlike the previous example, where we were looking for more contrast, here we are just trying to change color balance. Therefore, as shown in Figure 14.7, we reduce the amount of magenta and yellow contained in all reds in this image, and increase the cyan. As there is nothing other than the fleshtones that Photoshop will consider *red*, we are in business. The shadow above the lamp is not red. It is a

Figure 14.6 *Preliminary attempts to subdue the green cast. At left, after a correction in LAB. Right, a standard CMYK adjustment on top of this yields better highlights and shadows, but bright red flesh.*

neutral color. It will not be affected by what we are doing. The magenta and yellow in the fleshtone will come down but the shadow will hold its value.

Since there are areas in the flesh, particularly in the arm, that may be identified as being more yellow than red, a similar selective-color move is needed in yellow. The image is now approaching acceptability, but there is still not enough life in either the magenta or the yellow components of the faces.

There is good news and bad news

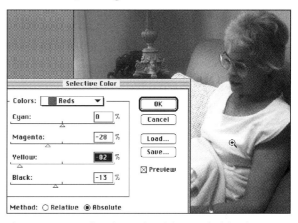

Figure 14.7 *Toning down the violent red of the face with selective color correction.*

about the black plate of this image. The bad news is, when this image was converted into CMYK, there was still a green cast. This turned the fleshtones gray, and when grays go into CMYK black gets generated—much more than we would like in this case.

This bad news also happens to be the good news, thanks to Photoshop 3. If the black is too heavy in the fleshtones, fine: we can reduce it with selective color correction. Meanwhile, although it is too heavy for now, it also carries a lot of contrast—more than in either the magenta or yellow plate. So, first we write a curve that exaggerates the contrast in the black even more, then we blend 25 percent of the black into both the magenta and the yellow plate. Finally, we go back to selective color correction, to drop the black almost completely out of all red areas.

Naturally, all this blending has its effect on highlight and shadow values. We will therefore have to adjust these with one last set of CMYK curves.

And there will be one final Photoshop 3 fillip. Despite all we have done, the lower half of the woman's face remains extremely hot. Needing to reduce the redness of this area, we turn to the new sponge tool. Choosing a large feathered brush, desaturation as the method, and 50 percent intensity, we brush over the hot spot. We do not particularly care about how dark it is: the problem is its redness, and desaturating it will take this away.

Having to go through all this rigmarole is tiresome, but a quick look back at Figure 14.4 reminds us of what it can accomplish. An original that seemed hopelessly bad has been converted into something that is professionally usable.

Where Is the Focus?

These sponge tool maneuvers could have been duplicated with a small amount of difficulty in Photoshop 2.5. There, with no sponge available, we could have activated the dodge tool, choosing midtones. We would have then opened the Channels palette and turned off writing capability to cyan and black. This would have allowed a reduction in magenta and yellow only.

In two variations of Figure 14.1, some more difficult sponging will be on display.

This is yet another example of the perennial problem of what the camera saw versus what a human observer *would* have seen. The riveting presence of the President of the United States would undoubtedly hold our attention, if we were present. Although the camera is focused on Mr. Clinton, causing the faces to his right to be blurry, they are still more pronounced and more colorful than we would actually see them ourselves.

That is, of course, if it was really Mr. Clinton we were concentrating on. Certainly that is the likeliest scenario, but circumstances clearly might arise where we wished to shift the emphasis away from the President and toward the listeners. Perhaps one of them is a relative of ours, or a political candidate for whom we are preparing advertising.

Figure 14.8 shows two interpretations. One is intended to subtly emphasize the President, one the audience.

To make corrections like this, we plainly have to select and save two paths, one for the President, one for the listeners. The method can be any one of those discussed in Chapter 6.

The next step is sabotage. On the assumption that Figure 14.1 is as good a

Figure 14.8 *Two more versions of the image of Figure 14.1. Above, emphasizing the President. Below, trying to accentuate the listeners. The most valuable tool in these moves is Photoshop 3's sponge.*

reproduction of both audience and President as can be had, the only way to emphasize one is to play down the other. We do it by selecting the area of the image that we want to deemphasize, then applying curves that make the faces more gray and thus, less lifelike. As a final insult, we run **Filter: Blur>Blur More**, to further defocus the undesired areas.

The most significant alteration is yet to come. Going all the way back to Figure 12.1, recall how much more powerful the image of the cheetah was once the background was changed from a shade of yellow to black and white.

If we were to make everything else B/W, the heads of either President or audience would appear much more pronounced. We hardly rate to get away with *that,* but there is no need to do anything so unrealistic. Just moving the background surrounding the heads in the *direction* of B/W will do the same thing. Here is where the sponge comes in.

For the version deemphasizing the President, we load the path isolating him, and, from the Paths palette, choose Make Selection. Then, we also load the path for the background images, and choose Make Selection: Add to Selection. With both President and audience selected, we **Select: Invert**. As we will be working on the area immediately bordering the heads, this selection method protects the faces from any change.

Activating the sponge tool, we choose a wide feathered brush, 50 percent opacity, and Desaturate as the method. Now, we gently trace the outline of the President's head. This done, we change the sponge method to Saturate, and stroke the outlines of the heads of the listeners.

For the version that emphasizes Mr. Clinton, we do just the opposite. We saturate the outside of his head and desaturate those of the audience.

Adjusting local saturation like this plays havoc with our depth perception. Compare the two halves of Figure 14.8 in the background next to the President's ear. In the top version, there is an area of dark green that is nearly colorless in the bottom one. Question: How far in back of Mr. Clinton do you perceive that green area to be? Because of the color contrast, I see him as being several feet further in front of the green than he is of the gray. In just the same way, when the area behind the audience is a bright blue, they seem much further in front of it than when it is more neutral. More important, perhaps, I see the President as standing several feet further in front of the audience in the top version as opposed to the bottom. This is saturation-related as well, although it is the result of curves, not the sponge.

The sponge's power is completely out of proportion to its visible effect. In first comparing the two images, you probably caught the curve-based variation in the various faces. Did you see the sponge maneuvers in the background? Yet the moves in the background are probably the more effective of the two.

The Lighting Effects Filter

This illusion of three-dimensionality is a fitting introduction to Photoshop 3's **Filter: Lighting Effects**, the program's first outright foray into this rapidly expanding area of image processing.

Action in this field has mostly been in dedicated 3-D programs that add the perception of depth to artwork, normally flat graphics of the kind generated by Adobe Illustrator and other such programs. The algorithms for this are fiendishly difficult and require massive amounts of computing time. The process of adding the look of three-dimensionality to an image is known as *rendering*. Until the advent of the PowerPC, it was absolutely commonplace in professional work for the rendering to take hours per image, and in some cases, days. This refers to raw number-crunching time: if you asked your computer to render, you could kiss the use of it goodbye for a considerable length of time.

The simple question that requires all this computing horsepower for an answer is: What happens to the light? Three-dimensionality is nothing more than its proper distribution. Shadows, reflections, hot spots, and color changes all have to be calculated.

These variables are vastly more difficult to deal with in photographic images than they are in line art, and Photoshop does not attempt a comprehensive solution, for the simple reason that it would be technically too difficult. Imagine trying to add depth to a group of individuals, such as the audience in the image we just worked with. An artificial light source can be introduced, but trying to calculate what would happen to that light once it hit would require more arithmetic than the current generation of computers can handle. To be accurate, we would need a reading on every fleshtone, every garment, that would define how much of each color it would reflect, and at what intensity, and how well it would accept a shadow.

Photoshop 3's capabilities in no way

approach this, but simple additions of a light source to a simple subject are now possible.

The controls for such lighting additions are flexible. We can fiddle with the color of the light, its intensity, the reflectance characteristics of what it hits, its angle, and how far away it is coming from.

There is obviously a lot of power here, and your guess is as good as mine as to what the major uses of it will be. Mine, for what it's worth, is that the big gain will be in merging two unrelated images. As discussed in Chapter 11, one of the major headaches in image merging is when the lighting of the two pieces vary. In Figure 11.1, an otherwise convincing merge was derailed by sunlight coming in from the right side in the background, but from the left side in the face of the young lady who was pasted into the foreground.

With earlier versions of Photoshop, attempting to correct this would be something best avoided. Fixing the background would be out of the question, so one would have to try to eliminate the sun's glare from the left side of the woman's face and introduce it on the right. This can be done, provided you are very good in Photoshop, have excellent aesthetic judgment, and nothing better to do with an afternoon. With Photoshop 3, it is still not easy, but it is at least reasonable. The bottom of Figure 14.9 is not an artistic prize, but it does represent approximately what would happen if light were really hitting the right side of the face. With color correction and careful use of layering options this effect could be incorporated into the original, and the result would be more convincing than by doing it the hard way.

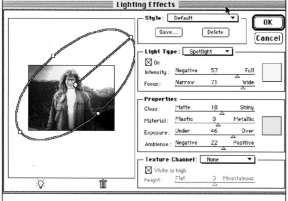

Figure 14.9 *In Chapter 11, the lighting on the left side of the face of the top image ruined a merge with a background in which the light was coming from the right. Middle, Photoshop 3's Lighting Effects filter introduces an artificial yellow light source coming in from the top right. The face in the bottom image can be used to merge with the top one, solving the lighting inconsistency.*

Layers Make Alterations Easier

If you do a lot of image merging, the layering capabilities will be the most exciting new feature of Photoshop 3. Getting them in was hard work for the programmers, but using them is very easy for us, requiring almost no explanation.

Layering in its simplest form was used in Figure 14.1 to deal with the problem of where to put the caption. There being no convenient place where type could be placed to be readable, I resorted to ghosting a rectangular area at top left of the image. Ghosting is the practice of drastically lightening an image, yet trying to retain some suggestion of detail. It is a popular design tool at the moment.

In earlier versions of Photoshop, this would have been done by selecting an appropriate rectangular area with the marquee tool and applying a lightening curve. Most likely, I would have just opened the master CMYK curve and brought 100 percent down to about 40. I would, of course, save the selection as a path, in case I thought, upon seeing the page proofs, that my ghosted area was still too dark for the type to be legible. I would, in this case, reload the path and apply a second curve.

Chances are that I would have gotten this part right the first time, so the precaution would be for nothing. A much more likely alteration, however, is one that I would not be protected against.

The size of the ghosted area plainly depends on how large the caption is. Having measured it, one could constrain the marquee tool to the desired size, or else watch the Info palette while drawing the selection, to be sure that the ghosted box is the right size, with adequate margins.

The problem is, I am basing the sizing

of this box on a *draft* version of the caption. I like it, but such are the vagaries of the publishing process that I am not the final word on it. My editor may be thickheaded enough to insist on changes, and, with my luck, they will alter the line count of the caption, and my ghosted box will be the wrong size.

In Photoshop 3, that is much less of a problem. Instead of curving an existing selection, we can make the ghosted area a layer by itself, fully editable in size and opacity. First, we select with the marquee tool in exactly the same way as before. To create the layer, we need to paste something on top of the background, so for want of anything more creative, we copy the selection to memory and then paste it back on top of itself. It is now a floating selection, which we can make into a permanent layer by means of the Make Layer command in the Layers palette, as shown in Figure 14.10.

As a new layer, the rectangular selection can almost be treated as a new Photoshop document. We now set the foreground color to white, and use **Edit: Fill** to replace the entire selection with white.

Now, it is just a matter of adjusting the sliding opacity scale in the Layers palette until we find a value that seems satisfactory. I chose 65 percent.

The layers have to be collapsed before saving the file in a printable form. To retain the ability to edit the layer, we must save in Photoshop 3 format. To print, we have to save a second version as a TIFF or EPS. Before doing so, we must go into the Layers palette and choose Merge Layers.

Having done this, we are well positioned to deal with unpleasant decisions by the editor. Suppose that the edited cap-

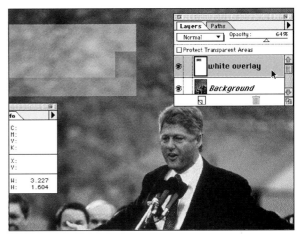

Figure 14.10 *Establishing the ghosted box that will hold the caption in Figure 14.1 as a separate layer.*

tion gains two lines, or that we are told that the ghosted area would look better a quarter-inch to the left, or that it is still too dark for easy legibility. I will merely go into the Photoshop 3 document, adjust the top layer as needed, resave, Merge Layers again, and save as a TIFF or EPS. If I were just trying to extend the depth of the white box, I would enter the layer, select the box, and do an anamorphic enlargement through **Image: Effects-Scale**, as discussed in Chapter 7.

It is true that this method is only slightly more efficient than redoing the job from scratch, which is what I would have had to do in earlier versions. The real productivity gain comes in more complex layering jobs. Any time there are three or more layers in a job, corrections are disastrously difficult without Photoshop 3, which supports 100 different layers per file, assuming that this does not fry your computer.

To see why, imagine a typical three-layer job. Suppose that in the macaw image of Figure 14.2, we learn that two macaws are not enough, and that we need to add a third, except that no third bird is available.

We will therefore have to clone one of the existing birds, plainly the one on the right, yet give it enough variation that the viewer will not realize it is a clone. Then, we will have to carefully paste it between the two original birds, so that it appears to be in front of one but behind the other.

In any version of Photoshop, we would start by isolating the right-hand bird, saving a path or a mask, and copying the entire document over for color correction, the idea being to make a bird of significantly different hues. Being in Photoshop 3 would already be a big help, because we would have made selective color masks using **Select: Color Ranges**, and these could be used to alter the plumage.

Once colors are satisfactory, we would resize, re-angle, and otherwise fool around with the macaw, in keeping with our wish to disguise the fact that it is a clone of the one on the right. Next, we would select it, paste it into the middle of the existing image, and adjust its position. We would arrange somehow for the original right-hand bird to come to the front, and presumably create some sort of shadow effect on the new, middle macaw, since the light is coming in from the right, and the right-hand macaw would be blocking some of it.

Again, these moves are easier in Photoshop 3. Getting the right-hand macaw in front would no longer be a problem. We would paste the new parrot in the middle and position it as before, but we would then save it as a layer. Then, returning to the background, we would load the path that isolates the right-hand macaw, copy

and paste in front, and save *that* as a third layer, in front of the new bird. The artificial shadow would go on a *fourth* layer, to cater to the possibility of a later move.

So far, we have made a modest case in favor of Photoshop 3 and its layers, but the real gain comes when we show a proof of what we did, and our client says, fine—except the new macaw should be moved one pica up and to the left, his beak should be open, and the right macaw should be enlarged and moved slightly to the right.

In Photoshop 3, having everything saved on its own layer makes this a snap. In previous versions, the situation is too nightmarish even to describe, since it calls for the restoration of background areas that have long since been obliterated.

Professional Color with Photoshop

Photoshop 3's efficiency in dealing with the specialized situations described in this chapter is undeniable. Now that we have reached the end of a long journey, however, it is well to point out that what governs the quality of the color will be you— far more than any program.

If you understand the basic principles of color correction, you will be able to achieve professional results with almost any software, almost any computer, almost any monitor. If you don't, a million-dollar dedicated system won't help.

General statements about color can be maddeningly easy to comprehend, yet just when you think you understand them they lead into dense and complex thickets of technique and exceptions. If you are not a professional, don't be intimidated. If you are a professional, you will know that most professionals don't understand many of the concepts enumerated here. For example, most professional scanner operators are familiar with the numerical color rules discussed in Chapters 4 and 5, but a majority of professional console operators are not. Competent handling of color to B/W conversion is virtually unknown in the professional world; if you apply the principles discussed in Chapter 12 correctly you will get much better black and whites than would be provided by 90 percent of color trade shops.

The reason for this is lack of experience. Digital color correction, even at the most prestigious color separation houses, is still relatively new. Several years worth of knowledge is not enough. We are always discovering new and better techniques. As we get more experienced, the learning curve gets a little bit flatter, but it never goes away. My own skills are somewhat better as a result of working on the example images in this book. They were adequate beforehand, but now I think in different ways. I have learned, for instance, to consider the use of the L channel in LAB to aid in correcting a CMYK image. This is a more effective way of adding sparkle, I have found, than the methods I used to employ.

Then again, two years from now, I expect to be much better at color correction than I am today. If you are uncomfortable with some of the methods discussed here, don't worry. The basics can be acquired. Improvement will never stop.

Photoshop evolves, gets faster, comes up with new techniques, becomes better in every way. With any effort, with any luck, so will we.

achromatic printing Term, used mostly in Europe, for making color separations with extensive use of GCR.

additive colors Red, green, and blue.

Adobe Adobe Systems Inc., the authors of Photoshop, the PostScript page description language, Adobe Illustrator, and several other important products in the digital imaging revolution.

alpha channel Any channel other than the ones minimally necessary in a particular colorspace. Normally, an alpha channel contains a mask or template.

analog The opposite of digital. Any device that measures information in a manner that is theoretically infinitely variable, as opposed to defining it as a series of numbers. A cassette tape player is analog; an audio CD is digital. The variable-voltage signal that comes off the photomultiplier tube of a high-end scanner is analog; when we import it into Photoshop, it is digital.

anamorphic A reduction or enlargement that reduces or enlarges width by a different proportion than depth.

anti-aliasing In importing an image into Photoshop or when making a selection, the process of reducing the jaggedness by only partially changing the edges of the selection or graphic.

base The nonemulsion side of film.

Bézier curve The basic mathematical curve model for PostScript graphics. Drawing paths using the pen tool will create this type of curve, which is governed by a series of anchor points and points that control the angle and intensity of the curve.

binary Said of a device, such as a computer, that uses a series of zeroes and ones as the basis of its arithmetic.

bit In computing, the smallest item that can be addressed, namely, a zero or a one.

bitmap A digital image form that is defined as a series of dots of specific size, as opposed to a continuous-tone file or a vector-based art file.

bitmapping Disastrous occurrence on output of film when the RIP cannot find a graphic or font that is being called for and substitutes a low-resolution version of it instead.

blanket On an offset press, the rubber layer that accepts the image from the printing plate and transfers it to the paper.

bleed 1) The practice of extending an image to the very edge of the printed page; 2) the additional image area outside of the page area that must be provided to ensure that the bleed will be successful.

blurring Reducing contrast, more or less the opposite of sharpening, for the purpose of making an image look less focused.

brightness Any one of several models that seek to measure luminosity in an image; roughly equivalent to a black-and-white rendition of a color image.

byte Eight bits of digital information, which happens to be the number necessary to describe either a letter of the alphabet or an individual color pixel.

capstan imagesetter An imagesetter that advances its film by pulling it out of a roll. Because of the possibility of stretch or other problems in transport, this type of device is generally not thought to be accurate enough for quality color separations.

cast An unwanted overall predominance of a given color. Casts are usually detected by examining the values in a color that is supposed to be a neutral gray.

catchlight See *specular highlight.*

CCD Charge-coupled device, an array of light-detecting sensors used in scanners.

CEPS A color electronic prepress system, customarily a proprietary system, such as those manufactured by Scitex.

channel One of the basic components of a Photoshop file. Channels can be viewed individually, copied, or transferred to other documents. Files for normal printing have four channels, one for each CMYK ink, but more channels can be added as masks or templates.

chokes and spreads See *shrinks and spreads.*

chrome A positive-film transparency, especially a 35mm shot.

chromatic adaptation Scientific term for the ability of human beings to adapt their vision to adverse lighting conditions. We see colors that we know to be neutral as gray even when the ambient lighting conditions are not neutral.

chromalin How Cromalin is customarily, and inaccurately, spelled in the graphic arts industry. See *Cromalin.*

CIE Commission International de l'Eclairage, (International Commission on Lighting), the major proponent of the L*a*b* colorspace.

CIELAB The iteration of the L*a*b* colorspace issued by CIE in 1975, which superseded earlier models. This is the version that is Photoshop's native colorspace, and when people speak of LAB, this is usually the one they mean.

clipping path A Postscript capability allowing an EPS file to contain an irregular border that defines its edges. If such a clipping path is defined, points outside it will be transparent if the file is imported into another application. Otherwise, the outside points will be white. Clipping paths tend to create technical problems and generally can be avoided, although there are exceptions.

colorspace A model that enables us to express colors in terms of some sort of numerical values. CMYK, HSB, LAB, and RGB are the colorspaces supported in Photoshop and files can be converted freely between them.

CMYK Cyan, magenta, yellow, and black—the inks that are universally used in color reproduction.

contacting Duplicating all or part of a piece of film by placing it in contact with an unexposed piece and exposing them to light. This is a standard operation in stripping.

continuous-tone Said of a photographic image that has not yet been broken into dots, as in an original photo or an image that has been scanned but not printed.

contone Continuous-tone.

contract proof A color proof of sufficiently high quality that printers will accept it as a guide to what the final printed product should look like. Traditionally, contract proofs have been generated directly from film, but digital proofs are now becoming more common.

contrast The overall differentiation of colors in the image. The further apart, in terms of lightness and/or color, that two objects are, the more contrast there is between them.

cool colors Blues and cyans.

CPU Central processing unit, the part of a computer that computes.

Cromalin A leading brand of film-based contract proof.

CT Continuous tone, frequently used to refer to a digital image that has not yet been output on an imagesetter. The terminology is especially common among users of Scitex equipment, and *Scitex CT* format is one of the many that Photoshop can read and write.

curve In Photoshop and all other image-processing applications, the most powerful means of correcting color.

DCS Desktop Color Separation, a variant of the EPS format proposed by Quark Inc. Instead of a single EPS file, DCS uses one file for each color, plus a placeholder file, making a total of five. Hence, the alternate name, *five-file EPS*. Although Photoshop supports this format, not every application does, nor does every output device.

defringe A Photoshop filter that tries to eliminate a perceptible edge on a selection area by pushing the interior pixels outward.

density 1) In image processing, a measurement of the dot values in a certain area; 2) in imagesetting and all other methods of generating a piece of film, an optical measurement of how black the unexposed areas are.

density mask A mask calculated by the computer to include areas of an image that are of a certain color or density.

despeckle A Photoshop filter that attempts to eliminate randomness in an image; it is roughly the opposite of noise, and tends to soften the look of an image.

device-independent color A chimera being chased by calibrationists.

dot etching The method used for color correction prior to the age of electronics. Craftsmen would reduce or increase the size of dots in existing film by photographic methods (dry etching) or through use of a solution of cyanide of potassium (wet etching).

dot gain Unavoidable phenomenon existing in all presses, whereby the printed dot will become larger than it is in the film. Knowing how much dot gain is to be expected in the printing process is a prerequisite for color correction.

double-dot printing A duotone in which both colors are black.

drum imagesetter An imagesetter that draws in its film and wraps it tightly around a drum before exposing it. This method minimizes motion during imaging and is considered the best way to produce high-quality color.

drum scanner A device that mounts original transparencies or reflective art on a drum that will spin at high speeds during scanning. Based on photomultiplier technologies, drum scanners at present yield the highest quality, provided the operator is competent.

duotone Strictly speaking, a halftone made with two colors only. However, using the four process colors to emulate the tinted effect of a duotone is frequently termed a *duotone* even though it is technically a quadtone, or occasionally a tritone.

dust and scratches A filter introduced in Photoshop 3.0, designed to eliminate obvious defects in an image.

E to E Emulsion to emulsion, the preferred way to duplicate images from film to film or from film to plate. Thus, the new original will have the opposite orientation of the old one. If that is not what is wanted, it is generally necessary to make an intermediate wrong-orientation piece to contact with, although occasionally, on lower-quality work, it is permissible to just go *B to E* (base to emulsion).

emulsion The side of the film or paper that is coated with light-sensitive materials, as opposed to the *base.*

enriched black The practice of using some undercolors as well as black in an area that is solid black. This gives a deeper, richer-looking black.

EPS Encapsulated PostScript, a major means of transferring graphic files from one application to another.

false duotone See *process duotone.*

false reseparation The practice of using intentionally ridiculous Separation Setups with the idea of using one or more of the resulting plates to aid another image.

feathering Increasing a selection area by one or more pixels, but having a small number of pixels on each side of the selection line be at less than full intensity. The purpose is to allow soft edges when changes are made to the selection area.

five-file EPS Another name for DCS, a format Photoshop fully supports.

filter A mathematical operation that in some way contrasts pixels to those adjoining them. Examples of the many filters that Photoshop supports are Unsharp Masking, Noise, Despeckle, Twirl, Zigzag, Dust and Scratches, Lighting Effects, and many others.

flat 1) an image or an area that lacks contrast; 2) a stripping makeready.

Focoltone A color designation and matching system, similar in conception to PMS, but not as widely used.

FPO For Position Only, a warning to all concerned that a placed image is not intended for final reproduction. The lack of these three initials, whether scribbled on a mechanical or in digital form, has caused many a catastrophic misunderstanding.

fractal A mathematically created image that is based on a single pattern that evolves through small variations and permutations. Fractals can be extremely lifelike, and can be generated to infinitely high resolutions, given the proper software.

gamma 1) Any input vs. output curve, such as the those used to color-correct in Photoshop, or to calibrate one's monitor; 2) Photoshop's monitor-calibration utility.

gamut The range of colors that can be reproduced by a given process. A color that cannot be represented in a certain colorspace, usually for technical reasons, is said to be *out of gamut.* Flourescent orange, for example, can be described in the LAB colorspace but is out of gamut in RGB or on a monitor. Bright blue can be shown on a monitor, but it cannot be printed by process inks, so we say it is out of gamut in conventional printing.

Gaussian Mathematical description of a certain type of noise or blur. Gaussian moves follow a bell curve, with points at the center of the selection receiving more weight than those at the edges. Photoshop users have the option of uniform or Gaussian noise and/or blurs.

GCR Gray component replacement, the practice of using black ink to some extent rather than cyan, magenta, and yellow in combination.

ghosting 1) In color manipulation, the practice of making an area of the image significantly lighter, usually so that black type can be placed over it and remain legible (see Figure 14.1 for an example); 2) on press, the undesirable appearance of a faint second version of an element, as if it were the ghost of the real thing.

gravure A type of printing. In gravure, as opposed to offset, the image gets transferred directly from plate to paper. The plate is an engraved copper cylinder. Ink resides in its valleys. Because of the great expense of making this cylinder, gravure is considered impractical for all but runs of over 100,000, but as the cylinder does not deteriorate the way offset plates do, the process becomes highly competitive the greater the pressrun.

grayscale A monochrome (black and white) image that has smooth gradations of gray, as opposed to having only two or slightly more tones available.

halftone An image that has been screened for printing.

high key An image where the most important areas are relatively light, e.g. a picture of a polar bear in a snowstorm.

highlight 1) Any value lighter than about 10 percent; 2) the brightest white area in an image that is not supposed to be a specular highlight.

histogram A graph indicating how many pixels in a given area have certain values.

HSB Hue, Saturation, Brightness, a major colorspace.

HSL Hue, Saturation, Lightness; see above.

Iris trade name of a color ink-jet printer generally accepted as producing output equivalent to that of a film-based contract proof. The line of Iris printers is marketed by Scitex.

JPEG Joint Photographic Experts Group, used to refer to the most common method of compressing image data. JPEG is a *lossy* compression routine, meaning that some data is discarded; so, in theory, the restored version will not equal the original. In most cases, however, the quality loss is minimal.

Julia set A stable fractal, a subdivision of the Mandelbrot set, which contains an infinite number of Julia sets.

Lab color See CIELAB.

L*a*b* See CIELAB.

linework Any graphic that does not have tone. Until recently, the term meant specifically artwork that could be photographed without a screen, such as company logos, but the term has become more vague with the advent of illustration programs.

lossless compression An image compression system that allows the original image to be reassembled with no loss of data. LZW is a lossless compression system.

lossy compression A method that actually discards certain information in the interest of greater compression. When reassembled, the image will not be quite the same as it was originally. The idea is that an intelligent algorithm can find and eliminate data that is really not necessary, and the viewer will not know the difference. JPEG is an example of a lossy compression system.

low key An image where the most important elements are dark; e.g., a picture of a black cat at night.

LUV A colorspace suggested by CIE. It is similar in conception to CIELAB.

LZW Lempel-Ziv-Welch, a type of lossless file compression. Photoshop allows TIFFs to be saved with this type of compression.

makeready The entire process of preparing a document for imaging or for printing. Frequently used specifically to refer to all the intermediate films and masks used by strippers to construct final film.

Mandelbrot set In fractal geometry, a set comprising repeating points of infinite complexity, based on equations relating only to the origin of the fractal and the current position of the point.

mask In stripping, an opaque sheet carefully cut and placed to prevent certain areas from changing when composite films are made. In electronic imaging, a separate channel, which can be temporary, that defines how a composite of two images will be constructed.

MatchPrint A leading film-based contract proof.

metamerism The visual phenomenon that two colors may appear to be the same under certain lighting conditions but different under others; when two colors have this relationship, they are termed a *metameric pair.*

mezzotint A screening technique using dots that are the same size or larger than in conventional screening, but of random sizes and frequencies. Used for artistic purposes to suggest an antique effect. Photoshop 3 has a special filter to make mezzotints; the technique is much more difficult in earlier versions.

midtone Areas of an image that are in the vicinity of a 50 percent dot value.

moiré An offensive interference pattern resulting from the juxtaposition of two or more subpatterns. Since color printing involves four such patterns (one for each process ink), moirés are possible, but generally manufacturers have been able to lick these problems. Nowadays, a moiré is much more likely when a part of the image itself contains a pattern that conflicts with one or more or the screens being used.

monochrome Having only one color or channel.

multisession Term used in referring to the Kodak CD format. If a CD is not full,

Kodak suppliers can write additional images to it at a later time. However, only a *multisession-compatible* CD drive can access these supplementary images.

multitone Inclusive term for any image printed with more than one ink, yet is actually based only on a single monochrome image (which can be altered by curves, however). Normal CMYK images are not multitones, since the individual channels are independent and not based on a single ancestor.

neutral color A white or gray.

Newton rings In high-end scanning, the undesirable appearance of large oval patterns in the scanned image, generally caused by the original not being in close enough contact with the scanning drum.

noise In a Photoshop pattern, pixels that vary randomly from their background. Noise is introduced by means of a filter. Small amounts may be used to cover up corrections, to enhance focus, to create a grainy effect, and so on.

out of gamut See *gamut.*

out of register In printing, where one or more color plates are slightly misaligned with respect to one another. This is adjusted mechanically on press.

Pantone The most widely known color reference company. Often the name is used as a synonym for PMS, but Pantone in fact has many other color-matching products.

PICT Short for *picture,* a graphics format that is now largely obsolete and seldom used in professional imaging.

pixel In scanning or imaging, the smallest dot that the process can address. The resolution of a Photoshop document is defined in terms of pixels per inch, and if you blow it up enough on screen, you will be able to see the individual squares.

pixelization Graphic effect when an image is of such low resolution that when it prints, individual pixels are perceptible. Unless there is an artistic reason for it, this practice is considered unacceptable.

plate 1) In multicolor images, a single color, as in a correction involving the cyan *plate* only; 2) in offset printing, the aluminum sheet that receives ink and transmits it to the printing blanket.

pleasing color Derisive term used to describe the sorts of images given to clients who either do not know the difference between good and bad color or who are unwilling to pay for the former.

PMS The Pantone Matching System, an industry-standard way of defining the color composition of specially mixed inks and also how best to match these colors using process inks only. Thousands of colors are so defined. PMS 199, for example, is a deep rose red. PMS gives the formula for mixing this color ink in case it is going to be an actual fifth color; if we have to match PMS 199 on press (and we can't; it is out of gamut), PMS tells us to use 0C100M65Y.

PMT 1) Photomultiplier tube, the image-sensing technology used by the best graphic arts scanners; 2) Photomechanical transfer, a two-step method of creating photostats.

PostScript The page description language that has become nearly universally accepted in desktop publishing. Introduced by Adobe, PostScript has a rich array of graphic commands. PostScript Level II, being introduced gradually, offers more efficient handling of complex color files during imagesetting.

preflight The practice of carefully examining a file prior to imaging it, hoping to save time in the long run.

prescreened original the unfortunate situation where we have to attempt to scan a printed piece rather than original art. Because of the presence of the screening pattern (and a much smaller dynamic range than would be the case in film), prescreened originals yield results that are mediocre at best.

process colors Cyan, magenta, yellow, and black.

process duotone Using the CMYK inks only to mimic the effect of a duotone.

prog or **progressive proof** Part of standard procedure in making a press proof of a job. In addition to the final printed sheets, for quality control reasons, the printer also prints sheets with each color alone and with each possible combination of other colors. These partial proofs are used as additional guidance by the final printer of the job.

quadtone Normally, a process duotone, but technically any image with four color plates that are based on a common ancestor.

quartertone Tonal values that are roughly in the range of 25 percent.

Quick Mask A Photoshop function. Any selected area can be converted instantly into a Quick Mask, which can then be saved as a separate channel or document or discarded after it is used.

QXP QuarkXPress, the favored page layout application among prepress professionals.

radiosity The study or description of, the manner in which an object reflects light.

RAM Random access memory, the amount of changeable information that a computer can store electronically as opposed to storage on a magnetic disk. RAM is accessed far faster than disk storage, but it is also many times as expensive. Programs like Photoshop that require large amounts of it to run efficiently are customarily referred to as *RAM hogs.*

range The difference between the lightest and darkest colors in a given area of an image.

reflective Description of any nonelectronic original that is not transparent, usually a photographic print or a hand-done piece of artwork.

register The process of keeping the various plates of a color image in precise alignment. In most printing applications, a variation of as much as .002 inch in the position of any plate is considered unacceptable. Strippers and pressmen ensure proper register in film and on press by carefully aligning thin crosshair targets known as *register marks.* It is the responsibility of the electronic artist to provide these marks in the film.

rendering The time-consuming computing process of evaluating an image and trying to recalculate it so that it appears more three-dimensional.

resampling Recalculating the number of pixels in an image by altering its size and/or resolution.

resolution The number of pixels per inch (or other unit of measurement).

RGB Red, green, and blue—one of the major colorspaces.

rich black See *enriched black.*

RIFF Raster Image File Format, the native image format for Fractal Design Corp.'s ColorStudio product, which competes with Photoshop. RIFFs cannot be opened directly in Photoshop.

RIP Raster image processor, a computer that converts PostScript into the bitmapped information needed to drive an imagesetter.

rosette Description of what is currently believed to be the optimal pattern of four-color screening. The term refers to the conjunction of the four printing dots around a central area that is blank. If you have a magnifying glass, you can find the rosettes in the color images in this book.

safety The space so close to the edge of a page that the printer does not allow graphic elements to appear there unless they are to bleed. The printer specifies the amount of safety required; a quarter-inch or less is standard.

saturation Measure of the relative purity of a color; how much it is tending toward gray.

scanning The process of converting an original image into an electronically readable form.

Scitex An Israeli company that is the leading supplier of dedicated professional color systems.

scitexing Magazine-production slang for the process of making artificial electronic improvements to a picture; generally used derisively to refer to the process of eliminating blemishes from the face of a female model.

screening The breaking down of an original continuous-tone image into a pattern of dots or lines so that it can be reproduced on press.

screen angles The relationship of the individual inking screens. Correct angling is necessary to avoid moiré. Normally, cyan, magenta, and black screens are placed at angles approximately 30 degrees apart from one another.

selection Defining and isolating a certain area of an image so that any alterations will affect that area only.

selective color Having the ability to make corrections to a certain color wherever it appears in an image, without affecting areas that are not of that color. By this term, professionals usually mean something similar to the Image: Adjust Selective Color command introduced in Photoshop 3.0, but the Image: Adjust Hue/Saturation command is also a means of selective color correction.

separation The process of converting an image into CMYK plates.

service bureau A company that sells imagesetting and related services, specializing in output of files their clients prepare.

shadow 1) Tthe darkest area of an image; 2) a literal shadow, as the term is commonly understood in English. Since control of both varieties of shadow is very important, the ambiguity is regrettable.

sharpness How well an image appears to be in focus.

sheetfed press A commercial press that uses precut sheets of paper rather than the continuous roll used on web presses. Sheetfed presses tend to have less dot gain. The shorter the pressrun, the more likely a sheetfed press will be used.

shrinks and spreads In stripping, making slight enlargements or reductions in the size of elements of an image for the purpose of creating trap.

Signature 1) The brand name of a contract proofing system marketed by Kodak; 2) the total contents of one press form, usually expressed in terms of the number of pages: this book was printed in 16-page signatures.

silhouette The complete elimination of a background so that a foreground object stands alone.

simultaneous contrast Technical term for an anomaly of human vision: when confronted with similar colors next to one another, our perception of them improves and we are able to see differences between them that we could not if they were far apart.

specular highlight An area of an image that is intended to portray a bright source of light, such as a reflection off a mirror, a streetlight at night, and so forth. Specular highlights should be ignored in setting minimum dot value. They are the only area of an image where it is professionally acceptable to have no dot at all.

spot color The use of a non-process color, usually a fifth or sixth color for emphasis.

stochastic screening A recently developed screening technology that uses very small, random spots of color rather than large dots in a repeating pattern. It is similar in concept to a mezzotint, but in a mezzotint the random dots are supposed to be large enough to be obvious, whereas in stochastic screening the randomness is intended to be invisible.

stat A black-and-white camera reproduction of a piece of art.

stripping Hand assembly of film into a final form suitable for printing.

subtractive colors Cyan, magenta, and yellow.

SWOP Specifications for Web Offset Publications, technical guidelines updated from time to time by an industry-supported nonprofit organization called SWOP Inc. SWOP standards are almost universally accepted in the magazine industry and are also widely used in commercial printing.

three-quartertone The range of tonal values falling approximately halfway between midtones and shadows.

TIFF Tagged Image File Format, a widely used digital image format.

transparency Positive photographic film, often referred to as a *chrome* if in 35 mm format.

trap The practice of intentionally overlapping touching objects, so that no blank area will appear between them if the job is printed out of register.

tritone A multitone that uses specifically three inks.

Trumatch A color designation and matching system, similar in conception to PMS, but not as widely used.

UCA Undercolor addition, the practice of adding cyan, magenta, and yellow to areas that are predominantly black, to achieve a richer and darker color.

UCR GCR that is confined to shadow areas only; generally used when one does not wish to use GCR yet has to meet a maximum ink density requirement, such as that laid down by SWOP.

unsharp masking A process that gives the illusion of making pictures better focused. Traditionally, this is done by comparing the original scan to a second scan that is out of focus, and exaggerating the regions in which they differ. In Photoshop, unsharp masking is a filter, done by mathematical algorithm.

vector Preparation of art files in a form that is independent of their resolution, meaning that they will be converted into bitmap form only when necessary and in the manner best suited to the resolution at that time. Adobe Illustrator and its competitors are examples of vector-based art programs.

viewing conditions The lighting under which artwork is evaluated. Drawing conclusions about color when viewing conditions are not standard is dangerous.

virtual memory In computing, the use of space on a disk as a substitute for RAM. Photoshop and other image manipulation programs must use this technique, because they frequently need more memory than is available in electronic form.

warm colors Reds and oranges.

waterless offset A relatively new printing technology that does not require the use of a dampening system during printing. In conventional offset printing, a mixture of ink and water hits the printing plate. Waterless printing appears to be able to support higher screen rulings and it is growing rapidly.

web press A high-speed printing press that takes its paper from rolls, as opposed to a *sheet-fed* press. Web presses are uneconomical for short runs because of large amounts of start-up waste; they are rarely used to print less than 10,000 pieces.

YCC Kodak's proprietary colorspace, similar to LAB.

THE SOURCES OF THE IMAGES

Several stock-photo firms and one independent photographer graciously gave permission for their images to be used in this book. Although each image is credited below, and is copyrighted by the firm or individual to whom it is attributed, here is a little more information on the firms involved and how you can acquire the images yourself, if you are so inclined.

As regards the stock-photo CDs, there is not very much uniformity in the industry as to how many photos are supplied per disk, and what formats they are in. Prices fluctuate and are therefore not listed here, but none of the CDs listed here cost more than $300 and some can be had for less than a tenth that. As the sample images used here indicate, quality is generally good enough for professional work.

Unless indicated otherwise, all of the CDs listed have very similar licensing terms. The standard terms are: unlimited use of the images in printing and multimedia for personal, professional or, commercial use. The user is never permitted to give or sell digital copies of the images to anyone else, except as necessary for permitted uses. Some companies also forbid use in advertising products that are direct competitors, in pornography, or in products where the image itself is the most important part of what is being sold, as in a calendar or greeting card.

In alphabetical order, the images were provided by:

- **Artbeats**, 800-444-9392 or 503-863-4429, or available from many mail-order sources. Artbeats specializes in backgrounds: textured images, such as marbled paper, wood, and stone. Images are provided at very high resolution, 30 mb or more, as RGB TIFFs, compressed losslessly.
- **Aztech New Media**, 800-361-0669, markets a 3,000-image collection, World-Bank, as a set of 24 CDs. Less than a full set is available at lower prices. The collection is organized country by country, with travel and culture shots dominating. Images are supplied as uncompressed CMYK TIFFs of around 5 mb, suitable for printing at approximately 20 square inches or less.
- **Cardinal Communications Group,** 212-489-1717, is one of New York City's most prominent prepress and digital communications facilities.
- **ColorBytes, Inc.,** 800-825-2656, markets two "Sampler" CDs with 100 JPEG-compressed RGB TIFFs. The files expand to nearly 20 mb apiece, yielding more than enough data for reproduction at full-page size. There are a number of interesting miscellaneous images, but wildlife and outdoor images are emphasized.
- **Corel Corp.,** 800-591-0010, also available from many mail-order sources. Corel has been the most aggressive vendor by far in terms of the breadth of its library, with well over 100 CDs currently available and more appearing every month, as well as its pricing. At this writing, Corel CDs are available for less than $20 apiece via mail

order. As against that, these are straight Photo CD scans, and they do not match the quality of the other vendors listed here. There are 100 images per disc; the topics range from broad ("People," "Food") to implausibly specific ("Tigers," "Doors of San Francisco," "Decorated Pumpkins.")

• The **Kodak** Photo Sampler CD, available at no charge to qualified graphics professionals, contains 24 colorful images that are intended to show the strength and versatility of the Photo CD process. This product is not licensed for commercial use, but "Authorized holders…may use, manipulate, store, transmit, reproduce and display the recorded images for any purpose associated with electronic imaging."

• **PhotoDisc, Inc.**, 206-441-9355, also available from many mail-order sources. The company sells individual CDs, most of which contain 336 images, an unusually large number. The images themselves are JPEG-compressed RGB TIFFs, expanding to about 5 mb apiece, suitable for printing to about 25 square inches. The number of titles is currently in the low teens, and expanding. Each disk has a theme, such as "Holidays and Celebrations," "Nature, Wildlife and Environment," "Food and Dining," etc., but with this many images on a disk, there are always a good number that do not exactly fit the category. License agreement prohibits use in products that are offered for sale. (Advertising in magazines, etc., that are offered for sale is permitted.)

• **René Suárez**, a professional photographer, specializes in images of Puerto Rico. He can be reached at Visual Producers Inc., PO Box 1962, Mayagüez, PR 00680; 809-832-8123; 809-834-3471 (fax).

INTRODUCTION

The favorite book on the first world of Photoshop that I was referring to is Dayton and Davis, *The Photoshop Wow! Book* (Peachpit Press, 1993). Descriptions of the experiments on animals showing a response to color can be found in Itten, *Kunst der Farbe* (Otto Maier Verlag, 1970).

CHAPTER 1

The frontispiece of the Grand Canyon is from Corel's "American National Parks" disk.

The camels image, Aztech New Media WorldBank Collection.

The Munsell color perception test is available from the Macbeth Division of Kollmorgen Corp., 405 Little Britain Rd., Newburgh, NY 12551; 914-565-7660.

The owl image is from ColorBytes Sampler One; photograph by Joe Lange.

The assertion that people with fair complexions and blond hair see color differently from the rest of us is found in Itten, *Kunst der Farbe* (Otto Maier Verlag, 1970).

CHAPTER 2

Copies of the full Specifications for Web Offset Publications are available for purchase from SWOP, Inc., 60 E. 42nd St. Suite 721, New York, NY 10165; 212-983-6042.

Information about the Pantone Matching System and other color-control products can be obtained from Pantone, Inc., 590 Commerce Blvd., Carlstadt, NJ 07072; 201-935-5500. Pantone swatch books may be purchased from many graphic sources.

The image of skiers demonstrating the problems of newspaper reproduction is from PhotoDisc 2, "People and Lifestyles."

Figure 2.4 comes from the QuarkXPress implementation of a calibration scheme known as EfiColor. Information may be obtained from Electronics for Imaging, 415-742-3400.

The image of the white shirt is from PhotoDisc 1, "Business and Industry." The burnt-out version was sabotaged to illustrate the point about trusting the monitor.

Image of Asian children, PhotoDisc 5, "World Commerce and Travel."

Chromatic adaptation as a phenomenon of human vision was noted in 1854 in Chevreul, *The Principles of Harmony and Contrast of Colors and Their Application to the Arts,* (Reinhold, 1967 reprint).

The quotation denigrating the importance of numbers comes from Billmeyer and Saltzman, *Principles of Color Technology* (John Wiley & Sons, 1981).

CHAPTER 3

The images of Tower Bridge, the castle in Spain, and Badlands National Park are the author's. The image of the package of chocolates was photographed digitally at Cardinal Communications Group.

The autumn leaves picture shown at different screen rulings is from ColorBytes Sampler Two; photography by Joe Lange.

For information concerning Scitex systems, contact Scitex America, Inc., 617-275-5150.

The image with an imagesetting moiré was provided by Cardinal Communications Group.

The image of Hong Kong is from PhotoDisc 5, "World Commerce and Travel."

CHAPTER 4

The image of the white building by the lake and of the horses are taken from PhotoDisc 5, "World Commerce and Travel."

The Russian winter scene is from the Aztech New Media WorldBank Collection.

The studio shot of the woman is from the Corel Professional Photos Sampler Disk.

The assertion that it is ludicrous to color-correct on an "uncalibrated" monitor was made by Paul Yi, in the August, 1992 edition of *Publish* magazine.

Ralph Viola, who did the color correction of Figures 4.1 (photograph by René Suárez, converted to PCD) and 4.8 (Corel "American National Parks" CD), has classic red-green color-blindness, and moderately deficient perception of yellows and blues. Before learning color correction, he was shown proofs of the uncorrected images in Chapter 4 and asked questions about them. In Figure 4.3, he could not see a color difference between the purplish trees to the right of the image and the green trees that surround it, even when the purple trees were specifically pointed out to him. In Figure 4.5, he identified the yellow cast in the highlights in the model's face and arms as being white. However, when shown an image very similar to Figure 4.4, he correctly perceived that there was a blue cast to the snow. In Figure 4.6 he did not detect any color cast to the pink horse. He sees reds that contain a yellow component as shades of brown, and can distinguish them from pure yellow.

CHAPTER 5

The images of the grasshopper, the welder, and the seal appear in the Corel Professional Photos Sampler.

The lobsters are taken from Corel's "Food" disk.

The smiling little girl is the author's niece, Rebecca, of whom the author is disgustingly fond. This is a Photo CD image.

The quotation alleging that bad originals cannot be compensated for is from Bridgewater and Woods, *Halftone Effects*, (Chronicle Books, 1993).

CHAPTER 6

The biker image comes from PhotoDisc 2, "People and Lifestyles." The horse image, repeated from Chapter 4, is from PhotoDisc 5.

CHAPTER 7

The fractal design of Figure 7.1 is one of the stock designs of Kai's Power Tools, a series of plug-in filters for Photoshop. Kai's Power Tools may be obtained from many graphic arts suppliers. For information, HSC Software, 310-392-8441.

A good disk of fractal images that could be used for the purposes explained in the chapter comes from Walnut Creek CDROM, 800-786-9907.

For further information on fractals and their properties, the seminal work is Mandelbrot, *The Fractal Geometry of Nature* (W. H. Freeman and Co., 1982), very deep, but worth the effort for those with a mathematical bent.

The biker's face, repeated from Chapter 6, is from PhotoDisc 2.

The image of Balancing Rock, Arches National Park, is from the Corel "American National Parks" disk.

The images of the walrus, Capitol Reef National Park, and the woman in the greenery are the author's.

CHAPTER 8

The images of the Asian children, the city nightscape, the coins, the statues of the Erechtheion, the Chinese tapestry, the rainy street scene, and the view of Hong Kong are all found on PhotoDisc 5, "World Commerce and Travel."

The GCR graphic of Figure 8.1 was constructed by the author. The background image is from Artbeats' "Marble and Granite" CD set.

The Scandinavian boat scene is taken from Aztech New Media's WorldBank collection.

The fruit basket photo appears in Corel's "Food" disk.

CHAPTER 9

The marbled paper pattern of Figure 9.1 is from Artbeats' "Marbled Paper Textures" CD. The artist is Phil Bates.

The Aruban dancer with the red feathers is from the Aztech New Media World-Bank Collection.

The studio picture of the model, repeated from Chapter 4, is from the Corel Professional Photos Sampler, as is the grasshopper, repeated from Chapter 5.

Old Faithful is from Corel's "American National Parks" CD.

The image of the tropical island is on the Kodak Photo Sampler disk; photograph by Don Cochran.

CHAPTER 10

The images of the pizza, the Photo CD and case, the shoes and watch, the chocolates, and the cardinal and tie were photographed digitally at Cardinal Communications Group.

The image of the cloud-shrouded

bridge in Figure 10.5 was photographed by René Suárez.

The image of Capitol Reef National Park used in Figures 10.6, 10.9, and 10.10 is the author's.

The Q–60 calibration set that was the source of the images of the grid and the musicians is officially known as the "Kodak Color Reproduction Guides" and is available directly through Eastman Kodak Co.

The LAB equations are quoted in several sources, e.g. Billmeyer and Saltzman, *Principles of Color Technology* (John Wiley & Sons, 1981).

The grasshopper image of Figure 10.14 is the same one from the Corel Professional Photos Sampler that has been appearing throughout the book.

The quotations attributed to Kodak CD spokespersons appeared in trade publications. The statement that scanning is a boring kind of operation was by Scott Brownstein, who led the team that developed Photo CD. Mr. Brownstein, who is no longer with Kodak, was so quoted in the January 1994 issue of *Advanced Imaging* magazine.

The quotation comparing PCD scan quality to that of professional operators is from Chris Heinz, manager of color characterization services at Kodak Electronic Publishing Systems (Billerica, MA). Mr. Heinz's remarks appeared in the May 1994 edition of *Graphic Arts Monthly*.

The photograph of the model with the red hat is from the Kodak Photo Sampler CD; photograph by Bob Clemens.

CHAPTER 11

All images in this chapter are the author's, except that the owl and the bricks are from ColorBytes Sampler One.

CHAPTER 12

The opening graphic of the cheetah: ColorBytes Sampler Two; photograph by Joe Lange.

The allusion to the artistic uses of black and white when color was available referred to Spielberg's 1993 film *Schindler's List,* and to Michelangelo's design and construction of the New Sacristy for the Medici Chapels in Florence.

The purple flower and the polar bear images are the author's. The building by the lake is part of Kodak's Q–60 scanner quality control kit; see notes to Chapter 10.

The Chart House image is from Aztech New Media's WorldBank collection.

The woman wearing the checked jacket is taken from PhotoDisc 1, "Business and Industry."

CHAPTER 13

All images are repeated from Chapter 12, except that the image of the brown bear with the fish is from ColorBytes Sampler One; photograph by Joe Lange.

The product that generates duotones by applying different curves to four channels is called TargetTones. It works, and is available from Graphic Systems Technology, 800-528-1851.

CHAPTER 14

The images of President Clinton speaking and of the woman holding a baby are from Corel's "People" CD.

The image of the tropical birds is from the Kodak Photo Sampler CD; photograph by Steve Kelly.

A Note on the Type

The letterforms used in this book are those of Utopia, designed by Robert Slimbach of Adobe Systems, Inc., and released in 1990. For this publication, all width data and kerning values were stripped out and new ones supplied by the author.

Though clearly based on classic principles, Utopia is a difficult face to classify. Its rounded letters, which are somewhat elliptical, are a nod in the direction of Hermann Zapf's Melior, but its slightly diagonal emphasis makes it technically a transitional face, in the same general grouping as Baskerville and Fournier.

Unlike those 18th-century types, however, Utopia has a large x-height. Moreover, it is sturdier, especially in the areas of the letter that are naturally thin. Often, the choice of type can help the color, and this is a good example. *Professional Photoshop* is printed on coated stock, which makes type look skimpier, and has images in which color fidelity is critical. Faces like Baskerville that have greater contrast in stroke weight tempt the pressman to increase the flow of black ink. This would play havoc with GCR decisions, as explained on Page 132.

3-D programs, characteristics of, 264–265
3M Co., Inc., 23
Adobe Illustrator, 42, 98, 265
Airbrush tool, 17, 105, 109–110, 118–119, 190, 195, 207
Aldus PageMaker, 24, 42
Anamorphic enlargement/reduction, 111–112, 122
Arches National Park, 205–206
Backgrounds, extensions of, 111–112, 122
Badlands National Park, 46
Beard, handling of, 54, 118–120
Bézier curves, 96–97
Black, uses of, *125–145, see also* GCR
    for deeper shadows, 10, 32
    defocusing a background with, 209
    in duotones, 244
    improving quartertone in, 117
    preparing for a grayscale conversion with, 221, 226–227
Black and white printing, 50, 217–231
Black and white, conversion into, *see* grayscale, conversion into
Blending channels:
    contrast enhancement through, 72–73, 185–189, 194
    to generate image that combines the strengths of two alternate versions, 103, 226
    to generate stronger unwanted color, 78, 134, 153, 162, 206
    method of, 19
    in preparation for grayscale conversion, 221, 225–226, 230
Blur filter, 19, 119, 209–210, 264
Blur/sharpen tool, 17, 109, 113, 118, 197
Brushes palette, 19
Bryce Canyon National Park, 204–206

Calibration and calibrationism, 20–39
    and conversion to grayscale, 229
    of imagesetting, 27
    inability to match results of intelligent correction, 91, 102
    insistence on LAB in, 180
    Kodak PCD as example of, 176
    of monitors, 62, 77, 79
    and predictability, 21–22
    of scanning, 28, 30–32, 177
    when it is not desirable, 38–39
Canvas size command, 111, 206
Capitol Reef National Park, 176
Cardinal Communications Group, 77
CCD scanning, 46, 60, 169, 179, 184, 198
Channels palette, 192, 199, 262
Chromatic adaptation, 37, 70
CIE, 180, 183
Clinton, Bill, 252, 262–264
Clipping path, 97, 211
Clone tool, 17, 96, 108, 109, 110, 112, 122
CMYK, 75, 193, 194
    ability to portray same color in more than one way, 125, *see also* GCR
    as standard, 8–10, 193–194
    controversy over conversion into, 32–34
    inability to portray certain colors with, 17–18, 28, 30, 38–39
    intuitive nature of, 180–181
    purpose of CMYK inks, 37–38
    when other colorspaces superior, 75, 190
CMYK, conversion into, *see also* GCR; Separation setup
    analogous to conversion into grayscale, 229
    black values, typical, 130
    criticism of Photoshop's algorithm, 31–33, 35–36

CMYK, conversion into *(continued)*
  delaying the changeover, 185, 190, 192
  false reseparation, 134
  GCR decision necessary in, 126, 128, 133, 135,
    142–144
  irrelevancy of perfection in, 32, 38–39
Color-blindness, 8, 77, 79
Color casts:
  correction by curves, 68–70, 77, 90
  correction by GCR, 134
  correction by plate blending, 73
  correction during scanning, 45–46
  defined, 5–6
  detection of, 68–70, 90, 154
  due to presswork, 238
  human ability to reject, 36
  in Kodak Photo CD, 160, 176, 179–180, 187
  relation to unwanted color, 155
  whether to retain in scanning, 31
Color perception, limitations of human, 12,
    92
Color printers, 23
Colorspaces, discussed, *see also* CMYK; HSB;
    LAB; RGB; YCC
  interchanging between, 33–36
  supported by Photoshop, 30
  three-letter nature of most, 125, 145
ColorStudio, 41
Composite command, 103, 192, 196, 200,
    207, 211, 214, 258–259
Contacting, 24, 26
Contract proofs:
  necessity of prior to printing, 38
  place in production cycle 23–24, 30, 173
  role in monitor calibration, 37
  and screening, 52
  when irrelevant, 132
Cromalin, 23
Cropping, 16
Crosfield Electronics, Inc., 45
Curves, *65–93*
  brilliant colors, handling of with, 256
  cannot alone generate unwanted color, 155

  to cleanse an image, 134, 142–143
  duotones, creating artificial with, 234,
    238–240
  duotones, custom-written 236, 239–244
  duotones, Photoshop preset, 239–245,
    248–251
  defined, 14–15
  to emphasize important details *81–93*
  to exaggerate black, 133, 135–136, 144
  to exaggerate unwanted color, 152–153,
    160–162
  eyedropper option, 194
  facial features, adjustment of with, 118
  necessity for proficiency in, 145, 251
  in scanner calibration, 171
  steepness of, impact on contrast, 82, 84, 127,
    142, 150, 157, 244
Cyan ink, deficiencies of, 23, 30, 32, 86, 128
Dainippon Screen, 45
Defects, inspecting for, 108, 122, 190
Defringe command, 208
Density mask, *see* Selecting a section of an
    image by color range
Desktop Color Separation format, 42
Despeckle filter, 19, 59, 119–120
Digital cameras, 44, 46, 58, 60, *164–199*
Dodge/burn/sponge tool:
  defined, 109, 254
  depth, creating illusion of with sponge tool,
    262–264
  in digital makeovers, 118, 122
  facial catchlights, repair of, 199
  facial hot spots, elimination of, 262
  generating a highlight or shadow with, 210,
    215
Dot gain:
  affected by paper, 27–30
  compensation for in contract proofs, 23
  effect of too fine a screen, 50
  in newspaper printing, 36, 133
  Photoshop approach to, 35
Double-dot printing, 236
Duotones, 131, 218, *222–251*

DuPont, 23, 45
Dust and scratches filter, 19, 109
Emulsion, 26
EPS, 42, 57
Eraser tool, 207
Erechtheion, the, 135–136, 138
Eyes, handling of, 118, 197
Feathering, 19, 100–101, 104, 110, 112, 118,
    190–191, 196–197, 200, 207–210, 214
Fill command, 210
Filters, 17
Fleshtones:
    appropriate values for, 78
    best scan resolutions for 54–55
    correction of, 187–189, 193
    cyan, role of in, 70–72, 147–148, 162
    as giveaways of problems in color reproduc-
        tion, 64–65
    merges, problems with during, 213, 215
    and selective color correction 259–262
Food shots, 90, 135
Four-color black and whites, 236–239
Fractals, 120–122
Gamut alarm, 38
Gamut, in offset printing, 127
GCR, 17, 124, *128–135*, 238, 240, 250
Ghosting, 266–269
GIF, 43
Goals in color manipulation, 5
Grain, handling objects with, 131, 157–160,
    162, 227
Grand Canyon, 2–4, 6, 74–76
Grayscale, conversion to, *217–231*, 245, 248
Grow command, 99
Hair, handling of:
    adding contrast to, 229
    in black and white, 221, 223, 230
    changing color of with LAB, 194
    difficulty of silhouetting, 99–101, 105, 191,
        210–212
    masks, use of in, 194
    placing highlights in, 195
Hell, Dr. Rudolf, 45

Highlight:
    blown-out (defect), 33, 35
    defined, 10, 78
    and dot gain in newspaper printing, 36
    effect of too fine a screen on, 50
    minimum value, 11, 13, 136
    setting to insure full tonal range, 65–68,
        70–74, 82
    specular, defined, 72
    in stochastic screening, 58
    values in duotones, 234, 241
    when image has none, 71–72
Hong Kong, 142–143, 145
HSB, 30, 125–126, 155–156, 181–182, 184, 254
Hue/saturation adjustment, 155–157, 159,
    162, 260
Image size command, 19, 48, 55, 112
Imagesetting, 24, 26–27, 55–58, 60–61
Info palette, 14, 19, 20, 23, 27, 36, 66, 172, 187
Iris, 23
JPEG, 43, 248
Kai's Power Tools, 121
Kodak:
    calibrationist views of, 171–172, 176
    and digital contract proofs, 23
    Photo CD marketing plan, original, 167–168
    position in graphic arts industry, 172–173, 177
Kodak Photo CD, *166–198*
    as alternative to high-end scanning, 43, 93
    at its best, 259
    format discussed, 43–44, 60, 168
    marketing plan, original, 167–168
    price of, 86, 93, 167
    problems with inadequate RAM, 43
    prone to color casts, 160
    unsharp masking required in, 115, 133
LAB, *179–185*
    as alternative to CMYK, 17, 190
    color correction using, 192–193, 198, 259, 269
    complexity of, 156, 171
    mathematical equations for, 180
    monochrome effects, use in, 117
    opponent-color nature of, 73, 75, 198

LAB *(continued)*
 Photoshop's internal colorspace, 165, 183
 preferred colorspace for Photo CD, 169, 189
 role in reseparation, 33, 61
 three-letter nature of, 125, 190
 use in reseparation, 134, 141
Lasso tool, 16, 97–98, 101, 103–104, 110, 112,
  190, 202, 206
Layer Options menu, 102, 123, 194, 196, 254,
  256, 258
Layers palette, 19, 102, 121, 185, 196, 254,
  256, 267
Layers, use of, 43, 102, 201, 254, 256,
  266–269
Least-common-denominator approach, 194,
  207–208, 210, 212, 214
Letterpress printing, 24
Lighting Effects filter, 254, 264–266
Lighting conditions, 5, 39, 70, 71, 203, 204,
  205, 210
Linotype, 24, 45
LZW compression, 42–43
Magazine reproduction, 50, 128–129, 171
Magic wand, 16, 97–100, 103–104, 118, 197
Marble, 136–138
Marquee tools, 16, 97
Masking, *see also* Quick Masks
 the advantage of editability, 191–192, 214
 merging two images with, 103–105, 206–207
 to protect complex objects, 191–192, 211
 selection by color range, 254, 257–259, 268
Matching the art, as a goal, 5, 6, 18, 31, 39,
  90, 171–177
MatchPrint, 23
Median filter, 59, 120
Merging unrelated images, 200–216, 265
Metallic colors, 88, 130
Metamerism, 182
Midtone:
 adjustment via curves, 82
 boosting black to add focus, 178
 defined, 11
 dropping to exaggerate darker tones, 150, 163

Moiré, 55–61, 143
Monitor, overreliance on:
 clues that artist has, 35–38
 impossibility of calibrating, 62
 need for calibration disproved, 77, 79
 as RGB device, 35
 screen resolution, 48
 why professionals avoid, 20, 23
Monitor Setup, 37
Multitones, 233, 236, 238, *see also* Duotones
Munsell test, 8–9
Neutral colors:
 additional cyan and magenta permissible in,
  88
 analysis of, 74
 and chromatic adaptation, 37
 control by curves 81, 89, 92, 136–138
 defined, 5, 10
 and GCR, 130–131
 as giveaways of poor reproduction, 64–66,
  187
 selective color correction, accessibility
  through, 254
Newspaper reproduction:
 appropriate highlight and shadow values in,
  65
 dot gain in, 36
 GCR techniques in, 133
 maximum screening values in, 50–52
 poor quality of, reasons for, 27–29
Noise filter:
 to add apparent sharpness, 115, 117–118, 122
 to add roughness, 204, 210
 to counter moiré, 59
 to disguise local corrections, 110
 monochrome option, 59, 61, 115, 117, 254
 similarity to stochastic screening, 57
Offset printing, 24–25
Old Faithful, 154–156, 159, 161
PageMaker, *see* Aldus PageMaker
Paintbrush tool, 109, 192
Pantone Matching System, 25, 38, 58, 242
Paths palette, 19, 97, 101, 191, 194, 264

Paths, use of, 97, 100, 103, 186, 190, 194, 197, 206, 210, 262, 268

Pen tool, 97–98, 104, 191

Pencil tool, 109–110, 118

Photoshop 3, new capabilities of, *253–269* *see also* Layering; Lighting Effects; Noise filter; Unsharp masking; Selecting a part of an image by color range; Selective Color

Photoshop 3 format, 42–43, 104, 258, 267

Photo CD, *see* Kodak Photo CD

PICT, 43

PostScript, 49, 52, 55–56, 97, 211

PowerPC chip, 253, 265

Prescreened originals, 58–59

Press characteristics, *see also* Dot gain:
    in duotones, 258, 267
    effect of excessive ink density, 128–129
    influence of paper, 27–28
    jobs requiring color flexibility, 132
    order of inks, 28
    screening values, 50–51, 60
    variability of entire process, 22–25, 30, 38

Press proof, 23

Printing Inks Setup, 37

Q–60 set, 173, 177, 223

QuarkXPress, 24, 42–43

Quartertone, 58, 74, 157, 163, 196
    adjustment via curves, 84–86
    black, role of in adding contrast, 117, 133, 178
    defined, 11
    in stochastic screening, 58

Quick Mask, 16, 102–104, 192, 206, 257

Registration, black as aid in, 133

Removal of objects from images, 212–215

Repeatability, 20, 28, 38, 133, 134, 172, 173

Resampling, 8, 53–54, 55, 60

Resolution, in imagesetting, 48, 52

Resolution of monitor, 48

Resolution, in scanning, 189, 190, 214
    optimal, 49, 53–55, 60–61
    overresolution, problem of, 53–54, 60
    relation to file size, 47–49

RGB:
    additive nature of, 30
    as alternate to CMYK, 17, 179, 182, 184–185
    conceptual perfection of, 32–36
    intuitive nature of, 156, 181
    three-letter nature of, 125–126

RIFF, 41

Right-reading vs. wrong-reading, 24–26

Rocky Mountain National Park, 200, 211

Rotating, 16

Rubber stamp tool, *see* Clone tool

Russia, lighting conditions in, 69–70, 73–74

Scanners:
    calibration of, 173, 177
    desktop and handheld, 46, 60, 114
    high-quality drum, 8, 40, 60, 93, 114, 166
    photomultiplier technology, 44–45
    proper resolution in, 49, 53–55, 60–61

Scanning, high-end:
    application of curves during, 166
    as "boring", 171–172
    different operators, different results, 166, 172, 174–175
    greater GCR flexibility in, 133
    introduction of hairs and dirt, 108
    mounting in oil or gel, 108
    prescan image analysis, 31–33
    produces CMYK files, 125
    selective color correction in, 60, 170, 173
    shortage of good operators, 46
    unsharp masking in, 113–115, 122, 166

Scitex, 52, 93

Scitex CT format, 43, 52

Scratches, 96, 107, 122

Screen angles, 56–57

Screening, 26, 27, 49–51, 56–58, 60, 238

Select similar command, 99, 191

Selecting a section of an image:
    defined, 15–16, 95
    by color range, 19, 254–255, 268, 257–259
    freehand lasso best in some cases, 110
    as last refuge of the incompetent, 78, 90
    methods of, 96–105

Selective color:
    defined, 254
    in fleshtone correction, 78, 259–262
    to reduce obtrusive colors, 90
    in scanning, 60, 170, 173
    where inappropriate, 259
Separation setup:
    duotones, recommended values in, 250
    in false reseparations, 134, 144
    GCR equivalency chart, 124
    maximum ink densities, 31, 129
    recommended values for, 8, 32–33
Shadow:
    analyzing for, 64–72, 74, 78
    appropriate values for, 33
    black, role of in, 133, 144
    in black and white, 221, 230
    as candidate for sacrifice, 139
    creating darker via multitoning, 234, 237, 241,
        250
    defined, 11–13
    effect of too fine a screen on, 50
    human insensitivity to color casts in, 130
    maximum values, 140
    stochastic screening, effect of on, 58
    and SWOP standards, 31
    three-quartertone boosts, 157
    treatment of very light, 74, 90, 140
    unbalanced shadows occasionally permitted,
        84–86
    weakness in CCD scans, 46–47, 184, 198
Sharpening, *see* Unsharp masking
Silhouetting, 15, 94, 96–99, 101, 104, 200, 204,
    208–212
Simultaneous contrast, 84, 114
Skin tones, *see* Fleshtones

Smudge tool, 17, 109, 207
Specular highlight, 72, 74, 78, 88
Sponge tool, *see also* Dodge/burn/sponge
    tool, 30, 38, 252, 262–264
Stochastic screening, 57–60
Stock–photo CD-ROMS, 8, 44, 60, 67, 74, 93
Stripping, 25–27
SWOP, 31, 33, 128–130, 144
Three-quartertone, 11, 130, 157
TIFF, 42–43
TIFF jaggedness in QXP, 42
Toolbox, Photoshop, 16
UCR, 126, 129, 144
Unsharp masking, *113–119*
    of black plate only, 59, 139, 143–144, 192
    as cause of moiré, 59
    when counterproductive, 59, 141
    and Kodak Photo CD, 133, 177–178, 169, 189
    of L channel in LAB, 193, 198
    of scans at too high a resolution, 54, 60
    technical explanation of, 116
    of unwanted color, 149
    variations among scanners, 45–46, 60
Unwanted color, uses of, *147–163*
    in brilliant colors, 256
    defined, 10, 147
    eliminating with GCR, 134
    generating heavier, methods of, 206–207
    in water, 161, 163, 248
USM, *see* Unsharp masking
Variations menu, 4
Video, 44
Viewing conditions, 7
Viola, Ralph, 77, 79
YCC colorspace, 125, 169, 183
Zion National Park, 203–205, 211